DEMOCRACY, POWER, AND LEGITIMACY:
THE CRITICAL THEORY OF JÜRGEN HABERMAS

Democracy, Power, and Legitimacy

The Critical Theory of Jürgen Habermas

Omid A. Payrow Shabani

UNIVERSITY OF TORONTO PRESS
Toronto Buffalo London

b 24411371

ISBN 0-8020-8761-2

Printed on acid-free paper

National Library of Canada Cataloguing in Publication

Payrow Shabani, Omid A.
    Democracy, power, and legitimacy : the critical theory of Jürgen
Habermas / Omid A. Payrow Shabani.

Includes bibliographical references and index.
ISBN 0-8020-8761-2

1. Habermas, Jürgen – Ethics.   2. Habermas, Jürgen – Contributions
in political science.   3. Democracy.   4. Legitimacy of governments.
I. Title.

JC423.S464 2003   321.8'01   C2003-900025-7

University of Toronto Press acknowledges the financial assistance to its
publishing program of the Canada Council for the Arts and the Ontario
Arts Council.

University of Toronto Press acknowledges the financial support for its
publishing activities of the Government of Canada through the Book
Publishing Industry Development Program (BPIDP).

To my parents

Contents

viii Contents

Acknowledgments

This book is a revised version of my doctoral thesis. The basic idea for the thesis emerged out of a reading group on Habermas's *Between Facts and Norms* with several graduate students and professors from Carleton University and the University of Ottawa. It is only appropriate, then, to thank these participants: Amy Bartholomew, Wade Diceman, Allen Hunt, Trevor Purvis, Peter Swan, and Melanie White. Then, during a summer program of the School for Theory and Criticism at Cornell University I had the good fortune of discussing some of my ideas with Professor Seyla Benhabib and Fredric Jameson. I would like to express my gratitude for their help and guidance. Later, at Northwestern University, I had the opportunity to discuss parts of my thesis with Professor Jürgen Habermas, who kindly commented on my work. He is the best teacher I have ever had.

I owe a special debt to my doctoral supervisor, Will Kymlicka, whose generosity, unfailing support, and unassuming fairness have helped my work throughout. I hope to do for my students what he has done for me. I am also grateful for the continuous support and guidance of my external examiner, Professor Thomas McCarthy, whose expert advice has improved the quality of my work. As well, I would like to express my appreciation to the members of my thesis committee, Hilliard Aronovitch, Denis Dumas, and Douglas Moggach, whose professionalism helped the development of my thesis project.

Thanks are also due to the following friends and colleagues for their support and friendship while I worked on this book: Paola and Simon Busse, Mark Raymond Brown, Frank Cameron, Roxana Kandel, Dean Lauer, Sascha Maicher, Jayson Mclean, and Dean Weston.

DEMOCRACY, POWER, AND LEGITIMACY:
THE CRITICAL THEORY OF JÜRGEN HABERMAS

Introduction

How can democracy and freedom be maintained in the long run under the dominance of
advanced capitalism?

Max Weber

The political changes that took place during the last two decades of the twentieth century contained important lessons concerning a viable socio-economic formation and its proper political structure. While the collapse of communism de facto proved the capitalist system of market economy the winner, the end of colonialism, apartheid, and numerous dictatorships opened the doors of many non-Western countries to the experience of democracy. Under these circumstances, with the peace processes under way in Ireland (following the Good Friday Agreement), in Sri Lanka, and in the Middle East (initiated by the Oslo Peace Accord – its recent setbacks notwithstanding), advocates of the project of modernity, as the pursuit of the ideal of free society by rational subjects, would contend that we are on the right track.[1] A prominent name among those who have tirelessly defended the viability of such a project is Jürgen Habermas. His long and fruitful scholarly life has been spent studying the strengths and potential ills of the ideals of Enlightenment. As a German philosopher, he not only has a native sense of appreciation for modernity's faith in reason as articulated by Kant and Hegel, but, growing up during the Second World War, he also is aware of the horror that same faith can provoke. While the maladies of modernity have, for some, proven sufficient reason to abandon the entire project altogether, Habermas has patiently laboured to diagnose modernity's limitations and free its potentials. His philosophical writings and political interventions have been aimed at providing a theory of justice[2] that tries to address the ethico-political concerns of our diverse, pluralist, and fragmented society. In recognizing the post-traditional character of our modern society, Habermas's critical theory opts for a mode of justification that seeks a middle ground between the foundationalism of the tradition and the contextualism of the sceptical position. The critical task of the theory consists in analysing the social reality with a normative yardstick of a 'moral point of view,'[3] which is inherent in our symbolic interaction, and our language, with respect to the ideal of a free society. But like any other Kantian morality, his theory, too, is haunted by the problem of how to bring the insight of the moral 'ought' to bear on the context of ethical life. In his most recent works, Habermas attempts to solve this problem by proposing that the concept of modern law can mediate between morality (*Moralität*) and ethical life (*Sittlichkeit*) by contextualizing the moral norm. As such, law would allow for public opinion and will formation to exert influence upon political power, giving the system legitimacy. Thus, in so far as the domains of economics, administration, and market in the constitutional states are open and submitted to discursive evaluation through law, the ideal of democracy as a norm-governed socio-political order has been realized.[4]

Habermas's project, as such, is aimed at articulating effectively and clearly the Enlightenment's interest in emancipation. His formulation of this unfinished project of modernity has created a great deal of interest among both its foes and friends, generating lively debates that have produced a vast literature and advanced the frontier of our knowledge in the area of social and political philosophy. Within this context, therefore, it is important for any change in his theory to be carefully examined with respect to its implications for research paradigms in morality and politics. The basic claim of this study, in conducting such an examination, is that Habermas's more recent works mark a turn toward a position that is inadequately critical of the existing political order in liberal democracies. In my view such an uncritical shift amounts to a complacency that is politically dangerous. To remedy this weakness, I propose to synthesize some insights of a different political theory, which aim to recognize and accommodate the complexity and diversity of our modern world, thereby recovering the critical tenor of Habermas's theory.

In confronting the challenges that one faces when writing on Habermas, one should note that his writing is overwhelming in terms both of its scope and volume. His insatiable appetite to digest diverse

philosophical insights and make them his own makes his writing ency-
clopedic, complex, and abstract. Add to this his high rate of productivity and the pace at which he actively contributes, and we can begin to
see how difficult it is to catch up with Habermas. He projects the
traditional image of a German philosopher who, during the course of
his investigation, does not leave any stone unturned. Such rigour in
turn requires critics to be patient and charitable. For without charity, as
the *sine qua none* of critique – an immanent attempt at understanding –
the critique will fail in achieving its goal. The task of critique is not
to disprove a theory but to show its limitations and the possibility of
overcoming them.

In the work of the early Frankfurt School philosophers, the idea of
critique acquires a social dimension and becomes a critical theory of
society, which through an interdisciplinary endeavour seeks to articu-
late the social interest in emancipation. Their overestimation of the
dominance of instrumental rationality, however, soon bestowed a pessimistic outlook upon their critical theory, leading their search for free
society into a cul-de-sac.

Habermas, thus, inherits the unfinished task of formulating a critical
theory of society. His first attempt, 'the theory of communicative action,' reveals the limitations of the philosophy of consciousness with
respect to the achievement of the modern ideals of freedom and autonomy. Habermas calls his rethinking of the relation between reason
and history, which would allow for a connection between reason and
concrete life to be established, 'desublimation of reason.' Desublimation
of reason is made possible by a move from philosophy of history to
philosophy of language, and a presentation of a communicative theory
of rationality and action. Such a theory neatly lends itself to a formulation of discursive ethics aimed at addressing questions of justice.

Translating the insight of discourse ethics into a socio-political theory
diagnoses the pathology of modernity as the domination of discursive
situations by systemic media of power and money, which Habermas
calls 'colonization of the lifeworld.' His analysis of the colonization of
the lifeworld, however, proves too restrictive to account for legitimate
power in modern society, since it focuses on the rationality of economic
and administrative systems. Coupled with an original tension between
morality and ethical life, or between the justification of moral principles
and their application, this restriction leads Habermas to consider legal
theory as a way out of the impasse created by the system-lifeworld
distinction. In *Between Facts and Norms* an elaborate attempt is made to

show how the institutionalization of discursive procedures allows for communicative insight to be translated into law, which, in turn, counteracts the colonizing effects of economic and political subsystems. This is where my main contention comes to the fore: an inadequate critical treatment of the actual institution of liberal democracies marks a shift to a more conservative position in Habermas's project, a shift that robs us of our critical ability to protest the remaining injustices in the system. Given the significance of Habermas's critical theory for the contemporary development of social, political, and moral theories, it is important to gauge carefully any new change that is introduced in the theory. Thus, in addition to locating precisely where the conservative shift occurs in Habermas and what it entails for the emancipatory promise of his theory, I also attempt to show possible ways of restoring the weakened critical thrust of his project by appropriating some insights from postmodern political theory. Such a recovery will, then, allow the theory to approach the ideals of democracy and justice by way of a universalization principle that has been made sensitive to the diversity of the forms of life. A brief description of my discussion follows.

To understand Habermas's philosophical orientation it is important to lay out its historical background and theoretical sources. To this end, in chapter 1 I recount Kant's formulation of modernity's problem of the subject's self-constitution as a moral agent. Kant's placing of the 'world-constituting ego' in the structure of mind, however, gives rise to the problem of self-grounding. That is to say, the 'knowing I' faces a problem of self-referentiality when it turns upon itself as the object of knowledge. Hegel's solution to this problem is to locate mind or spirit within history, proposing as absolute a notion of enlightened reason, which could resolve the problems of positivity and the subject's self-reassurance. Such a comprehensive appeal to reason, however, endangers modernity's principle of subjectivity or freedom, hence inviting a radical critique of absolute reason in Nietzsche, Heidegger, and the early Frankfurt School. My discussion at this point will be aimed at illustrating how Habermas preserves the ideals of 'emancipation' and 'rational society' along with the critique of instrumental rationality in order to solve the problems of modernity via a path shown in, but not taken by, Hegel, namely, communicative rationality.

Thus, the first chapter lays out the origin of Habermas's political and philosophical aspirations, namely, the formulation of modernity's principles of freedom and autonomy, which, in turn, defines his entire project. This outline tells a story of how modernity developed, who its protagonists were, and what ideals grew out of it. These questions are asked and answered to the extent that they make the origin and the goal of Habermas's work plain. This is a crucial point because, despite the prevalent position this view of modernity enjoys, there are other stories of modernity that, regardless of their validity, would not shed any light on the motivation for Habermas's project. Hence, when I say that the root of Habermas's philosophical ambitions is to be found in modernity, I have to state and show what modernity I am speaking of. Chapter 1 allows the reader to trace the history of Habermas's work, at different stages, back to the ideals of subjectivity and critique (i.e., freedom and autonomy) that drive his philosophy at all time. In fact, I try to mark the success of his work in each following chapter with respect to the pursuit of these principles. Chapter 1, therefore, *works as a benchmark against which Habermas's different doctrines can be measured with respect to their origin.*

In chapter 2, I give an account of how Habermas abandons philosophy of consciousness. He overcomes the philosophy of consciousness's subject-centred reason and its monological character by rationally reconstructing an intersubjective mode of reason as found in communicative interactions. This shift is made possible by way of 'the linguistic turn,' which is based on the belief in the emancipatory concept of reason latent in our linguistic interaction. Recognizing speech acts as basic units of such interactions, Habermas presents his theory of 'universal pragmatics,' whose task is to reconstruct the general structure of speech acts. The rational reconstruction of actors' communicative competence allows for agents' discursive claims to be argumentatively adjudicated, based on the generalizability of their interests. Such an account of communicative rationality allows Habermas to escape the fate of instrumental rationality and get the project of emancipation back on track. A detailed outline of Habermas's theory of communicative action at this point serves to establish the terminology and vocabulary of his architectonic, which will constitute the content of my later discussion.

The second chapter sets up the terminology of Habermas's philosophy without which his discourse would be inaccessible. It aims to present a lucid exposition of Habermas's architectonic and its basic terminology. Like Hegel and Heidegger, Habermas invents his own language, which differs from everyday speech – a loaded and technical language that introduces us to 'communicative action,' 'instrumental action,' 'purposive rationality,' 'discourse ethics,' 'linguistification,' 'universal pragmatics,' 'stages of moral consciousness development,' 'the lifeworld,' and so forth. All these terms will appear repeatedly in later chapters. Perhaps more importantly, the chapter links Habermas's background (i.e., modernity and its ideals) with his innovative approach in social and political theory – the link made possible by the linguistic turn. As a pragmatic and anti-foundationalist attitude in philosophy, the linguistic turn gives Habermas's later philosophical work, such as 'discourse ethics,' and political work, such as 'deliberative democracy,' their cutting edge in terms of their practical usefulness and policy applicability. Hence, chapter 2 works as a terminological key to the rest of the text. So, while it may not be 'topical' it serves a pragmatic purpose.

In chapter 3, and before turning to the political implications of communicative ethics theory, the strength and weaknesses of Habermas's theory are critically assessed. Here, a discussion of the Hegelian critique of Kant's moral theory will draw out the advantages of Habermas's discourse ethics over the Kantian morality. Subsequently, a selective survey of immanent critiques aimed at different aspects of his theory will reveal the insights we can keep for the purpose of critical social theory, and the oversights that need to be revisited. Specifically, an examination of Habermas's principle of universalization will show how it needs to be viewed in a weaker or concretized sense in order to avoid the Hegelian charge of empty formalism and, at the same time, be fruitful for the pursuit of the good life. Furthermore, a critique of the prominent role of the ideal of consensus, as the desired end of rational communication, reduces the efficacy of the charges of foundationalism and totalizing tendencies in regard to the theory. What remains is a critical theory that, based on a procedure of rational argumentation, makes an analysis of the pathologies of modernity and their remedy possible.

The third chapter thus serves to sum up the state of the debate on Habermas's theory of communication action and discourse ethics with respect to the insight that will be retained for the purpose of formulating a critical political theory. The chapter concludes that, in order to avoid the theory's traditionalist and foundationalist tendencies, the emphasis on the concept of 'consensus' as the ultimate telos of discourse should be weakened and instead be put on the procedural nature of the discursive situation that will remain open to future contestation. This insight is crucial not only to the development of Habermas's political theory but also to my final critique of its effectiveness.

Together these chapters make possible the formulation and development of my argument, namely, that the uncritical shift in Habermas's theory, which occurs as the result of an internal theoretical tension and external dialogue with his critics, can be remedied by an appeal to Foucault and Derrida's more radical political theory. The insight of chapter 3, which is to demote the ultimate status of consensus as the goal of discourse and instead emphasize the procedure, allows Habermas to develop his theory of deliberative democracy (chapter 5) and his doctrine of constitutional patriotism (chapter 7).

In chapter 4, I will discuss how the insight of Habermas's rational theory of communication is translated into a socio-political critique that theorizes the possibility of democracy in advanced capitalism. I argue that by acknowledging that capitalism and the market economy are here to stay, and by confirming that the logic of reproduction of such systems is different from the logic of reproduction of symbolic interaction, Habermas introduces the lifeworld-system distinction. The role of this distinction in his theory of social evolution is to separate the rationalization of lifeworld from the growing complexity of social systems, thereby overcoming the restrictive analysis of historical materialism. Next, a discussion of Habermas's theory of the evolution of society and the processes of legitimation crisis reveals the 'colonization of the lifeworld' as the primary danger to the achievement of the ideal of democracy. However, an analysis of criticisms aimed at the lifeworld-system distinction will divulge the theory's abeyance: there is no guarantee that the system would not completely colonize the lifeworld. The one-sided focus of the problem of colonization on economic and administrative systems results in the theory's inability to account for the possibility of legitimate power. The challenge, therefore, for Habermas's critical theory is whether, given the diversity of worldviews and the postmetaphysical character of our time, it will be able to present a theory of legitimate power in capitalism.

In chapter 5, we reach the main claim of this book with respect to Habermas's impressive attempt at theorizing deliberative democracy, which is supposed to enable his theory to account for, and distinguish, the kinds of power that need to be esteemed from those that need to be rejected. To this end, Habermas's attention turns toward legal theory and the role of law. In order to operationalize (i.e., make workable) the gap between the 'is' and the 'ought,' facts and norms, application and justification, and to account for legitimate power, Habermas turns to the concept of modern law, which, with its universal character and its orientation toward individual rights, can mediate between lifeworld and system. Such a concept of law will allow for communicative forces of the lifeworld to exert a certain influence on the systemic domains of politics and administration. It will be shown that this influence is made possible by a revision of Habermas's original concept of power.

Drawing on Arendt, Habermas distinguishes communicative power from administrative power, which has a strategic aim. Communicative power is generated through informal procedures of public deliberation that are aimed at rationally promoting the social agents' generalizable needs. Modern law translates the insight of communicative power into administrative power, thus counteracting capitalist domination of public deliberation. Yet, Habermas's revised model makes too many concessions to 'real-existing' capitalism, since it takes the existing institutions of liberal democracy as the starting point for its normative theorization. By aligning communicative power, legitimate law, and state power, Habermas legitimizes political power as exercised in Western democracies. For, tying the existing political and legal order so closely to communicatively generated power as their source of legitimacy compromises the critical ability of social actors to reproach the system for its failings. I will, therefore, argue that Habermas's *Between Facts and Norms* marks a shift in his critical theory towards a more conservative position. The work's inadequate critical assessment of the actual political order not only has the unfortunate effect of weakening the voices of protest and dissent, but also amounts to political complacency and a happy presentism.

Having shown the disabling turn in Habermas's more recent work, I will present, in chapter 6, the outline of a possible way of recovering the critical thrust of his theory. Given the pluralism of worldviews and the diversity of our modern society, James Bohman, a prominent critical theorist, has argued that 'we should abandon ... the very project of reconstructing an analogue to historical materialism as a comprehensive framework for critical social science: contemporary critical theory must be theoretically, methodologically, and practically pluralistic.'[5] While the eclectic approach of Habermas's theory has already drawn on many different traditions and trends of thought, I will propose to complement it further with insights of an unlikely source.

The deficiencies of Habermas's theory of power, I will propose, can be overcome to a great extent if we appropriate Michel Foucault's analysis of power, which goes beyond the restrictive consensus-coercion distinction of Habermas's juridical model of power by expanding the dimensions of the definition of power to a contestational network of relations that flow in all directions. In Habermas's juridical model, social injustices are recognized as either economic domination or illegitimate use of the sovereign right, which prescinds other forms of social inequalities. Thus, the symbolic force that governs the constitution and hierarchization of social identities is not understood as a form of political power. Foucault's analysis of power exposes a conflictual logic in the production of social structure that cannot be reduced to the analysis of power in the juridical model. Incorporating this insight would enable Habermas's critical theory to recognize other relations of power, which do not fit under the precept of the power of a sovereign or economic power, as political power.

With respect to overcoming the complacent political theory of the real-existing system, and the weakening of the critical voices of difference and dissent, I will draw upon Jacques Derrida's deconstructive strategy to highlight the distinction between law and justice. *Pace* Habermas, this distinction will show that a critical theory of democracy should not mistake the promotion of liberal-democratic institutions with the attainment of justice. Rather it should approach the goal of justice as an open-ended and incomplete task that requires constant examination and re-examination of our present. Justice conceptualized as what is always to come, *à-venir*, is not law. Law and its institutions can help us approximate justice, but its exercise is never the same as achieving justice. 'Giving injustice its due,'[6] to borrow a phrase from Judith Shklar, means injustice shouldn't simply be viewed as instances of the lack of justice or its violation, as temporary obstacles in the way of a just state. Derrida's deconstructive strategy allows for injustices to be seen as a central and immovable feature of the world that, as such, requires that contestation and dissent be viewed as democratic values, and not as anomalies that need to be eschewed.

To view the ideal of justice as *à-venir* instead of an institutional arrangement that can be achieved once and for all is, indeed, more consistent with the description of deliberative democracy as an enduring procedural argumentation among free and equal citizens with different world views. The synthesis of Derrida's insight with Habermas's theory will amount to changing the role of consensus as the ultimate telos of communication to being a critical principle of political engagement among differences. On this view, the defence of liberal democracy should not mean searching for an argument that is beyond argumentation. For what makes democratic politics persist is the irreducibility of difference. In the end, while the crux of my argument is to locate where the conservative shift in Habermas occurs, and while I acknowledge that my proposal to complement Habermas's critical theory with some insights of postmodern political theory is in need of further explication and elaboration, I believe that it suffices to show how we can recover the critical impulse of Habermas's theory that was weakened in *Between Facts and Norms*. The need for my proposed synthesis arises from the fact that the complex and rapidly changing reality of our modern society can no longer be investigated from the viewpoint of a single comprehensive theory, even if it has an interdisciplinary character.[7] A critical theory of society, therefore, should be able to draw upon the best insights of our contemporary social and political theories.

In such a refurbished critical theory, two conditions of modern democracies in advanced capitalism are emphasized: first, the recognition of the fact of pluralism; and second, the open-ended character of the discursive procedures of public deliberation. Here, the pursuit of the ideal of justice is envisioned as an enduring negotiation and contestation among diverse groups under the rule of law that is always renewed but never completed. Habermas's later book *The Inclusion of the Other* presents an auspicious instance of such a critical approach, whereby he develops his doctrine of constitutional patriotism to address the problem of social cohesion and political unity in diverse and multicultural states. Here the principle of universalization is reformulated so to allow a greater sensitivity to differences.

Chapter 7 will begin with an outline of constitutional patriotism as an alternative to the traditional bond of belonging and membership in the political community, where compatriots are united through their reciprocal allegiance to a set of laws embodied in a constitution. The ethnic bond of nationalism that has been under the pressure of globalization and multiculturalism is now envisioned to be replaced with the civic bond of constitutional patriotism, which is more consistent with the postmetaphysical conditions of our modern life.

Next, I shall discuss the criticism levelled against such a civic bond. Liberal nationalists allege that it is too weak to provide a sense of belonging and unity necessary for political legitimacy, while the advocates of republican patriotism argue that it is too dispassionate and thin to provide a shared sense of loyalty and identity. I respond to these criticisms by, first, arguing that while liberal nationalists conflate the concepts of 'nation' and 'state,' republican patriots overburden the task of political association with a loaded language nostalgic for past virtues. Second, I contend that the ideal of constitutional patriotism is capable of fostering a civic bond of belonging among citizens as a result of their allegiance to a set of laws that they simultaneously author and are subject to – the constitution.

Finally, and perhaps more importantly, in this chapter I argue that the critical spirit of political theory demands that constitutional patriotism not be viewed merely as replacing one fixed identity (traditional) with another (postconventional). To know that speed, technology, and globalization have shortened distances, increased complexities, and enhanced diversities is not just to concede that particular loyalties can no longer serve as the ground of political association, but also to realize that any identity suitable for a political life needs to be as flexible as are its surrounding conditions. Habermas's doctrine of constitutional patriotism, then, should be read radically as allowing for a reflexive, plastic, and transient sense of belonging that is consistent with the increasing hybridity and pluralism of our modern world.

Chapter 1

The Unfinished Project of Modernity and the Heritage of Critical Theory

In the battle against the traditional power of church and state, enlightenment requires the courage to make use of one's own reason, that is, autonomy and maturity.

Jürgen Habermas

Today, questioning the project of modernity, in a general way, constitutes the postmodern discourse. Despite this critical attitude, however, the fate of the ideals of modernity has not yet been definitely decided by the new discourse. Indeed, the debate over the viability of modern ideals is still a very open and heated one, in which Jürgen Habermas is enthusiastically advocating the feasibility of the unfinished project of modernity. To understand Habermas's philosophical and political convictions we need to begin by probing his philosophical heritage, which consists of modernity's roots, the formulation of Enlightenment's ideals in the tradition of German Idealism, and the critical appraisal of these ideals by the first generation of the Frankfurt School. For this purpose, first, I will give a brief account of what constitutes the Enlightenment. The problem of modernity will be construed as the problem of the human subject's self-grounding or self-constitution after appeals to external authorities such as God, myth, and religion have been abandoned. Second, in addressing this problem, I will show how Kant's and Hegel's contribution give expression to the ideals of modernity as freedom and autonomy, or as the principles of 'subjectivity' and 'critique.' Third, I will discuss the reaction to, and appropriation of, these ideals, first by Marx and then by the early Frankfurt School, which constitute a critical theory that views the attainment of the Enlightenment's ideals as possible only through emancipation from the domination of instrumental rationality. Such an inquiry will demonstrate both Habermas's philosophical inspiration and political motivation in maintaining the project of modernity, and his ambition to defend this project against any and all criticism. This explanation, later on, will also serve to give a critical account of Habermas's own project, which, in turn, will allow us to see whether his later work is still in line with the original architectonic. I should like to state that the initial narrative of modernity will be given from a Habermasian perspective, and also that the philosophical concepts of German Idealism are not discussed for their own sake but only in relation to what they mean for Habermas's project. Hence, the detail and depth of the discussion remain closely relevant to providing a sketch of Habermas's historical and philosophical background.

1. The Ideals of the Enlightenment

The modern[1] era, from the Renaissance to the middle of the nineteenth century, marks a distinctive epoch. This era is characterized by a move away from traditional thinking centred on a transcendent divinity towards a subject-centred philosophy. Cartesian rationality hypostatizes this move via its notion of the *cogito* as the inward self-understanding of the human subject. The turn from divinity to humanity, from God to the self, from faith to reflective reason, leading to a philosophy of consciousness centred on the human subject, constitutes the background of the Enlightenment as an awakening from a long slumber. The rejection of traditional assumptions about religion, art, and science, however, gave rise to the issue of 'foundations' as the most immediate problem of modernity: 'Once so much is put in doubt (once the world is lost) on what basis can the human subject "re-establish" a connection with the actual world? On what basis or foundation can a true "science" of reality be built?'[2] Descartes's answer to this problem was that the certainty of the scientific method cannot but be a self-certainty. That is to say, the subject's certitude of his existence as a self, capable of thinking, served as the foundation of Descartes's method. This presuppositionless beginning that characterized the modern subject's historical independence from the past, however, did not solve the problem of self-grounding. The self-understanding of the subject seemed still to beg the question of legitimacy, since there was a circular reference between the subject as the knowing subject and the subject as the object of knowledge. The first expression of dissatisfaction with the legitimacy of the modern subject's self-understanding took the form of aesthetic experience (i.e., French romanticism).[3] 'In the fundamental experience of aesthetic modernity, the problem of self-grounding becomes acute, because here the horizon of the temporal experience contracts to the decentered subjectivity that splits away from the conventions of everyday life.'[4] The aesthetic experience of modernity can be seen in French romanticism questioning the classic models of ancient art and beauty and replacing their eternal and absolute norm of imitating the form with the norm of a historical and context-bound beauty as the self-understanding of the new epoch.

On a general level, the use of the word 'modernity' here refers to an abstract opposition between tradition and the present. Hence, there are two major aspects to the problem of modernity: (a) the relation between the past, the present, and the future; and (b) the relation of modernity to a foundation – the need of the modern subject to provide the norms for its self-grounding from the inside. To connect (a) to (b), that is to say, to fashion the normativity of one's contemporary epoch as independent from the past and the future, the notion of *critique* is deemed serviceable. The philosophical paradigm of modernity begins with Kant's attempt to address these two issues by way of giving a critique. In connection to our present purpose, then, asking who we are in this concrete moment in time, and giving a critical analysis of our social life that is aimed at emancipation, is also what defines the starting point of Habermas's theory.

2. The Notion of Critique

Kant emphasizes aspect (a) – the relation between one's present and one's past and future – by pointing out the importance of the present as one's historical standpoint that grounds the critique. In other words, he connects the here-and-now of the modern subject to the power of critical reason. This connection brings Kant to the second aspect of the problem of modernity, for it marks the self-constitution of the rational subject whose self-grounding support cannot exist outside of itself. In his noted essay 'Was ist Aufklärung?'[5] Kant is concerned with the following questions: How do human beings relate to their present? What characterizes their period? How does the difference dividing the present moment from the past affect their lives? And, finally, who are we as *Aufklärer*? As Foucault notes, these questions are fundamentally different from the Cartesian question Who am I?[6] Unlike Kant's *Aufklärer*, who is historically concrete, the Cartesian 'I' as universal and ahistorical can be anyone, anywhere, at anytime. Kant's historical question allows for a critical twist to traditional philosophy. By relying on the faculty of reason, which offers a critical analysis of one's present – as a different epoch from those before and after – one can assume responsibility for one's cognitive and reflective power as a rational subject. For the first time, with Kant, reason becomes critical. He calls this ability to give a critical account of one's present *maturity*. Maturity involves employing our cognitive powers so as to take charge of our actions and judgments instead of referring the responsibility to an external authority of tradition (such as God, myth, religion). '*Sapere aude!* "Have courage to use your own reason!" – that is the motto of enlightenment.'[7]

Kant argues further that to achieve maturity we first need to separate the realm of reason from that of faith; secondly, we need to distinguish between the public and private use of reason. There is, therefore, enlightenment when philosophy's task, which is to determine 'the conditions of possibility of experience,' is achieved, not on the basis of some rationalist a priori givens, but by the legitimate use of reason. In short, there is a mutual relation or interdependency between Enlightenment and critique – in the sense of taking charge of one's rationality to respond to one's time. In Foucault's words, 'The critique is, in a sense, a handbook of reason that has grown up in Enlightenment; and the Enlightenment is the age of critique.'[8] Critique, however, according to Kant, is only possible because of 'the first principle of modernity': freedom. 'But that the public should enlighten itself is more possible; indeed, if only freedom is granted, enlightenment is almost sure to follow.'[9]

Hence, it is freedom of thought that allows the learned intellectuals (*Gelehrte*) of the Enlightenment to be radically critical. It is not, however, long before their critique is aimed at Kant himself, charging that his use of reason is still dogmatic and not critical enough. Fichte argues that if we are absolutely free, then instead of finding ourselves to be subject to the law, we ourselves determine what laws of reason we are subject to. That is to say, for him rationality is not prior to free self-determination but rather enfolds it. Self-determination, as the primordial activity that is free, necessary and independent of any external force, accounts for the possibility of all experience.[10] The activity of self-determination is structured by reason. To posit and impose unquestioned Kantian logical forms and categories on one's life-experience, instead of being free self-determination, is a critical failure that Hegel calls 'positivity.'

Positivity, as the dogmatic and uncritical acceptance of a set of absolute rules, is used to characterize religion,[11] against which enlightened reason waged a war. 'Yet seen in a clear light the victory comes to no more than this: the positive element with which Reason busied itself to do battle, is no longer religion, and victorious Reason is no longer Reason.'[12] In referring whatever it cannot understand to a realm *beyond*, 'a faith outside and above itself,' reason becomes more a receptive faculty than a legislative one. That is why, according to Hegel, the philosophies of Kant, Jacobi, and Fichte turn reason into a new positivity: 'a positive knowledge of the finite and empirical.'[13] This new positivity manifests a dominating characteristic of reason in the self-relation of a subject with its object. The structure of the self-relation of the subject is what, according to Hegel, marks modern times: 'The principle of the modern world is freedom of subjectivity.'[14] The principle of subjectivity entails four aspects of the modern age: individualism, autonomy, right to criticism, and idealism.[15] Demonstrating these characteristics is supposed to allow the modern subject to escape any dogmatism, grounding itself as a self-legislative and self-creating subject. Hence, subjectivity, as the spirit of the modern age, need no longer seek its justification outside of itself; instead, 'it has to create its normativity out of itself.'[16] In Hegel's words, 'That the world is the product of the freedom of intelligence is the determinate and expressed principle of idealism.'[17]

For Hegel, however, the principle of subjectivity still falls short of resolving modernity's need for self-reassurance, since its creation of norms out of itself appears to be self-referential. The division – of human agent as both the subject and object of knowledge – that results from the self-reflection of the subject reveals the repressive character of the principle of subjectivity as objectification – that is, externalization of human action in terms of the subject–object relation. The inability of the principle of subjectivity to unify and account for the knowing subject's constitution and its critical reassurance leads to what Hegel calls the subject's 'self-estrangement.' To overcome this diremption, Hegel attempted to work out a reconciling concept of reason that removes positivity. For him the origin of the objective world can be seen in the subject's activity of knowing, which suggests that there is a unity between subject and object. The gap between subject and object, and all other dualisms, is supposed to be overcome in Hegel's speculative notion of the World Spirit, *Zeitgeist*.

In order to overcome self-estrangement, and also to reconcile the opposite aspects of the modern subject as both knowing subject and empirical object, Hegel resorts to enlightened reason as the Absolute. In the concept of *Zeitgeist* the self-consciousness of intelligent human subjects is absolutized. Such an absolutization distinguishes the knowledge of the finite subject from the infinite. The Absolute Spirit's knowledge of itself – through knowing the world – overcomes all positivity and the dualisms of dogmatic thinking. However, such an all-encompassing appeal to absolute reason risks losing the critical aspect of our principle of subjectivity. That is to say, in Habermas's words,

> [A]s absolute knowledge, reason assumes a form so overwhelming that it not only solves the initial problem of a self-reassurance of modernity, but solves it *too well*. The question about the genuine self-understanding of modernity gets lost in reason's ironic laughter. For reason has now taken over the place of fate and knows that every event of essential significance has *already* been decided. Thus Hegel's philosophy satisfied the need of modernity for self-grounding only at the cost of devaluing present-day reality and blunting critique.[18]

Thus, after replacing the authority of myth, religion, and morality, reason itself has become a totality, losing its emancipatory character. The totalizing tendency of reason, as a new positive system, is what invites the radical critique of reason and its ideals of progress and emancipation, first by Nietzsche and Heidegger and later by the first generation of the Frankfurt School. In order to understand the orientation of the Frankfurt School, however, we need to mention briefly Marx's appropriation of Hegel. We can sum up the lesson of this section in the following way: the insight of Kant and Hegel that Habermas preserves in constructing his critical theory is the viability of the principles of maturity and subjectivity for the ideal of rational society. That is to say, the ideals of assuming responsibility for one's critical ability and the anti-dogmatic freedom and autonomy of one's self-creation fill in the concept of reason that Habermas obtains from Kant and Hegel. In their teachings, 'Reason is equated unquestionably with the talent for autonomy and responsibility and with sensitivity to the evils of this world. It has long since made its decision in favor of justice, welfare, and peace; the reason that resists dogmatism is a committed reason.'[19]

3. The Pessimism of the Early Frankfurt School

Having inherited the Enlightenment's ideal of progress and emancipation from Hegel, Marx attempts to provide an answer to modernity's problem of self-grounding by turning Hegel's philosophy upside down. Like Hegel, Marx too maintains that history is a dialectic. Unlike Hegel, however, he does not believe it is a dialectic of ideas, but rather a dialectic of classes. The French revolution crystallized the ideal of emancipation that was the promise of the class struggle as the genuine driving force of history. The new class of the bourgeoisie promised a reconstruction of society and liberation from the oppression of the aristocracy. According to Marx, however, 'This class emancipates all of society, but only on the condition that all of society is in the same position as this class, e.g., that it has money and education or can easily acquire them.'[20] In other words, members of the bourgeoisie only emancipated themselves and now were dominating a new oppressed class, the proletariat. For Marx, it is the material relations of production between the dominating and dominated class that map the road to a classless, and hence free, society. Moreover, since 'it is not the consciousness of men that determines their being but their being that determines their consciousness,'[21] modernity's principle of absolute freedom changes its focus with Marx from freedom of ideas to an objective freedom in a classless society. It is the task of philosophy to achieve that end by discovering and encouraging the objective (scientific) principles of historical materialism, which anticipate how progress will unfold. The objective of the theory of historical materialism, like any good science, 'is not to interpret the world, but to change it,'[22] whereby the dialectic of class struggle is converted into a revolutionary praxis (ibid., thesis III). However, like other philosophies of modernity, and in light of its emphasis on a predetermined path of historical class antagonism, Marx's theory, too, soon proved to be a closed philosophical system with totalitarian tendencies.

After the First World War the intellectuals who inherited the tradition of German Idealism were faced with the task of re-examining the project of modernity and, in particular, the Marxist proposal for revolutionary struggle that changed the political map of Europe at that time. The most crucial task was to re-evaluate the relation between theory and practice. In Marxist literature, this relation was referred to as 'praxis' and connoted what the term 'maturity' did for Kant. 'Loosely defined, *praxis* was used to designate a kind of self-creating action, which differed from the externally motivated behavior produced by forces outside man's control. Although originally seen as the opposite of contemplative *theoria* when it was first used in Aristotle's *Metaphysics*, *praxis* in the Marxist usage was seen in dialectical relation to theory. In fact one of the earmarks of *praxis* as opposed to mere action was its being informed by theoretical considerations.'[23] The goal of revolutionary activity was to bring *theoria* and *praxis* together. The dogmatic demands by political parties to keep everyone within the orthodoxy were not serving this goal. Hence, the need for theoretical innovation and independence was made concrete in the founding of the Institut für Sozialforschung (Institute for Social Research) at Frankfurt University. Among the many names that contributed to the life of the Institute the names of Max Horkheimer, Theodor Adorno, and Herbert Marcuse resonate most strongly because of their prominent impact on the social and political theories that followed in the second half of the twentieth century. Critical Theory's main catalyst was its revolutionary perspective of providing a radical critique of dominant conditions.

Philosophers of the Frankfurt School inherited the critical theory of German Idealism at a time when the ideals of Kant's liberalism, Hegel's idealism, and most recently Marx's materialism were faced with severe scepticism as a result of the bleak socio-political reality. Unlike the time of the early critical theorists, when it was hoped the proletariat would be a revolutionary force, by the time of the Second World War the proletariat increasingly began to show signs of integration into society. Martin Jay, in his history of the Frankfurt School, concludes from this fact that '[i]t might be said of the first generation of critical theorists in the 1840's that theirs was an "immanent" critique of society based on the existence of a real historical "subject." By the time of its renaissance in the twentieth century, Critical Theory was being increasingly forced into a position of "transcendence" by the withering of the revolutionary working class.'[24]

Keeping within the humanist tradition of German culture, Horkheimer and Adorno did not view their philosophy as an independent *Wissenschaft* (science) that aimed to discover perpetual truths but as a materialist theory that would bring to bear the methods of empirical social research. The use of empirical methods encouraged an interdisciplinary approach[25] to the various projects of the Institute. Statistics, polls, and questionnaires issued in the service of sociological, economical, and psychological interpretations and analyses soon suggested that socio-political events were not shaping up in the way Marx had predicted. The Institute was initially reluctant to use the orthodox Marxist theoretical tools, such as the concepts of revolution and class, to prove the historical determinism of the Marxist view. But after the National Socialists came to power in Germany, this initial reluctance deteriorated into a downright scepticism of any all-encompassing system of justice and emancipation such as Marx's and Hegel's. Against the totalizing tendencies of these systems to uncover the 'immutable truth,' Horkheimer argued that the image of complete justice 'can never be realized in history because even when a better society replaces the present disorder and is developed, past misery would not be made good and the suffering of surrounding nature not transcended.'[26] Consequently, 'philosophy as [Horkheimer] understood it always expresses an unavoidable note of sadness, but without succumbing to resignation.'[27]

This critical attitude was based on the Enlightenment's faith that rationality was at the base of any social progress. Recalling Hegel's distinction between *Verstand* (understanding) and *Vernunft* (reason), Horkheimer wanted to restore the primacy of the role of reason in any social progressive theory. Critical Theory's appeal to *Vernunft* was still within the Hegelian horizon of reconciliation of social and political contradictions. But Horkheimer radicalized Hegel's notion of critique by giving it a materialist interpretation. Arguing that the realization of progress depends on the activity of historical subjects, he relinquished the theologically derived idea of ensured progress. Furthermore, abandoning the idea of universal history, he embraced a more limited view of history that was time-bound and culture-dependent. According to this materialistic twist, then, we can say that *critical theory*, for Horkheimer, was a theory of the modern epoch that was oriented towards the future via an interest in reaching a rational society where humanity attained emancipation. Real freedom would be achieved only in a rationally organized society. In Marcuse's words, 'We know that freedom is an eminently political concept. Real freedom for individual existence (and not merely in the liberal sense) is possible only in a specifically structured polis, a "rationally" organized society.'[28] The faith in the possibility of a free society and the belief that such a political endeavour necessarily has a rational character are convictions that later would resonate strongly in Habermas's project.

Critical Theory's faithfulness to the questions of social justice and truth marked its loyalty to the ideals of modernity: true society (democracy) is achieved when enlightened subjects follow their own reason. So, unlike Weber, the founders of Critical Theory refused to accept capitalist society as the highest socio-economic formation,[29] precisely because it lacked any rational socio-economic plan. The Frankfurt School philosophers argued that while society is ultimately the result of human activity, at the same time it prescribes the limits of this activity. In

Horkheimer's words, critical theory 'considers the overall framework which is conditioned by the blind interaction of individual activities ... to be a function that originates in human action and therefore is a possible object of planful decision and rational determination of goals.'[30] Indeed, Marcuse went so far as to argue that '[t]he turn from the liberalist to the total-authoritarian state occurs within the framework of a single social order. With regard to the unity of this economic base, we can say it is liberalism that "produces" the total-authoritarian state out of itself, as its own consumption at a more advanced stage of development.'[31]

The events of the Second World War made the viability of the initial project of the Frankfurt School, which was to mediate between critical theory and revolutionary practice via empirical research and political praxis, even more doubtful than before. The post-war reality demanded a new theoretical response that for the School could not but be bleak. Indeed, its major publications after the war, such as *Dialectic of Enlightenment*, *Eclipse of Reason*, and *Minima Moralia*, presented a severe critique of modernity that destroyed any hope in the idea of progressive rationality. As Horkheimer wrote in the preface to the *Eclipse of Reason*, 'progressive rationalization tends ... to obliterate that very substance of reason in the name of which this progress is espoused.'[32] Hegel's system, which conceived of human history as progressive, was perhaps the foremost expression of such rationalizing systems. Against the optimism of this system, which claimed that 'the truth is the whole,' Adorno, in an aphorism entitled 'Dwarf fruit,' replied, 'The whole is the untrue.'[33] The engine of history is neither Hegel's dialectic of the Concept nor Marx's dialectic of classes. The real conflict that has led to the crisis of Western society lies somewhere else: man's alienation from nature.

In its post-war analyses, the Frankfurt School shifted its focus concerning the conflict so as to replace the orthodox concept of class conflict with an enlarged one. The range of the conflict was now seen to extend beyond capitalism and to explain the totalitarian tendencies of instrumental rationality. In Horkheimer's words: 'The human being, in the process of his emancipation, shares the fate of the rest of his world. Domination of nature involves domination of man. Each subject not only has to take part in the subjugation of external nature, human and nonhuman, but in order to do so must subjugate nature in himself. Domination becomes "internalized" for domination's sake.'[34] For Horkheimer, then, the Enlightenment's notion of nature as the object of manipulation was connected to the idea of political domination that separated human beings as both objects and subjects of domination. Reason was in eclipse. According to *Dialectic of Enlightenment*, the major collaboration of Horkheimer and Adorno, the prognosis of the modern age was an unpromising one, for the crisis of Western civilization, as crystallized in human alienation from nature, appeared to be insoluble. The optimism of Christianity, of idealism, and of materialism was rejected as illusory.[35] 'Hope for better circumstances – if it is not mere illusion – is not so much based on the assurance that these circumstances would be guaranteed, durable, and final, but on the lack of respect for all that is so firmly rooted in the general suffering.'[36]

Perhaps the only factor that prevented Horkheimer and Adorno from complete resignation, despite their overwhelmingly pessimistic view, was their faith in *Vernunft* as being capable of reconciling the opposition between man and nature. They never, however, attempted to devise a use of reason that could address this crisis. In fact, the Frankfurt School viewed any attempt at achieving the project of modernity as instrumentalization. They were suspicious that any instrumental, subjective, and coercive use of reason was in the service of the dominant means of production devoted to the interests of control and manipulation. This despairing view colours the first generation of the Frankfurt School's treatment of modernity and its ideals. And it is this view that concerns the School's notable second-generation thinker, Jürgen Habermas, and calls forth his orientation towards restoring faith in the Enlightenment's project. Against such a background in the 1950s, Habermas defines his original problem as 'a theory of modernity, a theory of the pathology of modernity, from the view-point of the rationalization – the deformed rationalization – of reason in history.'[37] This would suggest that, agreeing with Nietzsche in this rare case, Habermas accepts that the project of modernity in its original formulation by the philosophy of consciousness is doomed, and requires that the idea of subject-centred reason be reconstructed and rehabilitated by way of a communicative rationality that attributes an emancipating character to language. The subject/object dualism of the philosophy of consciousness that leads to an instrumental understanding of reason needs to be reconstructed along the lines of a philosophy of intersubjectivity. Habermas believes that such a paradigm shift from the philosophy of consciousness to the philosophy of language will successfully address modernity's problem of self-grounding vis-à-vis a critical social theory based on communicative action. By attributing an emancipatory character to the communicative competence that is constitutive of the rational subject, Habermas rejects the claim that the sole mode of rationalization is an instrumental one. The next chapter will explicate in detail Habermas's theory of communicative rationality, which is aimed not only at providing an account of how human subjects are constituted within the space of their symbolic interaction, but also at showing how the process of deformed intersubjectivity can be diagnosed and remedied by an appeal to the emancipatory ideals inherent in the linguistic core of human interaction.

Chapter 2

Communicative Action Theory and the Rational Reconstruction of Linguistic Interaction

Being, in so far as it can be understood, is speech.

Hans-Georg Gadamer, *Wahrheit und Methode* (1965), xxxiv

The preceding discussion reveals that Habermas sees his philosophical project as situated within the Enlightenment tradition. Still, he conceives the Enlightenment as an incomplete project whose ideals are yet to be realized. Drawing on Kant and Hegel, he too believes that in order to achieve *maturity* and *freedom* the enlightened subject needs to become self-reflective so as to provide its normativity out of itself: *the ideal of grounding or foundation.* And like Marx, Habermas believes that the task of philosophy is to give a critique of one's time so as to allow for the reconstruction of society to overcome domination: the ideal of emancipation. Working as Adorno's assistant, he witnesses how the Frankfurt School devises Critical Theory as a response to the challenge of this task. Habermas inherits Horkheimer's and Adorno's faith in the role of *Vernunft* to rationally reconstruct a true society. However, he parts company with them when they abandon hope in progressive rationality and view all use of reason as instrumental and in the service of technological domination. Given the ideals of grounding and emancipation, the problem of modernity, for Habermas, consists in yielding *a critical account of the possibility of unconstrained communication that would make the self-constitution of modern subjects as social and moral agents possible.*

The aim of the present discussion is to mark where Habermas's approach branches off from that taken by the Frankfurt School, and to lay down and explicate his appropriation of the problem of modernity in terms of an intersubjective rationality. As such, the thrust of this chapter is more explanatory than argumentative. In what follows I will first discuss some of Habermas's earlier works that share with the Frankfurt School a commitment to social justice and an anti-positivistic aim. Then his departure from the conclusions of the Frankfurt School will be examined in view of his linguistic turn, which, in addition to instrumental reason, allows for another mode of rationality, *communicative rationality*. It will be made plain that, according to Habermas, the linguistic turn and the theory of communicative rationality reveal the emancipatory character of language. In view of this recognition of the emancipatory potential of linguistic communication, Habermas reformulates the problem of modernity, providing an account of modern subjects' self-constitution that is based on the critical analysis of communicative interaction. Finally, the architectonic of both communicative action theory and discourse ethics will be reconstructed in view of Habermas's ambition of solving modernity's problem.

1. Critique of Positivism and the Linguistic Turn

In the twentieth century many philosophers have been forced to re-examine the power and limitation of reason because of the severe attack on the rationality of cultural modernism. The dualism of subject/object at the core of the philosophy of consciousness amounted to an unsatisfactory and limited version of reason that could only be instrumentally conceived. Habermas initially sees his project as an attempt to present a more comprehensive conception of reason that is intersubjectively established and, as such, allows for a critical social theory with the added practical goal of emancipation from domination. The self-reflection and self-understanding that are the integral parts of this theory are undermined by positivism's one-sided emphasis on pure reason and pure facts as independent from the knowing subject's socio-cultural life context. Therefore, Habermas's attempt to re-evaluate the conception of reason and rationality is primarily realized as a critique of positivism. Like Horkheimer and Adorno before him, he sets out to show how scientific research is closely related to the world of conflicting social interest. Against the positivistic claim that the validity of scientific knowledge is independent of any normative presupposition, Habermas argues that knowledge is historically rooted and interest-bound.

Investigation of the relation between knowledge and human activities and interests is what motivates one of Habermas's earliest works,

Knowledge and Human Interest.[1] There, he acknowledges the fact that positivism began as a scientific response to all ideological dogma, be it religious, metaphysical, or otherwise. But this emphasis on scientism is taken to the extreme when 'we no longer understand science as *one* form of possible knowledge, but rather identify knowledge with science.'[2] Against this view of science, Habermas proposes a theory of 'knowledge-constitutive interest,' in which the validity of scientific claims is inseparably tied to human interests. These knowledge-guiding interests are the ground upon which reality is revealed and appropriated. For him to argue that there is a basis of interests in the formation of human knowledge implies an understanding of the knowing subject as (a) capable of using tools, (b) capable of using language, and (c) capable of employing reason. From this understanding of the human subject he respectively infers three non-reducible cognitive interests: the technical, the practical, and the emancipatory. He writes: 'The approach to the empirical-analytic sciences incorporates a *technical* cognitive interest; that of the historical-hermeneutic science incorporates a *practical* one; and the approach of critically oriented sciences incorporates the *emancipatory* cognitive interest.'[3] These knowledge-constitutive interests are rooted in three different dimensions of our social life: work, power, and language.

At the time, Habermas believed that the arguments of *Knowledge and Human Interest* could be epistemologically grounded. Such an ambition, however, invited the charge of foundationalism. Thus, he shifted his focus from epistemology to a theory of language in order to avoid this charge levelled against his critique of positivism.[4] The critique of scientism is then formulated in terms of what his colleague Karl-Otto Apel calls the 'a priori of communication' – as the other aspect of rationality missing in positivism's understanding of science. That is to say, science cannot be understood merely in terms of an abstract system of formal rules, but must be viewed also as a product of human interaction and language. It is here that Habermas's attention comes to focus on a theory of language as the motive and context of human activity. 'What raises us out of nature is the only thing whose nature we can know: *language*. Through its structure, autonomy and responsibility are posited for us. Our first sentence expresses unequivocally the intention of universal and unconstrained consensus. Taken together, autonomy and responsibility constitute the only Idea that we possess a priori in the sense of the philosophical tradition.'[5]

The language of a community constitutes tradition as the context of human activity. Consequently, Habermas endorses Gadamer's critique of positivism in which he claims that the concept of a neutral and independent observer is a myth. For Habermas also believes that understanding (*Verstehen*) requires the mediation of tradition. But he is critical of Gadamer's dogmatic acceptance of tradition, arguing that language, in addition to being the matrix of our activities, also contains relationships of coercion and domination. That is why he contends that to understand fully human social interaction we need a theory that is 'constituted conjointly by language, labour and domination.'[6] Habermas views language as a universal medium in which our social life unfolds. Thus, he believes that any critical social analysis should be grounded in a theory of language.[7] He sees formal capacities required for our emancipation inherent in language. With such a promise, he turns his attention to developing a theory of linguistic interaction.

In contributing to the development of this theory, Habermas's linguistic turn makes the tripartite knowledge–constitutive interests (technical, practical, and emancipatory) correspond to a tripartite symbolic interaction (instrumental, strategic, and communicative). The technical interest, which aims at the production of technically exploitable knowledge, is parallel to instrumental action, while the practical interest, which aims at the clarification of practically effective knowledge, is associated with communicative action. Instrumental and strategic interactions both aim at success, but in different domains. The former needs a non-social context or objective realm (technical), while the latter takes place in a social domain. Finally, the emancipatory interest, which Habermas describes as seeking to reach understanding in the form of rational consensus among social agents, also corresponds to communicative action. In order to recover communicative action from other social interactions Habermas re-evaluates the concept of praxis.

Following Marx and his own predecessors in the Frankfurt School, Habermas considers practice or *sensuous human activity* as the groundwork of his critical theory. However, unlike Marx and the Frankfurt School, he does not view practice primarily as instrumental action or human labour, but rather as symbolic interaction within language. Habermas argues: 'Marx does not actually explicate the interrelationship of interaction and labour, but instead, under the unspecific title of social praxis, reduces the one to the other, namely communicative action to instrumental action.'[8] It should be noted, however, that the proposed dichotomy between work and interaction used to criticize Marx has provoked enthusiastic responses from Marxist theorists. For example, Anthony Giddens has questioned the fruitfulness of breaking the unity of Marx's concept of praxis into two elements, work and interaction. More importantly, he charges that Habermas's theory of communicative action is too strongly centred on language and normativity at the expense of adequate attention to the conditions of production and reproduction of society.[9] In respect to the first objection, as Hans Joas and Thomas McCarthy have pointed out,[10] Habermas's labour/interaction distinction serves to call attention to a fundamental difference regarding the actor's attitude and orientations in social and non-social situations. As for the second objection, this distinction also later allows for a further differentiation between the 'lifeworld' and the 'system' that enables Habermas to account for the material and social processes of reproduction of society. I will return to the system/lifeworld distinction in chapter 4. Perhaps a more serious critique is that of Axel Honneth, who charges that Habermas's work/interaction distinction is insensitive to a kind of 'practical rationality' that coincides neither with that of communicative action nor with the logic of instrumental action.[11] He gives the example of workers' resistance to the external pressure of rationalization of the workplace (e.g., Taylorism). While it is clear that Habermas introduces the distinction in order to revive communicative action as the neglected aspect of praxis in Marx, the categories of instrumental and strategic action do not seem to completely recover the concept of work. Honneth concludes: 'The formulation of historical materialism upon communication theory has at least the advantage of diverting attention to the structures of an evolutionary process of communicative liberation which is no longer attributable to a specific class. But its categorical weakness, as I see it, is that its basic concepts are laid out from the beginning as though the progress of liberation from alienated work relations, which Marx had had in mind, were already historically complete.'[12]

Habermas, however, believes that for the purpose of developing a critical theory of society it is important that we distinguish between different dimensions of social interaction. The interconnection of human interactions is understood only when their boundaries are drawn explicitly. Habermas contends that in their examination of human practice, both Marx and the Frankfurt School philosophers universalize the role of instrumental reason, reducing the notion of praxis to *techne* or technical action. Thus, since the problem for the Frankfurt School philosophers is with the domination of instrumental or purposive rationality, they see the solution to be a radical break with the domination of purposive rational action. Habermas, however, believes that we can utilize technical knowledge with its claims to empirical truths for the maintenance of social systems without privileging or universalizing it over other forms of rationality. 'If Marx had not thrown together inter-action and work under the label of social practice (*praxis*), and had he instead related the materialist concept of synthesis likewise to the ac-complishment of instrumental action and the nexuses of communica-tive action then the idea of science of man would not have been obscured by identification with natural science.'[13] This means that, for Habermas, '[a]lthough [Marx] himself established the science of man in the form of critique and not as natural science, he continually tended to classify it with natural sciences.'[14] Thus, against this one-sided emphasis on in-strumental action Habermas proposes to split Marx's notion of sensu-ous human activity into two separate actions: work, or purposive action, and symbolic interaction, or communicative action. The rationalization of the former is aimed at success, augmentation of the productive forces, and technical control as in instrumental action. He writes: 'By *work* or *purposive-rational action* I understand either instrumental action or rational choice or their conjunction. Instrumental action is governed by technical rules based on empirical knowledge.'[15] The rationalization of social interaction, by contrast, is aimed at consensual communication free from domination. Indeed all speech, Habermas claims, is oriented toward the idea of consensus.[16] He explains: 'By "interaction," on the other hand, I understand *communicative action*, symbolic interaction. It is governed by binding *consensual norm*, which defines reciprocal ex-pectations about behaviour and which must be understood and rec-ognized by at least two acting subjects.'[17] Habermas's shift towards a philosophy of language is, therefore, inspired by the promise of an emancipatory concept of reason latent in our linguistic interaction. In formulating a theory of communicative action, he first wants to clarify the nature of his theory.

At the end of *Knowledge and Human Interest* Habermas notes that his emphasis on the importance of self-reflection as a necessary part of critique that will anticipate freedom needs to be refined, since the concept can connote more than one self-constituting activity. So, in his postscript he distinguishes between two modes of reflection: *rational reconstruction* and *self-reflection* or *self-criticism*.[18] A rational reconstruc-tion is aimed at explaining the rules in different areas of human compe-tency, which means that the reconstruction depends on reflection though the reflection itself is not dependent on a specific subject. Habermas's plan is to 'reconstruct the possible condition of human understanding,' which is the aim of communicative action.[19] His theory, therefore, would take the form of a reconstructive science that differs from ordinary sciences in being a blend of empirical scientific investigation and philosophical generalization aimed at uncovering the universal basis of human action.[20] To put it differently, in the domain of human sciences reconstruction means 'taking a theory apart and putting it back together again in a new form, in order to attain more fully the goal that it has set for itself.'[21] Habermas employs such an approach to construct a theory of communicative interaction that intends to reveal a more comprehensible concept of reason for the purpose of formulating a critical social theory.

2. Communicative Rationality and Moral Discourse

It is not until 1981 that Habermas fully develops his theory in a two-volume text entitled *The Theory of Communicative Action*. The task of the book is to present a social and critical theory of rationality. Habermas introduces the concept of 'communicative rationality' as the link between rationalist philosophy and social theory. That is, communicative rationality connects the appeal to critical reason with social intersubjectivity, allowing him to go beyond subject-centred reason. He contends that in language our practical interests reveal a level of intersubjectivity, which allows us to communicate and become social-cultural agents. That is, since in communicative interaction we can examine validity claims of a socio-cultural nature through reflective argumentation, then 'through this connection with cultural tradition and social institutions the concept of communicative action becomes serviceable for social theory.'[22] Communicative action is presented as embodying a form of rationality that is basic to our social interaction. Habermas believes that modernity's 'philosophy of the subject' needs to be linked with the social sense of rationality. That is to say, the monological character of the philosophy of the subject, which could not support the self-grounding of the knowing subject – because it was self-referential – needs to be replaced by the dialogical character of social life, whereby the problem of self-referentiality is resolved. The reconciliation of the mediated subject via the structure of intersubjectivity takes the form of language or communicative interaction, which Habermas believes offers a way out of subject-centred reason. He contends that within the confines of language our practical interest communicatively achieves intersubjectivity. The theory of language, which was deemed the ground of social theory at the beginning of the linguistic turn, now needs to be complemented by a theory of action. Habermas suggests that by studying human language and human action we can formulate a theory of communicative action that, as a social theory, can give us a means for normative judgment that guarantees universal validity while remaining critical. The insight of such a theory, then, can be applied to the moral and practical dimension of our lives.

Universal Pragmatics

In turning his attention to the study of everyday language, Habermas recognizes the importance of analytic philosophy as a starting point. He writes: 'Analytic philosophy, with the theory of meaning at its core, does offer a promising point of departure for a theory of communicative action that places understanding in language, as a medium for coordinating actions, as the focal point of interest.'[23] Before turning to a discussion of Habermas's appropriation of the insight of analytic philosophy, however, it is important to note that he begins by opposing the widely accepted formal separation of language as an abstract knowledge from speech as its practical use. The pure linguistic separation of language from speech, which starts with Saussure and is repeated and reinforced in Chomsky as competence and performance, rests on the idea that the competence of the ideal speaker can be reconstructed in a formal manner through linguistic analysis of phonetics, syntax, and semantics. Habermas finds this separation of *langue* (competence) and *parole* (performance), in terms of the analysis of the meaning, unacceptable. He maintains that 'linguistic competence' includes not only formal aspects relating to phonetics, syntax, and semantics but also communicative or pragmatic competence as well. He explains:

> The separation of the two analytic levels, language and speech, should not be made in such a way that the pragmatic dimension of language is left to exclusively empirical analysis – that is, to empirical sciences such as psycholinguistics and sociolinguistics. I would defend the thesis that not only language but speech too – that is, the employment of sentences in utterances – is accessible to formal analysis. Like the elementary units of language (sentences), the elementary units of speech (utterances) can be analyzed in the methodological attitude of a reconstructive science.[24]

In other words, for a phrase to be meaningfully rendered, we need not only to consider its formal aspects as a sentence, but also to know its pragmatic meaning as an utterance. The formal and pragmatic competences together constitute *communicative competence*:

> By 'communicative competence' I understand the ability of a speaker oriented to mutual understanding to embed a well-formed sentence in relation to reality, that is:
> 1. To choose the propositional sentence in such a way that either the truth conditions of the proposition stated or the existential presuppositions of the propositional content mentioned are supposedly fulfilled (so that the hearer can share the knowledge of the speaker);
> 2. To express his intentions in such a way that the linguistic expression represents what is intended (so that the hearer can trust the speaker);
> 3. To perform the speech act in such a way that it conforms to recognized norms or to accepted self-images (so that the hearer can be in accord with the speaker in shared value orientations).[25]

A speaker's communicative competence is made up of three minor competences: cognitive competence, speech competence, and interactive competence. Briefly, the first is the knowledge of formal and logical structure, the second is abstract linguistic knowledge, and the third is the mastery of participating in social interaction.

This communicative competence is a part of Habermas's *universal pragmatics* theory, which is inspired by Austin and Searle, whose 'theory of speech acts marks the first step toward a formal pragmatics that extends to noncognitive modes of employment.'[26] Habermas's universal pragmatics is supposed to capture the universal and necessary conditions under which utterances are formed and used in interaction. 'In the present context, the main advantage of a formal pragmatics is that it highlights, in the pure types of linguistically mediated interaction, precisely those aspects under which social actions embody different sorts of knowledge.'[27] The theory of universal pragmatics thematizes the basic units of speech in the same way that linguistic does sentences as the units of language. Recognizing speech acts as the primary units of linguistic communication, Habermas describes the task of universal pragmatics as the reconstruction of the general structure of speech acts. This formulation of the universal communicative competence of human beings involved in speech acts is what Habermas calls the 'reconstruction of universal competence.' Thomas McCarthy explains this phrase as follows:

Like Kant's transcendental philosophy, universal pragmatics aims at disclosing conditions of possibility, but the focus shifts from the possibility of experiencing objects to the possibility of reaching understanding in ordinary language communication. Moreover the strong a priorism of the Kantian project (the transcendental deduction) is surrendered in favour of a 'relativized a priori,' one that recognizes empirical boundary conditions, the phylogenetic and ontogenetic development of universal structures, and the structural interconnection of experience and action. Kant drew a sharp distinction between transcendental and empirical analysis. Rational reconstruction, by contrast, is dependent on a posteriori knowledge.[28]

Habermas claims that the aim of Kantian transcendental philosophy is to build 'reconstructive sciences' as opposed to empirical-analytic sciences. Reconstructive sciences rise to the level of reflection that is pre-theoretical, formal, and innate knowledge of the deep structures informing our cognitive ability. They are concerned with communicative experience or understanding, while empirical-analytic sciences are concerned with sensory experience or observation. Habermas explains:

> The tolerant sense in which I understand formal analysis can best be characterised through the methodological attitude we adopt in rational reconstruction of concepts, criteria, rules, and schemata ... [R]econstructive procedures are not characteristic of sciences that develop nomological hypotheses about domains of observable events; rather, these procedures are characteristic of *sciences that systematically reconstruct the intuitive knowledge of competent subjects.*[29]

Thus, we can say that the knowledge of 'reconstructive sciences' is 'knowing how' as opposed to normal sciences' empirical knowledge of 'knowing that.' Austin's and Searle's works in universal pragmatics, Chomsky's work in generative grammar, and Kohlberg's and Piaget's work in developmental psychology are examples of the 'reconstructive sciences' in which Habermas is interested.

A Theory of Types of Linguistic Interaction

Focusing on speech acts, Habermas reformulates his earlier distinction between purposive and communicative rationality in terms of different uses of language. He distinguishes between a communicative use of

language aimed at attaining common objectives through mutual understanding, and a language use that aims at producing success, and as
such has strategic motives. Communicative speech, for him, has primacy over strategic language use because he sees the former to be 'the
inherent telos of human speech.'[30] Again, looking at Austin's work in
formal pragmatics, Habermas initially finds the distinction between
illocutionary act – doing something by saying something – and perlocutionary act – producing certain effects by saying something – to be
reflective of the communicative/strategic action distinction.[31]

Like the work/interaction distinction, Habermas's typology of communicative and strategic action has attracted important critical reaction. Jonathan Culler, among others, has argued that Habermas's attempt
to attribute to communicative action an 'originary' priority over the
'parasitic' strategic action is an unconvincing move, since it is based on
the problematic analogy between the illocutionary/perlocutionary and
communicative/strategic distinctions.[32] Erling Skjei, too, questions
Habermas's distinction as it applies to perlocutions and illocutions,
arguing that if the distinguishing feature of perlocutions, according to
Habermas, is their unavowed or strategic intention, then the distinction
seems to be more intentional than formal concerning the types of speech
acts.[33] In connection with this unavowed feature of perlocutions, Allen
Wood argues that generally it is false to say that in order for perlocutions
to work they need to be concealed; hence latency or covertness of
strategic action is not the demarcation criterion of perlocutions.[34] Yet
perhaps the most cogent attempt at critical reconstruction of Habermas's
communicative/strategic distinction is presented by James Bohman,
who attempts to respond to the above criticism by arguing that
Habermas's distinction should not be seen as essentialist and real, the
way Habermas himself presents it, but as an analytic distinction that
allows overlapping areas between the two types of interaction. Otherwise the distinction would deny the theory's emancipatory character as
a critical social theory. He explains: 'I want to show that the strong
distinction Habermas wants to make creates difficulty for understanding the sort of activity he uses speech act theory to describe and justify:
that of the social critic. I shall argue that, as emancipator, the social critic
performs speech acts that are neither strictly perlocutions nor illocutions,
but an important hybrid type that Habermas' "real distinction" dis-
allows. This hybrid I shall term "emancipatory speech."'[35] Instead of
separating perlocutionary and illocutionary acts as two pure types that
are in contrast to each other like two branches on a tree diagram,

Bohman proposes that we view them as different circles that overlap and allow for speech acts that combine features of both. Emancipatory speech, the act of the social critic, is a perlocutionary act with communicative aims; 'it is of this class that we can say that success is equivalent to understanding.'[36] However, Habermas himself seems to realize that the respective mirroring of the communicative/strategic versus illocutionary/perlocutionary is too strong and needs to be weakened. He admits that there are perlocutionary effects that are not strategic and need not conceal their intentions, while there are illocutionary acts that are strategic.[37]

In connection with the rational reconstruction of linguistic interaction, Habermas proceeds to classify the speech acts according to their produced illocutionary effect. He contends that utterances manifest the relation of sentences as pure linguistic units to three other realms: the external world, the inner world, and the normative or social world. This suggests that to engage in a speech act, besides the formal linguistic claim to comprehensibility, one is making three kinds of 'validity claims': to truth, to truthfulness, and to rightness. 'A validity claim is equivalent to the assertion that the conditions for the validity of an utterance are fulfilled.'[38] That is to say, an utterance (a) has to be *well formed* (grammatically) as a sentence, (b) has to make a *correct* statement about the external world, (c) has to express *truthfully* the speaker's belief and desire that reflect their inner world, and (d) has to raise the *right* claim with respect to the normative world. It is under these conditions that a speech act is recognized by a hearer as raising validity claims.[39] The pragmatic functions of the last three validity claims correspond to what Habermas calls a 'commonly supposed system of worlds.' There is a relation between each validity claim and its corresponding reality or world. The pragmatic function of a claim to truth is raised in relation to the objective world. This constitutes a representative relation (science). The claim to truthfulness in a speech act is raised in relation to one's inner world.[40] This constitutes an expressive relation (art). Finally, the pragmatic function of a speech act, whose validity claim is to rightness, is connected to the social world and, as such, constitutes an interactive relation (morality). These relations are concerned with the analysis of the universal and necessary conditions for the validity claims raised in their respective worlds that allows Habermas to distinguish four models of action.

In the teleological model of action, language is oriented toward the achievement of success. Habermas talks about strategic action when the domain is social, and when the domain is non-social (nature), he speaks of instrumental action under the teleological model of action.[41] In the normative model, language is 'a consensus that is merely reproduced with each additional act of understanding.'[42] The dramaturgical model of action embodies a view of language as oriented toward self-expression. These models of action, Habermas tells us, are one-sided in that they only emphasize one dimension of the relation of the agent to the world; 'in each case only one function of language is thematized: the release of perlocutionary effects, the establishment of interpersonal relations, and the expression of subjective experience.'[43] However, in the fourth model of action, communicative action, all these functions are brought together. Habermas explains: 'Only the communicative model of action presupposes language as a medium of uncurtailed communication whereby speakers and hearers, out of the context of their preinterpreted lifeworld, refer simultaneously to things in the objective, social, and subjective world in order to negotiate common definitions of the situation. This interpretive concept of language lies behind the various efforts to develop a formal pragmatics.'[44] Habermas's first sketch of the types of action (*TCA* 1, 85–95) describes communicative action as a model of action on its own as opposed to the teleological, normatively regulated, and dramaturgical. However, in his fuller account of models of action (*TCA* 1, 325–30) he first talks about communicative action as a subclass of regulative action, then puts it under the category of conversational action – which happens when the action does not 'serve the carrying out of the purposive activities of the participants.'[45] This discrepancy is never explained. (See table 1.)

It is in this model of communicative actions that actors, through speech acts, show their potential rationality latent in language. Habermas demarcates communicative rationality with an attitude that is oriented towards reaching understanding (*Verständigung*) as opposed to any instrumental orientation. He explains the process of reaching understanding as one of reaching agreement (*Einigung*) among the participants in a dialogue. Such a communicatively achieved agreement has a rational basis that cannot be induced by outside influence. 'Agreement rests on common *convictions*. The speech act of one person succeeds only if the other accepts the offer contained in it by taking (however implicitly) a "yes" or "no" position on a validity claim that is in principle criticizable. Both ego, who raises a validity claim with his utterance, and alter, who recognizes or rejects it, base their decision on potential grounds or reasons.'[46] Habermas contends that the success or failure of

Table 1 Pure types of linguistically mediated interaction

Types of action	Formal pragmatic features					
	Characteristics of speech acts	Functions of speech	Action orientation	Basic attitudes	Validity claims	World relations
Strategic action (teleological)	Perlocutions Imperatives	Influencing one's opposite number	Oriented to success	Objectivating	Effectiveness	Objective world
Conversation or communicative action	Constatives	Representation of states of affairs	Oriented to reaching understanding	Objectivating	Truth	Objective world
Normatively regulated Action	Regulative	Establishment of interpersonal relations	Oriented to reaching understanding	Norm-conformative	Rightness	Social world
Dramaturgical action	Expressive	Self-epresentation	Oriented to reaching understanding	Expressive	Truthfulness	Subjective world

Source: TCA 1, 285, 329.

the illocutionary force of speech acts depends not only on their comprehensibility but also on their *acceptability*. By acceptability he means a serious offer on the part of the speaker to commit herself to the hearer. Habermas here again relies heavily on Austin's and Searle's account of the necessary conditions for the success of illocutionary acts, which are propositional content and preparatory, essential, and sincerity rules: *'We understand a speech act when we know what makes it acceptable.* From the stand point of the speaker, the conditions of acceptability are identical to the conditions for his illocutionary success.'[47] In other words, a speech act is accepted if the hearer can take a 'yes' position to the performative proposition of the speaker. The criteria of acceptability are important for Habermas, because by alluding to the mechanism of the coordinating character of the speech act they help in the construction of a sociological theory of action. At this point Habermas asks, What is the force of illocutionary acts that cause the hearer to accept the speaker's commitment? In his attempt to answer this question, he attributes the mutual recognition and commitment of speaker and hearer to a rational basis. 'A hearer understands the meaning of an utterance when, in addition to grammatical conditions, he knows those *essential conditions* under which he could be motivated by a speaker to take an affirmative position. These *acceptability conditions in the narrow sense* relate to the illocutionary meaning that S expresses by means of a performative clause.'[48]

Thus, what Habermas seems to be doing in formulating universal pragmatics is reconstructing the general conditions and rules of social relations and linguistic interactions, whose aim, in turn, is understanding based on the rational ground of the comprehensibility, acceptability, and testability of the validity claims. By attributing a cognitive character to the validity claims of illocutionary acts, he also distinguishes his cognitivist concept of rationality from any other notion of the rationality. Indeed, the presupposition of cognitive capacity of human agents is what for Habermas constitutes another interaction adjunct to communicative action. He calls a mode of communication where we can test the normative claims instead of uncritically accepting them *discourse*. What is important in this typology of linguistic interaction for Habermas's universal pragmatics is the communicative/strategic distinction, since it would ground the normative force of the discourse.

If we accept, with Habermas, that the true purpose of language is communicative rather than instrumental, then, as he goes on to claim, the same emancipatory potential can be used to reconstruct a practical morality. Formulation of a theory of an emancipatory rationality latent within everyday language was the first stage of Habermas's social theory, which is to be complemented by developing a theory of *discourse ethics*.

3. Discourse Ethics: Justice and the Good Life

To start the discussion of Habermas's discourse ethics and see how this moral theory is developed out of communicative action theory, we need to begin with his distinction between action and discourse. In a general way, we can say that this distinction reflects the traditional one between mere opinion and knowledge. That is to say, while the claims to validity in communicative action are uncritically accepted so as to bring about an agreement, those same claims are only hypothetically assumed in discourse, and as such have to be justified with an appeal to the force of argumentation and reason. In Habermas's words:

> In action, the factually raised claims to validity, which form the underlying consensus, are assumed naively. Discourse, on the other hand, serves the justification of problematic claims to validity of opinions and norms. Thus the system of action and experience refers us in a compelling manner to a form of communication in which the participants do not exchange information, do not direct or carry out action, nor do they have or communicate experiences; instead they search for arguments or offer justifications. Discourse therefore requires the virtualization of constraints on action.[49]

It is the role of argumentation, and the rational constraints imposed by it, that elevates a mode of communication from action to discourse. While communication remains tied to the context of action, discourse transcends the constraints of action. It is 'the condition of unconditioned.'[50] The validity of an argument, for Habermas, resides not in a deductive validity that holds between the linguistic units, but rather in a 'non-deductive relation between the pragmatic units.'[51] The logic of argumentation, therefore, can provide us with the reason needed as the means of testing the validity claims raised in communicative action. It can confirm or reject their claim to truth or legitimacy in a discursive process. In his words:

> The discursive process of reaching understanding, in the form of a co-operative division of labour between proponents and opponents, is normatively regulated in such a way that participants
> – thematize a problematic validity claim and,

- relieved of the pressure of action and experience, in a hypothetical attitude,
- test with reasons, and only with reasons, whether the claim defended by the proponents rightfully stands or not.[52]

Thus, the goal of any participant in discourse is to reach a rational consensus that is based on the normative acceptance of a specific validity claim. Habermas believes that for discourse to function as the domain of testing validity claims, individuals who enter into discursive argumentation need to have reached a certain level of linguistic and psychological maturity in order to recognize and accept their responsibility and autonomy in communicative interaction. So, just as Habermas uses Chomsky, Austin, and Searle to develop theories of linguistic and pragmatic competences at the disposition of a mature actor in communicative action, he uses Piaget's and Kohlberg's developmental psychology to show the different levels of cognitive and psychological competence required to participate in discourse. Such competence requires basic mastery of the notions of time, space, substance, causality, and cognitive and moral judgment. The importance of the Piaget-Kohlberg system of cognitive developmental psychology for Habermas becomes clearer when he divides the discursive argumentation into two domains: theoretical discourse and practical discourse.

To explain Habermas's appropriation of developmental psychology, we need to begin with his distinction between theoretical and practical discourse in terms of their different validity claims. The former is concerned with truth claims, being 'the form of argumentation in which controversial truth claims are thematized,' while the latter is concerned with legitimacy claims, being 'the form of argumentation in which claims to normative rightness are made thematic.'[53] Thus, practical discourse is 'an exacting form of argumentative decision making'[54] concerned with the domain of practical questions of morality and politics. It is in this respect, the normative evaluation of legitimacy claims in practical discourse, that the study of developmental competence within Kohlberg's schema of the stages of moral consciousness becomes important for Habermas. (See table 2.) Kohlberg distinguishes three general levels, each containing two stages of the development of the ego's interactive competence. Habermas views these stages as 'the gradual approximations' to a discursive procedure required for a moral judgment at the post-conventional level.[55] In order for an individual to

Table 2 Stages of moral consciousness development

Levels of interaction	Actions	Actors	Ethics	Stages of moral consciousness
Pre-conventional	Particular expectation of behavior	Natural identity	Magical ethics	Punishment and obedience
				Instrumental hedonism
Conventional	Norms	Role identity	Ethics of the law	Mutual interpersonal expectation
				Law and order orientation
Postconventional	Principles	Ego identity	Ethics of conviction and responsibility	Social-contract legalistic orientation
				Universal and ethical principles

Sources: McCarthy, Critical Theory of Habermas, 344–5; TCA 2, 175; MCCA, 122–4.

engage in discourse, her interactive capacities, her motivations and affects, need to have achieved a certain level of development and maturity. Interactive competence is, thus, essential to both ego identity, since 'it liberates the individual from the egocentrism of early childhood,' and moral consciousness, since it allows 'rational autonomy.'[56] The derivation of the stages of moral consciousness from the degrees of interactive competence amounts to 'Habermas' thesis that "moral consciousness" is at the bottom only the ability to employ interactive competence for a conscious resolution of morally relevant conflicts.'[57] Transition from the earlier stages to the more complex ones constitutes learning, at the end of which we have a *discursive procedure* at the postconventional level.[58] This procedure is characterized by three presuppositions: *reversibility* – the role exchange of the participants; *universality* – the inclusion of all concerned; and *reciprocity* – participants' mutual recognition. Habermas calls the presence of these conditions in every discursive argumentation 'the fact of reason.'[59]

The rational aspect of discursive argumentation frees the dialogue from specific external or internal limitations, and guarantees the reciprocity of discourse. Habermas believes that moral and political questions (the realm of practical discourse), like theoretical discourse, fall within the scope of reason as the force of the better argument, and as such they too admit of 'truth' as the condition for validity claims. We can, then, say that linguistic, theoretical, and practical expressions can be adjudicated in terms of the truth of their validity claims. Habermas writes:

> Only the truth of propositions and the rightness of moral norms and the comprehensibility or well-formedness of symbolic expressions are, by their very meaning, universal validity claims that can be tested in discourse. Only in theoretical, practical, and explicative discourse do the participants have to start from the (often counterfactual) presupposition that the conditions for an ideal speech situation are satisfied to a sufficient degree of approximation. I shall speak of 'discourse' only when the meaning of the problematic validity claim conceptually forces participants to suppose that a rationally motivated agreement could in principle be achieved, whereby the phrase 'in principle' expresses the idealizing proviso: if only the argumentation could be conducted openly enough and continued long enough.[60]

It is this rationalization of normative claims in practical discourse that provides the ground for *communicative* or *discursive ethics*, which, like any Kantian cognitivist moral philosophy, is formalistic and universalistic. That is to say, 'moral judgements have a cognitive content.'[61] The task of discourse ethics is to provide a test for the validity of normative claims in the light of justice. Such an ethic is formalistic in the sense that it distinguishes 'moral questions,' which can be 'decided rationally in terms of justice or the generalizability of interests,' from evaluative questions, which 'present themselves at the most general level as the issues of the good life or of self realization.'[62] The claim of discourse is that the important quality of valid norms is their impartiality and fairness, that this quality can be universalized, and that the universalized principle can be rationally justified. Habermas writes: 'I have introduced U (the principle of universalization) as a rule of argumentation that makes agreement in practical discourse possible whenever matters of concern to all are open to regulation in the equal interest of everyone.'[63]

The Principle of Universalization

The principle of universalization supports a rational justification of a generalizable need that generates agreement. Habermas further explains that, just as normative claims in communicative action protect an actor's interests, they also work to the satisfaction of an actor's needs. By 'need' Habermas does not mean a universal biological need, but rather what he calls an 'interpretive need,' that is, what, in a given society and culture, is necessary to the flourishing of human life. That is why he discusses 'need interpretation,' which not only includes the material needs of an agent in a poor country but also the intellectual (spiritual) needs of an agent in a rich country (i.e., the need for adequate social and political information). In order to see how actors interpret their needs in a discursive situation, one requires a reciprocity test, which assesses how others can be affected by normative claims of one's interpretive needs. That is to say, the test aims to determine whether the need in question is a *generalizable interest* or not. To make the point plain by way of an example, suppose in a discursive situation an interpretive need of a citizen of a rich country is a recreational activity (e.g., hunting wildlife), which can be provided only at the cost of another actor's suffering in a poor country (i.e., destabilizing the ecology of the region). The function of the reciprocity test, then, would be to show whether satisfying the need, in so far as it affects all the participants, can form a generalizable interest. The latter is not the result of comparing needs and deciding which is of a greater importance, but rather a matter of judging that a need is not justified in so far as it does not serve, and provide for, the interest of everyone involved in the discursive situation. A discursive will-formation is legitimate when it deliberates on *common interests* and is *constraint-free*. 'The discursively formed will may be called 'rational' because the formal properties of discourse and of the deliberative situation sufficiently guarantee that a consensus can arise only through appropriately interpreted, *generalizable* interests, by which I mean needs *that can be communicatively shared*.'[64] Generalizable needs tie actors' expectations of behaviour intersubjectively and reciprocally, and as such give the achieved consensus a quality of fairness. In Habermas's words, 'The need interpretation which is implied in a normative claim thus must be one that can be "universalized" – that is "communicatively shared" – if that claim is to withstand discursive testing and thus be acceptable.'[65]

Unlike in the domain of theoretical discourse, in practical discourse the relation between the descriptive result of agreement about generalizable needs and interests and their normative force to back up the consensus is not,

> and cannot be, a deductive relation. But as centuries of debate have shown, neither is the relation between observational-experimental evidence and general laws deductive. In both cases we have to do with 'casuistic' evidence that renders a statement more or less plausible. We are dealing here with the pragmatic modality of cogency and not with the logical modality of necessity: casuistic evidence, in the form of cogent arguments, provides good reason or grounds for accepting a proposed explanation or justification. In theoretical discourse the logical gap between evidence and hypothesis is bridged by various canons of induction. The corresponding function in practical discourse is filled by the principle of universalizability: 'only those norms are permitted which can find general recognition in their domain of application. The principle serves to exclude, as not admitting of consensus, all norms whose content and range of validity are particular.'[66]

Furthermore, Habermas's universal competence theory entrenches the idea of cooperation in discourse based on generalizable needs. It points to the important role of reciprocity for interaction and moral judgment. That is to say, it places emphasis on an actor's capacity, her pragmatic competence, which allows her to build, and when necessary to mend, the process of understanding in communicative action. This capacity, then, serves as a basis for a cooperative search for truth in social interaction. It is this presupposition of reciprocity that leads to cooperative interaction – namely, that what goes for you must go for me, and conversely. Habermas's point is that reciprocity promotes free cooperation of communicative action toward reaching a rational agreement, as opposed to the coerced cooperation of strategic action aimed at domination. However, when interests conflict, effort should be made toward a *compromise*, which has to be legitimate.[67]

Transcendental Pragmatic Argument

It is the presupposition of the principle of universalization (which belongs to the communicative competence of any actor involved in normative argumentation) that prevents actors from falling into a 'performative contradiction.' This is Habermas's *transcendental pragmatic argument*, which has two parts.

First, Habermas wants to show how the transcendental argument manifests that 'the principle of universalization, which acts as a rule of argumentation, is implied by the presuppositions of argumentation in general.'[68] The principle of universalization (U), Habermas tells us, is presupposed by each actor who accepts the universal and necessary rules and presuppositions of speech acts, and implicitly knows how to justify a norm within a discourse.[69] Following Aristotle, Habermas divides the process of presupposition of argumentation into three levels: the logical level of products, the dialectical level of procedures, and the rhetorical level of process. The presuppositions of argumentation at the first two levels are not adequate for a transcendental-pragmatic argument, since the first is the domain of logical and semantical rules with no ethical content, and the second arranges the pragmatic presuppositions, necessary for a search for truth, in the form of a competition. It is only at the third level of the process that argumentative presuppositions in speech acts, whose goal is understanding, present a structural design capable of hosting an ethical content. 'In argumentative speech we see the structures of a speech situation immune to repression and inequality in a particular way: it presents itself as a form of communication that adequately approximates ideal conditions. This is why I tried at one time to describe the presuppositions of argumentations as the defining characteristics of an ideal speech situation.'[70] The term 'performative contradiction,' which Habermas borrows from Apel, is meant to explain the innate presupposition of these argumentative rules in every speaker's universal pragmatic competence who will, at the same time, want to contest the hypothetical reconstruction of the rules. To put it differently, performative contradiction applies to those who want to question the status of the argumentative rules while their very act of engaging in discourse presupposes those rules. The function of discursive rules at this level of process is to prevent the influence of any external motives on discourse except 'that of the cooperative search for truth.' These rules are as follows:

1 Every subject with the competence to speak and act is allowed to take part in discourse.
2 a) Everyone is allowed to question any assertion whatever, b) everyone is allowed to introduce any assertion whatever into the discourse, c) everyone is allowed to express his attitudes, desires, and needs.
3 No speaker may be prevented, by internal or external coercion, from exercising his rights as laid down in (1) and (2).[71]

Thus, the recognition of argumentative presuppositions and rules implies that every speaker who enters into a discourse implicitly knows and accepts the principle of universalization. The conjunction of the ideal structural design that argumentative rules and presuppositions provide and the acceptance of the principle of U allows Habermas to formulate his principle of discourse ethics (D): '[O]nly those norms can claim to be valid that meet (or could meet) with the approval of all affected in their capacity as participants in a practical discourse.'[72]

The second part of the transcendental-pragmatic argument provides it with the status of justification, which, Habermas tells us, cannot be an ultimate justification but 'a recognition of something that is presupposed.'[73] He explains that the necessity of accepting rules and presuppositions of argumentation arises out of the lack, for a speaker, of any other alternatives for engaging in discourse ethics without falling into a performative contradiction. In that sense it is the necessity of the rules that is being proved, which is different from their status being justified. In Habermas's words:

> Demonstrating the existence of performative contradictions helps to identify the rules necessary for any argumentation game to work; if one is to argue at all, there are no substitutes. The fact that there are no *alternatives* to these rules of argumentation is what is being proved; the rules themselves are not being *justified*. True, the participants must have accepted them as a 'fact of reason' in setting out to argue. But this kind of argument cannot accomplish a transcendental deduction in the Kantian sense.[74]

Therefore, Habermas continues, the justification of discourse ethics does not need to be an infallible one. It needs to be no more than a *programmatic* justification that has the status of an assumption and, as such, requires the following rules:

1   A definition of a universalization principle that functions as a rule of argumentation.
2   The identification of pragmatic presuppositions of argumentation that are inseparable and have a normative content.
3   The explicit statement of that normative content (e.g., in the form of discourse rules).
4   Proof that a relation of material implication holds between steps (3) and (1) in connection with the idea of the justification of norms.[75]

The transcendental-pragmatic argument thus provides ideal conditions for discourse ethics. That is to say, when these discursive presuppositions and rules govern a speech act, we have what Habermas calls an *ideal speech situation*.

Ideal Speech Situation

The most adequate statement of the ideal speech situation is given in a paper entitled 'Wahrheitstheorien.' While the paper is not available in English, the relevant passage is quoted by McCarthy. It is so important that it is worth reproducing here in its entirety:

> The ideal speech situation is neither an empirical phenomenon nor a mere construct, but rather an unavoidable supposition reciprocally made in discourse. This supposition can, but need not be, counterfactual; but even if it is made counterfactually, it is a fiction that is operatively effective in the process of communication. Therefore I prefer to speak of an anticipation of an ideal speech situation ... The normative foundation of agreement in language is thus both anticipated and – as an anticipated foundation – also effective ... To this extent the concept of ideal speech situation is not merely a regulative principle in Kant's sense; with the first step toward the agreement in language we must always in fact make this supposition. On the other hand, neither is it an existing concept in Hegel's sense; for no historical reality matches the form of life that we can in principle characterize by reference to the ideal speech situation. The ideal speech situation would best be compared with a transcendental illusion were it not for the fact that ... [in contrast to] the application of the categories of the understanding beyond the experience, this illusion is also the constitutive condition of rational speech. The anticipation of the ideal speech situation has ... the significance of the constitutive illusion which is at the same time the appearance of a form of life. Of course, we cannot know a priori whether that appearance [*Vorschein*] is a mere delusion [*Vorspiegelung*] – however unavoidable the suppositions from which it springs – or whether the empirical conditions for the realization (if only approximate) of the supposed form of life can practically be brought about. Viewed in this way, the fundamental norms of rational speech built into universal pragmatics contain a practical hypothesis.[76]

Habermas has already explained that actualizing the principles U and D would amount to an ideal condition for discursive ethics in which the potential ideas of truth, freedom, and justice, latent in the communicative competence of every actor, are realized so as to guarantee a rational consensus regarding the participants' needs and interests. These rules create an environment of fairness and impartiality, thus treating each and every actor justly. The idea is that since the ideal speech situation is this model of fair and just communicative interaction, we can employ it to address practical issues. This is not to say that these rules govern our linguistic communication a priori, but that, potentially, they are present in discourse; and since their nature embodies the ideas of truth, freedom, and justice, they seem best to address the issues of our social and moral life.

Justice, as Habermas defines the principle of universalization, requires all actors to accept norms (and act freely according to them) that would result in impartial, fair, and rational satisfaction of their interests. The connection here is not between consensus and truth, but between consensus and rightness or fairness. On this point McCarthy writes:

> The principle of universalization gives expression to this connection: if there is to be a rationally motivated agreement concerning the 'worthiness to be recognized' of a recommended norm or standard, then the pattern of legitimate chances for need satisfaction that it represents must be something that all those potentially affected by it could want. In fact argumentatively achieved consensus is nothing other than a procedural realization of universality.[77]

Minimal Character of Discursive Ethics

Habermas's discourse ethics limits itself to the questions of justice, thus avoiding evaluative issues of what constitutes the concept of the good life. The reason is that evaluative questions are always biased towards a primary set of goods in a specific form of life. This, however, does not mean that discourse ethics disregards concrete situations. Habermas believes that universal pragmatism allows the principle of justice to apply to concrete situations in the form of the generalizability of particular interests. He writes:

> Thus the development of the moral point of view goes hand in hand with a differentiation within the practical into *moral questions* and *evaluative questions*. Moral questions can in principle be decided rationally, i.e., in

terms of justice or the generalizability of interests. Evaluative questions present themselves at the most general level as issues of the *good life* (or of self-realization); they are accessible to rational discussion only within the unproblematic horizon of a concrete historical form of life or the conduct of an individual life.[78]

Thus, decisions about justice, while based on concrete situations, should be generalizable, suggesting that the conception of universalization be a pragmatic conception. Nevertheless, pragmatic universalization, according to Habermas, still has universal validity, which 'extends beyond the perspective of a particular culture' and 'is based on a transcendental-pragmatic demonstration of universal and necessary presupposition of argumentation.'[79] In contrast to issues of justice, questions concerning the good life resist such universalization, and hence remain out of the range of discourse ethics.

Habermas thinks of his ethics as minimal, not only because it limits itself to questions of justice leaving questions of the good life out, but also because he admits the incapacity of discourse ethics to provide us with 'substantive norms of justice.' What this ethics can do, however, is to lead us toward a kind of thinking that can rationally justify normative claims in procedural discourse:

> The discourse theory of ethics, for which I have proposed a program of philosophical justification, is not a self-contained endeavour. Discourse ethics advances universalistic and thus very strong theses, but the status it claims for those theses is relatively weak. Essentially, the justification involves two steps. First, a principle of universalization (U) is introduced. It serves as a rule of argumentation in practical discourse. Second, this rule is justified in terms of the substance of the pragmatic presuppositions of argumentation as such is in connection with an explanation of the meaning of normative claims to validity.[80]

This universal yet weak status of the principles of discourse ethics nevertheless seems vulnerable to the charge of emptiness. That is to say, one could ask what practical insight such abstract principles can offer beyond the boundary of discourse they regulate. I will return to this question in the next chapter.

To sum up: according to communicative action ethics, human interests and needs, not with respect to the question of the good life but with respect to the question of justice, can be rationally pursued in real discourse. Real discourse involves actors' universal competences, including the mastery and recognition of universal principles, discursive rules, and presuppositions of mutual accountability and recognition of legitimacy. These competences allow each agent's normative claim to be adjudicated through argumentative assessment of its potential effect on others involved in the discourse. Such a discursive ethics would produce rational consensus. Habermas believes that he has resolved modernity's problem of self-referentiality by moving the rationality of solitary subject-centred reason to an intersubjective domain of social interaction. His version of critical theory discerns in Hegel's early writings a path alluded to, but not taken, namely, that of intersubjective understanding. Communicative reason, in turn, allows him to escape the fate of instrumental rationality – so bleakly predicted as dominant by the Frankfurt School – and account for human interaction in a rational society. Situating an intersubjective concept of reason at the core of language, Habermas believes that he has escaped the boundary of the philosophy of consciousness, grounding a critical social theory that paves the way to a true society. However, before moving on to discuss the political extension of his critical theory, we first need to give a critical assessment of communicative action theory and its achievement.

Chapter 3

The Communicative Ethics Controversy: Insights and Oversights

It is necessary to distinguish power relations from relationships of communication which transmit information by means of a language, a system of signs, or any other symbolic medium. No doubt communicating is always a certain way of acting upon another person or persons. But the production and the circulation of elements of meaning can have as their objective or as their consequence certain results in the realm of power; the latter are not simply an aspect of the former. Whether or not they pass through the system of communication, power relations have a specific nature. Power relations, relationships of communication, objective capacities should not therefore be confused.

Michel Foucault, 'Structuralism and Post-Structuralism' (*Telos*, Spring-Summer 1983: 217)

My preceding discussion illustrates that from the vantage point of the linguistic turn, Habermas's theory of communicative action is able to address the problem of modernity from an intersubjective perspective, showing that human subjects are constituted as a result of their linguistic interaction. The situation most conducive to emancipation, it is suggested, is the discursive situation as outlined in Habermas's theory of discourse ethics. Habermas claims that discourse ethics is a genuine descendent of Kantian moral philosophy, since, like Kantian morality, discourse ethics is deontological, cognitivist, formalist, and universalist. It is deontological in that it rejects any material ethics (i.e., ethics based on self-interest) by refusing to favour one form of life over other forms. In discourse ethics the validity of moral norms of action is determined by the truth claims of their discursive proposition. 'A deontological ethics conceives the rightness of norms and commands on *analogy* with the truth of an assertoric statement.'[1] Discourse ethics is cognitivist because, beyond any 'expression of the contingent emotions, preferences, and decisions of speakers,' it conveys a cognitive content. This cognitivism for discourse ethics means that the moral and practical question can be decided based on reason. Discourse ethics is also formalist in that it formulates a rule (of the procedure of moral argumentation) that explains the moral point of view for all rational beings. Finally, discourse ethics is a universalist ethics since its principle of (U) is valid, not just with respect to a set of preferences or intuitions of a particular culture, but universally. Yet it is only natural that any attempt at universalization of rational norms in a Kantian formal vein would invite a communitarian critique, anticipated by Hegel, which would insist that the valid norms should be drawn from within the concrete context of a community. Aware of this critique, Habermas attempts to avoid it by arguing that discourse ethics has made important improvements upon Kantian morality. In what follows, I will first discuss these improvements. Next, I will submit the project of communicative ethics to a critical analysis, namely, an examination of whether the identity of modern subjects as moral agents can be adequately accounted for via the theory of communicative action. Finally, marking the theory's limitation, we can move on with what Habermas keeps from discourse ethics for the purpose of formulating a critical political theory.

1. Habermas's Improvement upon Kantian Ethics

Despite the commonalities between discourse ethics and Kant's moral philosophy, Habermas is anxious to draw three important differences between his and Kant's theory. He believes that these differences have enabled discourse ethics to improve upon Kant's morality to the extent that any Hegelian critique of discourse ethics would prove ineffective. Habermas discusses Hegel's objection to separating moral theories of *duty* from theories of *right*. While Kant's ethics of duty puts the emphasis on the principle of justice, Aristotelian theories of right concentrate on the common weal. Aristotle's *Nichomachean Ethics* does not appeal to any meta-ethical norms or principles of universalization, since virtue is deemed to be a practice embodied in actual life. Kant's ethics of duty, however, is achieved precisely by an appeal to an abstract universalization. On Hegel's position concerning these two models, Habermas writes:

Hegel was the first to argue that we misperceive the basic moral phenomenon if we isolate the two aspects, assigning opposite principles to each.
His concept of ethical life (*Sittlichkeit*) is an implicit criticism of two kinds
of one-sidedness, one the mirror image of the other. Hegel opposes the
abstract universality of justice manifesting itself in the individualistic
approaches of the modern age, in rational natural right theory and in
Kantian moral philosophy. No less vigorous is his opposition to the concrete particularism of the common good that pervades Aristotle and Thomas Aquinas. The ethics of discourse picks up this basic Hegelian aspiration
to redeem it with Kantian means.[2]

Habermas believes that, while being oriented toward the principle of
justice, discourse ethics surpasses Kant by including 'the structural
aspects of the good life that can be distinguished from the concrete
totalities of specific forms of life.'[3] This ambivalence concerning abstract universalization, on the one hand, and providing insight for
issues of the good life, on the other hand, constitutes a tension that will
surface later. The tension arises out of Habermas's desire to overcome
the Hegelian critique by improving upon Kant's ethics, while remaining faithful to the general Kantian framework.

To get back to the differences that Habermas wants to outline, the
first difference between discourse ethics and Kant's moral theory is
discourse ethics' rejection of the Kantian dual world. The implication of
abandoning this dichotomy in discourse ethics is that for actors the
necessity of taking part in discursive argumentation arises from their
rational competences and the generalizability of their interpretive needs
and not from their assumed freedom:

> [D]iscourse ethics gives up Kant's dichotomy between an *intelligible* realm
> comprising duty and free will and a *phenomenal* realm comprising inclina-
> tions, subjective motives, political and social institutions, etc. The quasi-
> transcendental necessity with which subjects involved in communicative
> interaction orient themselves to validity claims is reflected only in their
> being *constrained* to speak and act under idealized conditions.[4]

In Kant, the dichotomy between the sensible and the intelligible world
provides the framework for explaining the autonomy of the moral
agent. The core of Kant's third antinomy is that while the moral agent,
as a part of the sensible world, is bounded by natural laws, she is free in

so far as her actions are objectively determined by an *ought* that expresses the connection between her ideas, as belonging to the intelligible world, and the faculty of reason. The actions of rational beings, 'so far as they are appearances ..., are subject to necessity of nature; but the same actions, as regards merely the rational subject and its faculty of action according to mere reason, are free.'[5] In other words, for Kant, morality is made possible by the fact that the solitary agent, a member of the intelligible world, can appeal freely to its faculty of reason. By saying that the free and autonomous agent belongs to the intelligible (noumenal) world, Kant also means that the motivation of moral acts is not that of satisfying self-interests or inclinations rooted in the phenomenal world, but that which arises out of duty. Thus, the dichotomy between the world of appearance (phenomena) and the real world (noumena) provides the moral agent with duty as her orientation point, and closes the door to any phenomenal orientation as the determining ground of a moral maxim. For Habermas in discourse ethics, by contrast, the opposition between the dual worlds is resolved in everyday communication, wherein the empirical structure of communicative interaction anticipates an idealized situation. He writes: 'The unbridgeable gap Kant saw between the intelligible and the empirical becomes, in discourse ethics, a mere tension manifesting itself in *everyday communication* as the factual force of counterfactual presuppositions.'[6]

Having explained this difference, Habermas goes on to say that Hegel is wrong to think that the formalism of Kantian ethics only leads to tautologies. Here, the formalist feature of the theories does not mean only a semantic or grammatical consistency; it more importantly reveals the binding force of a given norm that results from its universal acceptance by the participants. Thus, this formalism, Habermas argues, is not an artificial creation of philosophers, but is derived from actual everyday life: 'The content that is tested by a moral principle is generated not by the philosopher but by real life. The conflicts of action that come to be morally judged and consensually resolved grow out of everyday life. Reason as a tester of maxims (Kant) or actors as participants in argumentation (discourse ethics) *find* these conflicts. They do not create them.'[7]

The second difference is the test for Habermas's universalization principle and Kant's categorical imperative or any abstract principle of universalization as such. The test for Kant's imperative, by its very subject-centred nature, is monological. That is to say, it can be performed by an individual. Habermas's universal test, by contrast, is the result of a collective and 'actual argumentation' (the force of the better argument) among those involved and affected by the norm that targets their interests. In his words:

> Discourse ethics rejects the monological approach of Kant, who assumed that the individual tests his maxim of action *foro interno* or, as Husserl put it, in the loneliness of his soul. The singularity of Kant's transcendental consciousness simply takes for granted a prior understanding among a plurality of empirical egos; their harmony is preestablished. In discourse ethics it is not. Discourse ethics prefers to view shared understanding about the generalizability of interests as the *result* of an intersubjectively mounted *public* discourse. There are no shared structures preceding the individual except the universals of language use.[8]

The communicative character of his discursive ethics enables Habermas to leave the solitude of Kant's moral agent, and its individualistic frame of reference, and move to the intersubjective domain of society. While preserving the rationality and universality of the moral imperative, Habermas appeals to communicative interaction, where the frame of reference is intersubjective. This allows discourse ethics to escape Hegel's charge of rigourism (referring to any strict procedural ethics, such as Kant's) which ignores the possible consequences of its rationally defended moral maxim. Habermas explains the difference as follows:

> The charge of rigorism applies to Kant. It does not apply to discourse ethics, since the latter breaks with Kant's idealism and monologism. Discourse ethics has a built-in procedure that insures awareness of consequences. This comes out clearly in the formulation of universalization (U), which requires sensitivity to the results and consequences of the general observance of a norm for every individual.[9]

The third difference concerns the extent to which Kant's and Habermas's principles of universalization are effective. Hegel's criticism is that any Kantian principle of universalization is so abstract that it loses its practical effect and as such is empty. But Habermas believes that discourse ethics has overcome this problem too: 'Discourse ethics improves upon Kant's unsatisfactory handling of a specific problem of justification when he evasively points to the alleged 'fact of pure reason' and argues that the effectiveness of the "ought" is simply a matter of experience. Discourse ethics solves this problem by deriving (U) from the universal presupposition of argumentation.[10] That is to say, the monological character of Kantian ethics, when forming a moral imperative, universalizes the free will of a concrete situation of a solitary subject. This abstract universalization separates the agent's personal orientation from her sense of duty, weakening the practical force of the moral 'ought.' In fact, the Hegelian critique gains most weight against this separation of duty and inclination, because no concrete norm of action can be derived from this abstract rationality of the intelligible world. Hegel argued that the Kantian dual world separated an agent's personal orientation (needs and interests) from her moral action and thus made morality impossible. Unlike Kant's pure rationality, which could not provide a satisfactory answer to why we should be moral, the rationality of discourse ethics appeals to a pragmatic use of reason (practical discourse), allowing for the consideration of needs and interests insofar as they are generalizable. Indeed, individual needs and interests cannot be excluded because the rational consensus (the moral maxim) is based on the process of the generalizability of, and argumentation for, those needs and interests:

> Kant is vulnerable to the objection that his ethics lacks practical impact because it dichotomizes duty and inclination, reason and sense experience. The same cannot be said of discourse ethics, for it discards the Kantian theory of the two realms. The concept of practical discourse postulates the inclusion of all interests that may be affected; it even covers the critical testing of interpretations through which we come to recognize certain needs as in our own interests.[11]

Relying on his model of developmental psychology, Habermas claims that most people are capable of distinguishing questions of moral justification from contextual ones. However, as indicated earlier (see note 58 in chapter 2), the validity of the developmental model itself does not enjoy certainty. Hence, the question of what issues can be decided by discourse ethics seems to be relative to the uncertain question of how many subjects can achieve stage six of their cognitive development so as to be capable of entering the discursive situation.[12]

Having established these differences with Kant, however, Habermas thinks that he has improved upon Kantian ethics so as to overcome most of Hegel's objections. Of course, one can take issue with the selective nature of this reading of Hegel's critique of Kant. One could argue that there is much more to Hegel's critique of Kant than Habermas makes us believe.[13] For instance, Habermas's account of this critique may give the mistaken impression that the move toward intersubjectivity is original to discourse ethics, when in fact Hegel's chief philosophical discovery, against the Kantian dualism between moral action and moral intention, is that human action unfolds in the intersubjective realm of the social world. The debate concerning the weaknesses and strengths of this discovery, however, goes beyond the immediate concern of my project here.[14] For my purposes, it should suffice to focus on the efficacy of Habermas's alleged improvements upon Kant's ethics in the face of Hegelian objections, the major objection being that any Kantian moral philosophy with its formalist and universalist features is forced to address a constricted and abstract domain of moral action that is far removed from the world of everyday life.[15] Having appealed to the communicative rationality of social interaction, Habermas claims to have escaped this charge. But this seems to depend to a large extent upon the status of the principles of discourse ethics. That is to say, to the degree that these principles are formalized the effectiveness of discourse ethics would depend on the extent to which the proposed formalization and universalization can reflect the specific cultural and historical values and the conceptions of moral reasoning. This problem, however, is only a by-product of the kind of status that discourse ethics claims for itself and for its justification of moral intuitions.

2. The Status of Discourse Ethics' Claims

The vast literature on communicative action theory, to which Habermas still continues to make his contribution, has greatly enriched the debate about human interaction in the social, political, and philosophical domains. At the same time, despite the theory's increased sophistication and complexity, it still appeals to common sense. Everyone recognizes the dignity, satisfaction, and safety that result when social conflicts or disputes are resolved through dialogue as opposed to coercion, deception, or the use of force. Its tenor provides Habermas's project with *prima facie* plausibility. However, Habermas's writing has attracted lively and fruitful critical reaction, which in turn has created a vast body of literature that cannot completely be accounted for in the present space. The more important and sustained criticisms, perhaps, can be generally grouped around three main topics: (a) a Hegelian critique of the project's emptiness and ineffectiveness;[16] (b) a critique of the ethnocentrism of communicative rationality as arising out of the specific historico-cultural context of European rationality;[17] and (c) a feminist critique of communicative action as being within the tradition of a morality of justice that excludes other forms of rationality and morality (e.g., morality of care).[18] These charges generally have been made from two different perspectives: (1) an examination of the theory's practical impact, which may reveal undesirable implications (e.g., ethnocentrism, the exclusion of weaker voices in society, etc.) and (2) the criticism of its formal composition, which alludes to theoretical deficiencies and ambiguity (e.g., labour/interaction distinction, system/lifeworld distinction, his reading of Hegel, Weber, and Marx, etc.).[19] Despite the overwhelming force of some of these criticisms, both quantitatively and qualitatively, Habermas's estimable attitude has been to incorporate their insights in order to further improve and refine his theory. Given such an extensive critical exchange, my contribution in this chapter will not be aimed at formulating a new criticism of the Habermas corpus, but rather at highlighting the aspects of a gradual change toward a more conservative position in Habermas that culminates in *Between Facts and Norms* (later, in chapter 5, I will develop my criticism of a political complacency that results from this uncritical shift). Thus, my discussion of some of the more important of these debates and controversies here will be tailored to revealing the contributing moments to this shift in Habermas's theoretical development.

I will begin by tracing a tendency in Habermas's theory, reminiscent of his epistemological ambition in *Knowledge and Human Interest*,[20] that has direct implications for the topic of my inquiry – namely, the fact that his most recent works tend to compromise the critical heritage of his philosophy. This tendency arises out of a strong version of the status of discourse ethics and the assigned ground of justification for our moral intuitions. I shall, therefore, discuss how Habermas draws a set of moral intuitions by way of drawing an alleged analogy between them and communicative competences. This account, then, will help to reveal an a priori and foundationalist tenor to his project that, if left unchecked, will jeopardize the critical vigour of Habermas's social theory.

As stated from the outset, Habermas's goal in presenting the theory of communicative action was to resolve modernity's problem of the subject's self-constitution and self-reassurance by providing a determinate character of judgment that would function as a normative source of orientation. Communicative action theory creates norms according to which a modern subject can interpret and analyse itself critically.

At the same time, it provides standards allowing for normative self-reassurance. Accordingly, maturity as critical self-constitution is achieved, Habermas argues, via communicative action, which 'is intended to make possible a conceptualization of the social-life context that is tailored to the paradoxes of modernity.'[21] It was through the 'reconstruction of universal pragmatics' that Habermas accounted for communicative rationality. Communicative rationality, in turn, allows the reintegration of the three cultural spheres of modernity and grounds a universalist discourse ethics that closes the door to any value scepticism. Discourse ethics is oriented towards moral questions, which 'can in principle be decided rationally, i.e., in terms of *Justice* or generalizability of interests,'[22] leaving evaluative questions of the good life to rational discussion of concrete historical forms. The architectonic of discourse theory, as the space where human subjects produce their truth, uniquely intertwines the problem of self-constitution with the problem of justice: human subjects' identities are formed within a communicative space where their validity claims to truth and normative rightness are argumentatively assessed. The structure of communicative rationality, furthermore, serves to demonstrate the modern subject's relation to its past and its future as a progressive process that is based on learning and the accumulation of knowledge.

By drawing a map of affinities and differences between Kant's moral theory and discourse ethics, Habermas has argued that a Hegelian critique does not have the same force against discourse ethics as it did with Kant's theory. Despite his effort one still may ask, Does Habermas's theory completely overcome the Hegelian critique? Granted that the dialogical nature of discourse ethics greatly improves upon Kantian solitary morality, does discourse ethics then become an attainable ethics (*Sittlichkeit*) in the Hegelian sense, capable of addressing the practical issues of a situated agent? How, in other words, does this highly elaborated system of abstract thoughts and arguments help us to live a good life? Or to put it differently, Is a formalist and universalist morality such as Habermas's discourse ethics, capable of providing one with concrete insights as to how one should live one's life?

Habermas seems ambivalent in regard to these questions, and ends *Moral Consciousness and Communicative Action* with the recognition of the limitations of his communicative action theory. He confesses that an important objective of his theory has been to overcome value scepticism and thus to defend the universal rationality of moral judgments. In order to achieve this end, Habermas has constructed the theory of universal pragmatic competence, whose basic features, in turn, represent moral ideas. In doing so, Habermas relies on P.F. Strawson's article 'Freedom and Resentment,' which 'develops a linguistic phenomenology of ethical consciousness.'[23] Claims concerning moral issues cannot be decided as true or false in the same way as descriptive sentences can, yet

> if normative sentences do not admit of truth in the narrow sense of the word 'true,' that is, *in the same sense* in which descriptive statements can be true or false, we will have to formulate the task of explaining the meaning of 'moral truth' or, if that expression is already misleading, the meaning of 'normative rightness' in such a way that we are not tempted to assimilate the one type of sentence to the other. We will have to proceed on a weaker assumption, namely that normative claims to validity are *analogous to truth claims*.[24]

By giving an account of the presuppositions and principles of universal pragmatic competence, Habermas is hoping to show the potential rationality of our communicative action as a basis for our moral judgment. 'The moral principle can then be derived from the content of these presuppositions of argumentation if one knows at least what it means to justify a norm of action.'[25] It seems, however, legitimate to ask, Is Habermas justified in reconstructing moral ideals as the features of universal pragmatic competence? After all, what does the principle of charity as a pragmatic principle, for example, have to do with any moral maxim? Habermas's reply would be to argue that the questions of truth and rightness are similar but not identical; they both have a cognitive context that allows them to be decided by reason. He also has told us that

> pure intersubjectivity exists only when there is a complete symmetry in the distribution of assertion and dispute, revelation and concealment, prescription and conformity, among the parties of communication ... (1) In the case of unrestrained discussion (in which no prejudiced opinion can be taken up or criticized) it is possible to develop strategies for reaching an unconstrained consensus; (2) on the basis of mutuality of unimpaired self-representation ... it is possible to achieve a significant rapport despite the unavoidable distance between the partners, ... (3) in the case of full complementarity of expectations ... the claim of universal understanding exists, as well as the necessity of universalized norms. *These three symmetries*

represent, incidentally, a linguistic conceptualization of what are traditionally known as the ideas of truth, freedom, and justice.[26]

That is to say, the pragmatic motives and principles of our communicative competence stand as analogous to the moral ideas of truth, freedom, and justice in discourse ethics. The features of communicative competence are universal and context-independent, which, by analogy, means that so are the moral ideals. Such a universal character allows for a formalization through which discourse ethics gains a transcendental range.

> There is only one reason why discourse ethics, which presumes to derive the substance of a universalistic morality from the general presuppositions of argumentation, is a promising strategy: discourse or argumentation is a more exacting type of communication, going beyond any particular form of life. Discourse generalizes, abstracts, and scratches the presuppositions of context-bound communicative actions by extending their range to include competent subjects beyond the provincial limits of their own particular form of life.[27]

This means that Habermas's efforts to provide an ethical theory aim to supply a transcendental imperative by showing that the foundations of our moral judgment – what he calls our 'moral intuition' – are necessary and universal. Kant, too, in the second chapter of the *Groundwork of the Metaphysics of Morals* declared that the aim of his theory was to provide our moral intuitions with an a priori foundation. Habermas, however, is quick to distance himself from Kantian a priorism. For him the reconstructive science of communicative rationality 'is based on a transcendental-pragmatic demonstration of universal and necessary presuppositions of argumentation. We may no longer burden these arguments with the status of an a priori transcendental deduction along the lines of Kant's critique of reason.'[28] Habermas believes that to formulate a transcendental theory that accounts for universal conditions of possible experience, one does not need to follow the Kantian synthetic a priori doctrine. The necessary conditions of such experience can be accounted for a posteriori, that is to say, pragmatically as general conditions of experience that go beyond any particular instance of it. Even though Habermas does not give an a priori account of moral intuitions – but instead derives them by way of an analogy with principles of universal pragmatics, which themselves are empirically arrived at – the way he extracts them still resembles a priorism because of the role that he assigns to them. According to Habermas, what makes a discursive situation possible is the presupposition of these moral ideals. The already pre-established validity of these ideals is where the Kantian a priorism surfaces, whether Habermas wants it or not. He is aware of such a risk and characterizes the universality of his theory as fallibilistic and not absolute. Such an understanding of fallibilism, however, as Wolfgang Kuhlmann has pointed out,[29] may cause a further dilemma for the theory of communicative action; namely, that the principle of fallibilism itself cannot be justified since it cannot be applied to itself. Habermas contends, however, that we cannot maintain 'the division of theoretical statements into two groups: those with a hypothetical status and others by means of which we justify the fallibilist nature of that status.'[30] This is because he understands the principle of fallibilism simply as a grammatical 'explanation which must itself naturally be justified and is therefore in principle itself open to revision. Again, each is part and parcel of the other in such a way that a dilemma of self-application cannot arise.'[31] Thus, for Habermas the justification for the transcendental-pragmatic principle is not absolute but hypothetical, which means that the principle can be amended as soon as new data arises that falls beyond the range of the theory:

> The *certainty* with which we put our knowledge of rules into practice does not extend to the *truth* of proposed reconstructions of presuppositions hypothesized to be general, for we have to put our reconstructions up for discussion in the same way in which the logician or the linguist, for example, presents his theoretical descriptions. No harm is done, however, if we deny that the transcendental-pragmatic justification constitutes an ultimate justification. Rather, discourse ethics then takes its place among the reconstructive sciences concerned with the rational basis of knowing, speaking, and acting. If we cease striving for the foundationalism of traditional transcendental philosophy, we acquire new corroborative possibilities for discourse ethics.[32]

To emphasize this transcendental-empirical character of the theory, Habermas calls universal pragmatics 'quasi-transcendental.' The problem, however, is that if we grant his approach the empirical character that improves upon Kant's transcendentalism, there appears to be a circular reference between the presupposition of the rules of argumentation and moral ideals in the discourse and their extraction from the discursive argumentation. In other words, the presupposition of the rules of argumentation allows us to take part in a discursive situation aimed at resolving practical issues, but the very presupposition is based on the structural design of the discourse itself that has been discovered empirically. To overcome this problem, however, Habermas is explicit about his disillusionment with transcendental attempts at justification. In his *Postmetaphysical Thinking*, he contends that appeals to metaphysics are no longer feasible. If one understands metaphysics as a kind of philosophy in search of a unifying, 'universal, eternal, and necessary being'[33] that is the foundation of everything, the problem at the level of practical philosophy, according to Habermas, is that metaphysics cannot recognize the individual as an autonomous being but only as an accidental aspect of a universal unity.[34] That is why Habermas is sceptical about a fundamental grounding of discursive presuppositions. For, to have already accepted the presuppositions of argumentation that analogously implicates moral intuitions is the same as Kant's a priorism, which Habermas dismisses. But to say that the presuppositions are empirically arrived at – via the reconstruction of universal pragmatics – as Habermas does, and then are presupposed, is precisely what constitutes the problem of circularity.

3. The Justificatory Role of 'Performative Contradiction'

In his more recent works Habermas has turned away from attempts to provide justification for discourse ethics either transcendentally or empirically. That is to say, instead of appealing to deductive or inductive arguments, Habermas once again draws on Apel's notion of 'performative contradiction' as a justificatory argument. In his 'Discourse Ethics: Notes on a Program of Philosophical Justification'[35] he argues that questioning the pragmatic presuppositions of argumentation constitutes the actor's performative contradiction. For example, if somebody states, 'I doubt that I exist,' she raises the truth claim with the propositional content 'I do not exist.' At the same time, the utterance of the former statement is based on an existential assumption with the propositional content that states, 'I exist,' where the personal pronoun in both statement refers to the same person. Thus, the cognitive proposition of the actor's speech act requires her to presuppose the discursive rules for her utterance to avoid self-contradiction. Habermas writes:

Apel turns this form of performative refutation of the skeptic into a mode of justification, which he describes as follows: 'If, on the one hand, a presupposition cannot be challenged in argumentation without actual performative self-contradiction, and if, on the other hand, it cannot be deductively grounded without formal-logical *petitio principii*, then it belongs to those transcendental pragmatic presuppositions of argumentation that one must always (already) have accepted, if the language game of argumentation is to be meaningful.'[36]

While employing the concept of 'performative contradiction' is an improvement upon both deductive and inductive modes of justification, its justificatory power is effective only in so far as the presupposition of universal pragmatics is concerned, and not necessarily for what it analogously implies in terms of the presupposition of moral intuitions. That is to say, the fact that we already have accepted the rules of argumentation does not justify the moral ideals of discourse ethics. For even with such a presupposition, there can be other moral interpretations than the one suggested by discourse ethics (i.e., care, responsibility, happiness, etc.).

This tension in the quasi-transcendental status of discourse ethics causes Habermas's ambivalence. He knows that in order to reject value scepticism the theory needs to have a universal and transcendental reach, but he also wants to avoid foundationalism, because a foundationalist theory claims an absolute status – maintaining that the theory can justify the absolute, necessary, and universal validity of its respective conception of knowledge or morality. Habermas has tried to answer accusations of the foundationalist tendencies of his theory of communicative action itself by arguing that, unlike the roots of his theory (in Kant, Hegel, Marx), the theory itself is not playing the role of an 'usher' among the sciences by showing their ultimate limitations. It tries rather to demonstrate the conditions under which meaningful actions are rendered valid in different disciplines by way of what he has described earlier as reconstructive sciences.[37] Habermas claims that he has replaced traditional Kantian foundationalism with a reconstructive approach that accounts for the pre-theoretical knowledge of the agent's pragmatic competence. He emphasizes the pragmatic aspect of his theory by saying that the empirical 'limitation of practical discourses testify to *the power history has over transcendental claims and interests of reason.*'[38] Moreover, he reminds us that the validity claims of communicative action or discourse ethics have a hypothetical, and not an absolute, status. Still, Habermas believes that this does not prevent reconstructive sciences from constituting cognitive, interactive, and linguistic competences as the quasi-transcendental conditions of possible experience:

> It is important to say that rational reconstructions, like all other types of knowledge, have only a hypothetical status. They may very well start from a false sample of intuitions; they may obscure and distort the right intuitions; and they may, even more often, overgeneralize particular cases. They are in need of further corroboration. What I accept as an anti-foundationalist criticism of all strong a priori and transcendentalist claims does not, however, block attempts to put rational reconstructions of supposedly basic competences on trial and to test them indirectly by employing them as input in empirical theories.[39]

Habermas thinks that his explanation helps avoid the charge of foundationalism. But if this explanation is accepted, then it will, at the same time, weaken the status of his moral claims and narrow the moral perspective of his theory. He confesses: 'Any ethics that is at once deontological, cognitivist, formalist, and universalist ends up with a relatively narrow conception of morality that is uncompromisingly abstract.'[40] Here Habermas tries to make it clear that discourse ethics does not claim to be able to provide concrete and substantive solutions to moral issues of our time, which is one weakness of his theory. But in explaining this shortcoming, he emphasizes an aspect of the theory that is reminiscent of Kant's foundationalism:

> What moral theory can do and should be trusted to do is to clarify the *universal core of our moral intuitions* and thereby to refute value skepticism. What it cannot do is to make any kind of substantive contribution. By singling out a procedure of decision making, it seeks to make room for those involved, who must then find answers on their own to the moral practical issues that come at them, or are imposed upon them, with objective historical force. Moral philosophy does not have privileged access to particular truths ... Philosophy cannot absolve anyone of moral responsibility.[41]

Even if we accept Habermas's minimalist ethics, 'it runs the risk of falling into a certain rationalistic fallacy of the Kantian sort, in that it ignores the contingent, historical, and effective circumstances which made individuals adopt a universalist-ethical standpoint in the first place.'[42] In other words, how can a formalist and universalist theory, which does not take into account the concrete issues of one's specific context as distinct and relevant to one's identity, provide guidance to problems of who one is and how one should live one's life? However, if we accept the minimal character of Habermas's theory, then it seems that the theory falls short of addressing the self-constitution problem of the modern subject. For the identity formation of subjects also has to do with their life context. To put it in Habermas's words, '[T]he identity of a nation or of a region is always something concrete, something particular ... which can never consist merely in general moral orientations and characteristics, which are shared by all alike.'[43] Granted that, generally speaking, in moral and political theories the issue of justice does not necessarily entail the problem of subjects' self-constitution and vice versa. Still, in Habermas's theory, as mentioned earlier, the two are different faces of the same coin. For the ideal of justice, along with truth and freedom, forms a moral competence that is constitutive of rational subjects (see quote on page 68). Given this connection between justice and self-constitution, the theory's one-sided emphasis on the question of justice that leaves out considerations of the good life (with respect to who we are as individual subjects) is also indicative of a failure to successfully account for subjects' self-formation.

Once again, to spell out this connection is not to burden Habermas with a task that he does not set for himself. His theory, rather, incorporates the goal of addressing problems of both justice and the self-constitution of the subject when it defends 'an outrageously strong claim' that locates the core of our rationality and morality in a cognitive competence that is definitive of our interaction in all times and all societies.[44] Since Habermas sees his theory as being in line with 'the project of modernity,' which has been defined as an account of the identity formation of the modern subject as a rational and moral agent, his effort is aimed at both universal reconstruction of the subject's communicative competence (which constitutes morality) and the actual influence of the moral theory's insight for the ideal of a free society in real life. Depending of course on the force and direction of the criticism levelled against him, Habermas has shown ambivalence towards the respective importance of these two aspects of his theory. Up to the end of MCCA he insists that his moral theory of discourse ethics cannot take on concrete issues of ethical life. Yet shortly thereafter, and as a result of Hegelian critique of his discourse ethics, he begins to look for ways to say something about the contentful life. He writes: 'I am not claiming here that questions of justice are the only relevant questions. *Ethical-existential questions are usually far more urgent – questions which oblige the individual or the collective to get clear about who they are and would like to be.* Such problems of self-understanding can oppress us far more than questions of justice.'[45] The two problems of identifying principles of justice and accounting for the subjects' self-understanding entail the further problem of an application of the insight of moral norms, since the abstraction that happens as the result of the formal and universal character of discourse ethics empties the moral norms from the content that gives them meaning.

Discourse ethics's narrow conception of morality focuses on questions of *justification* and leaves aside the problematic of *application*, since Habermas believes that 'the process of application escapes the procedure of universalization.'[46] As various critics have pointed out, the separation of justification from application *à la* Kant remains a constant source of tension in Habermas.[47] Any specialized ethics as such leaves an account of how to undo the abstract moral maxim, with respect to a particular context, that is desired. Habermas recognizes this problem at the end of *MCCA* when he writes:

> No norm contains within itself the rules for its application. Yet moral justifications are pointless unless the decontextualization of the general norms used in justification is compensated for in the process of application. Like any moral theory, discourse ethics cannot evade the difficult problem of whether the application of rules to particular cases necessitates a separate and distinct faculty of *prudence* or judgment that would tend to undercut the universalistic claim of justificatory reason because it is tied to the parochial context of some hermeneutic starting point.[48]

In a series of articles thereafter, however, Habermas acknowledges the need to bridge the gap between justification and contextualization of discourse ethics. If discourse ethics is to be fruitful, it needs to bring the insight of our moral ideals to bear on what is permissible in actuality. In an interview entitled 'Discourse Ethics, Law and *Sittlichkeit*' he states that 'only with reference to concrete individuals cases will it become apparent which of the competing principles is the appropriate one for the current content. That is the task of the discourses of application.'[49] The need for the reference to concrete individual cases arises because 'knowledge of which norms and principles are valid is not yet sufficient for knowing how I shall act in a particular situation.'[50] Here Habermas is explicit about how we should avoid 'a one-sided concentration on questions of grounding' over questions of application, since there exists a relation of 'complementarity' between them.[51]

That is why, in *Justification and Application: Remarks on Discourse Ethics*, Habermas distinguishes three domains of use for practical reason: a pragmatic, an ethical, and a moral use. The first two, according to Habermas, do not admit of universally valid norms, while the third, the issue of justice in social interaction, can be decided on a basis of a universal norm of judgment. In the book's-second essay, 'Remarks on Discourse Ethics,' he introduces 'a two stage process of argument consisting of justification followed by application of norms.'[52] Borrowing from Klaus Günther's *Der Sinn für Angemessenheit*,[53] Habermas continues, '[I]n discourse of application, the principle of *appropriateness* takes on the role played by the principle of universalization in justificatory discourse ... What must be decided is not the validity of the norm for each individual and his interests but its appropriateness in relation to all of the features of a particular situation.'[54] These remarks are indicative of a newly found interest in Habermas, namely, to provide discourse ethics with a theoretical ability to account for the application of moral law to the actual life. The separation of justification from application in practical discourse ethics still means that programmatic, hypothetical reasoning for the justification of norms leaves out the consideration of contextual institutions. In other words, discourse ethics is still not able to bridge the gap between practical issues and their respective moral norms, on the one hand, and what Hegel calls the substantive ethics (*Sittlichkeit*) of the subject's self-realization, on the other. As Habermas himself puts it, '[U]nless discourse ethics is undergirded by the thrust of motives and by socially accepted institutions, the moral insight it offers remains ineffective in practice.'[55] In other words, the efficacy of a moral norm depends on whether it can be correctly applied to a practical context. An effective application, in turn, can provide motivation for moral action. The problem of motivation, therefore, is related to that of application. For as much as a clear account of an effective application of a moral rule can strengthen the motivation of an agent to act upon it, a theory devoid of such an account can weaken the agent's motivation and disturb her moral decision.

The separation of justification from application also suggests that there is a residue of a Kantian dichotomy left in Habermas's account.[56] Earlier I discussed how, from a Hegelian perspective, the separation of the phenomenal and noumenal world, duty and inclination, rendered Kant's ethics untenable. What creates the same difficulty for Habermas is, on the one hand, his belief in the evolutionary 'universal core of our moral intuition' and, on the other, his further belief in contextual socio-cultural factors as important in the formation of our identity. To put it more clearly, evaluative issues of the good life can be seen as issues concerning the empirical context involved in human subjects' self-formation, which determine who we are. These issues, however, will require more than is allowed by the formalist distantiation between the ideal situation and the participants required by discourse ethics. As Habermas himself later confesses, 'Moral judgments, decoupled from concrete ethical life (*Sittlichkeit*), no longer immediately carry the motivational power that converts judgments into actions.'[57] Hence, for Habermas's theory, as for any other morality, it is important to be able to answer why it is good to be moral. For discourse ethics would be of little use if it ignores questions of motivation and application, which have to do with the content of one's life. Ethical questions, as opposed to moral questions, are context-dependent and as such do not comply with the idealized distantiation that is needed as a condition of rational argumentation. Regarding one's life, one cannot simply make a leap to a decontextualized situation because, then, the validity claims of one's particular needs that are to be submitted to argumentation will lose their meaning. Consequently, with respect to the Hegelian distinction between morality and the ethical life, *pace* Habermas, discourse ethics may still be seen as 'an empty formalism' that 'does not represent much of a gain for the real concern of philosophical ethics.'[58]

On the topic of Hegel's critique of Kant, Gordon Finlayson notes that while the term 'empty formalism' has generally described Hegel's critique of Kantian morality, it is an effective criticism only in so far as it refers to a more sophisticated point that Hegel made in his *Elements of Philosophy of Rights*, namely, the 'indeterminacy' of moral judgment in Kant. Whereas the earlier[59] charge of formalism can be deflected by showing that not all formal principles are empty, Hegel's later[60] statement of this charge makes a different claim – 'that the indeterminacy of the moral standpoint results from the attempt to settle the question of the validity of moral laws formally – that is, prior to and independent of their relation to a possible content.'[61] As a result, very few moral maxims are sufficiently determined to be applicable to a particular context. Finlayson wants to argue that Hegel's objection to the 'abstract indeterminacy' of Kant's moral theory can be extended to Habermas's discourse ethics: '[I]n Hegel's eyes Kant is guilty of separating universal from particular content, whereas the procedural principle U separates universalizable content from particular content. The result, however, is equally incapacitating.'[62] Discourse ethics decidedly does not embrace the contextual factors since they are assumed to be biased; instead, it is apt to settle the general issues of justice (morality) rationally. And since only few moral laws pass the filter of its U principle as the test of their validity, moral discourse is rendered of little use for our moral lives. Thus, given that the identity of the individual is formed within the context of ethical life, such minimal insight would not provide any meaningful answer to the problem of self-constitution and of self-realization of the modern subject.

Moreover, the communicative rationality that gives rise to the basis of moral ideals through analogy is only one factor involved in the self-constitution of the moral subject. Other factors involved in this process, such as normative obligations, relations of production, and power relations, are context-dependent and as such defy discourse ethics's formalism. On the basis of a rationality that is interior to communicative interaction, Habermas has given a privileged status to discursive rationality over the other ingredients of the social reproduction of life, even though this privileged status is not actual, but an ideal status that requires a formal and universal reconstruction of the humanist ideals of justice, freedom, and truth inherent in language. Thus, one may still argue that a Hegelian critique of discourse ethics would persist: insofar as its formalist and universalist character of hypothetical justification go, discourse ethics does not offer us a substantive knowledge of ethical norms. And insofar as it wants to claim such an insight, through the emancipatory force of the idealization of the discursive situation, it runs the risk of foundational a priorism. It appears, then, that Habermas's theory is lost between a Scylla of foundationalism and a Charybdis of the context of the good life. In order to avoid traditional foundationalism, his reconstructive sciences cannot claim strong status. Then, however, the theory as such is unable to effectively address its target of ethical constitution of the modern subject, thereby strengthening the Hegelian criticism of emptiness and ineffectiveness. It is one thing to claim the innateness of argumentation for speech acts, but it does not thereby follow that everybody, all the time and everywhere, is both *able* and *willing* to engage in argumentation. Indeed, '[t]he ability and the motivation for reason have their genesis in conditions which reason does not control, but out of which it itself emerges.'[63] The unintended infallibilism of discourse ethics is not in its mode of justification – which has already been secured by Habermas as hypothetical and not absolute – but in its privileged status as emancipatory idealization. This would be the implication of the strong status that Habermas's moral theory claims. But what if we weaken the claim so that it does not appear to claim an *a priori* ground for our moral intuition but just propose a procedural requirement for a fair social interaction? In this respect, communicative ethics definitely has something to contribute to a critical social theory.

4. The Minimal Contribution of Communicative Ethics

If we reject Habermas's claim that the moral ideals of modernity are always already present in the discursive situation as a kind of communicative intuition, does it mean that we have to give up his entire theory? An affirmative answer would mean throwing out the baby with the bathwater. For we can read Habermas in the following way: realizing the metaphysical inadequacy of the foundationalist philosophy, he attempts to avoid the a priorism of transcendental approaches by appealing to the method of 'reconstructive sciences,' which are only pragmatically – a posteriori – universal. The theory of formal pragmatics accounts for a formal structure of rational communication that is common to all speech acts. The structural logic of this universal competence permits a fair and impartial adjudication of all validity claims raised in a discursive situation. The establishing of the mutual recognition and normative evaluation of validity claims based on the force of the better argument is a valuable contribution of discourse ethics to any critical social theory. Reformulating this modest insight, we then can say that if in specific cases participants are serious and rationally motivated, there will be enough 'quasi-transcendental' constraints that could lead to a possible consensus.

Thus, discourse ethics stands or falls depending on whether we accept or reject the following two assumptions: '(a) that normative claims to validity have cognitive meaning and can be treated *like* claims to truth and (b) that the justification of norms and demands requires that a real discourse be carried out and thus cannot occur in a strictly monological form.'[64] The universalization required to carry out the real discourse does not need to be a Kantian one, for '[t]he emphasis shifts from what each can will without contradiction to be a universal law to what all can will in agreement to be a universal norm.'[65] However, as critics of the Kantian interpretation of the principle of universalization (U) have shown,[66] *the justification of the moral insight is not the arrived consensus but the rational procedure that brings such a consensus about.* The reason, as Seyla Benhabib states it, is that '[c]onsent alone can never be a criterion of anything, neither of truth nor of moral validity; rather, it is always the rationality of the procedure for attaining agreement which is of philosophical interest.'[67] Albrecht Wellmer, in his *Ethik und Dialog,* cogently criticizes Habermas's account of the relation between truth, rationality, and consensus. He argues that since we cannot formally characterize the rationality of a consensus, the rationality of a consensus does not entail truth. For him the idea of an ultimate consensus pollutes Habermas's pragmatic philosophy of language with the objectivist illusions of logical empiricism.[68] The ideal of agreement, therefore, needs to be viewed as a regulative principle rather than a constitutive one. Hence, in order to overcome the above criticisms, principles of discourse need recourse to actual practices of a context rather than an abstract universalization. The principle (U) should be necessitated by the context of practical issues, since the very introduction of the concept arises from within the modern culture of pluralism. Seeing (U) in such a way allows for overcoming the restriction of discourse ethics only to questions of justice. Questions of the good life, too, can be effectively decided by being submitted to the procedure of discursive argumentation. The importance of discourse ethics is precisely in providing us with such a procedural deliberation on practical issues. Seyla Benhabib explicates this view of the theory as follows:

> Discourse ethics does not simulate a thought experiment for all beings capable of speech, and establish what norms they ought to accept as binding. It requires that controversies over the validity of contested norms be settled through an argumentative process in which the *consensus of all concerned* decides upon the legitimacy of the controversial norm. *Participation precedes universalizability.*[69]

This proposed shift in emphasis from the ideal of consensus to the deliberative procedure also resolves the problem of circularity, since we agree to submit even the presuppositions of discourse, if necessary, to the conversation, in which the burden of proof would be on the side of anyone who wants to challenge the validity of discursive presupposition. Furthermore, stressing the procedure allows for participants' awareness of the historico-cultural context to be taken into account, thereby dissolving the danger of ethnocentrism by making the discourse conscious of where it is situated. As Benhabib explains:

> When we shift the burden of moral test in communicative ethics from consensus to the idea of an ongoing moral conversation, we can begin to ask not what all would or could agree to as a result of practical discourses to be morally permissible or impermissible, but what would be allowed and perhaps even necessary from the stand point of continuing and sustaining the practice of the moral conversation among us. The emphasis is now less on *rational agreement*, but more on sustaining those normative practices and moral relationships within which reasoned agreement *as a way of life* can flourish and continue.[70]

To sum up, we can say that a critical social theory aims to provide a normative ground for the study of human interaction, its distorted forms under domination, and the possibility of its emancipation. For this critical purpose, Habermas's theory of communicative action is serviceable because it accounts for the conditions of deliberation about human interests as a structural procedure of communication. Thus far, we have seen how this theory explains the capacity of human subjects for such a procedural deliberation. In the next chapter I will discuss the appropriation of this insight on engaging in the discursive situation for the purpose of giving an account of the evolution of society and the legitimation of its political order, which is the next step in formulating a normative theory of society.

Chapter 4

Discourse Ethics and Legitimation Problems in Advanced Capitalism

As traditional 'lifeworld' horizons disintegrate, individuals find themselves burdened with new demands, choices, and freedoms. And as societies become more complex, individual find themselves inhabiting multiple and pluralistic roles for which traditional identities are unsuited. Under these circumstances, new identities must be generated by individuals themselves. Moreover, the performance of complex institutions increasingly requires that identities be discursively negotiated, which in turn requires appropriate institutional spaces. In political language, this means that democratic empowerment – a condition of discursively formed identities – is increasingly necessary for modern societies to function.

Mark E. Warren[1]

The foregoing discussion has illustrated how Habermas's concept of reconstructive sciences enables him to abandon the monological and self-estranged voice of the philosophy of consciousness in favour of a consensual understanding of an intersubjective rationality. Formal reconstruction of such a rationality yields a communicative theory capable of resolving the problem of modernity by accounting for the constitution of modern subjects as mature, critical, and autonomous agents via their linguistic interaction. Communicative action theory, in turn, leads to an ethics of discourse, wherein competent subjects can test one another's validity claims by norms of argumentation. Anticipation of such an ideal situation is the condition of achieving maturity as one of the original ideals of modernity. However, the task of emancipation further requires drawing on the relation between reconstructive sciences and the notion of critique so as to produce a critical social theory that accounts for the possibility of solidarity in a true society. To demonstrate the possibility of democracy in modern societies, Habermas's critical theory must show how the damaged intersubjectivity and deformed lifeworld can be repaired and overcome. And to do so, he needs to explicate what his theory of communicative action and discourse ethics implies for the political dimension of our social interaction. Having shown the evolutionary character of the human subject's communicative competence with its normative core that constitutes a theory of morality, Habermas is able to move to the next stage of his project: constructing a theory of justice capable of diagnosing the maladies of our modern society. Henceforth, the focus of Habermas's project comes to the fore as the pathology of the social order and of political power in the Western world in relation to the possibility of social justice and emancipation.

In what follows, then, (section 1) I will discuss Habermas's analogy between the individual's learning and society's development that grounds the formulation of his theory of the evolution of society and the crisis of legitimation; (2) the topics of evolution and the crisis of society will be examined as framed within the context of the lifeworld/ system distinction; (3) the logic of systemic and lifeworldly reproduction in society will bring to the fore the problem of the possibility of legitimate political power; and, finally, (4) Habermas's argument that a normative social theory requires the institutionalization of discursive procedures will be assessed. I realize that these topics, if treated on their own, require a much more detailed examination. However, my discussion is restricted to their relevance to the development of Habermas's later view of a political theory of democracy. With this goal in mind, then, the following is a selective treatment of these topics.

1. Social Evolution and the Problem of Legitimation

In discussing Habermas's project thus far, I have only examined the theory of communicative interaction that grounds a moral theory of discourse without drawing out the social and political implications of Habermas's universal pragmatics. Since *Legitimation Crisis* (*LC*) and *Communication and the Evolution of Society* (*CES*), however, Habermas has been eager to complement his moral philosophy with a social and political theory. For while his initial attempt at solving the problem of modernity takes the form of communicative theory, his ambition is to appropriate that insight for the purpose of providing a critical social theory. He wants to apply the insight of the discursive situation, where modern subjects anticipate the ideal state of emancipation, in order to theorize the possibility of a free society, that is, democracy.

For Habermas the reconstruction of universal pragmatics is dependent upon human subjects acquiring the communicative competences not only on an individual level, but on a social level as well. The following question of his brings to focus this point: 'Could a universalistic linguistic ethics no longer connected to cognitive interpretations of nature and society (a) adequately stabilize itself, and (b) structurally secure the identities of individuals and collectives in the framework of a world society?'[2] At the core of this question lies the idea that the social context of the individual's learning in the form of developmental psychology suggests an analogous level of social learning.[3] The main point of Habermas's essay 'The Development of Normative Structures' in *CES* is that the evolution of human society can be reconstructed as a learning process. He sees a parallel between social and individual development, or to put it in his words, between 'the reproduction of society and the socialization of its members.'[4] In appropriating the model of developmental psychology of Piaget and Kohlberg, Habermas uses the ordering of stages of moral consciousness to describe the individual's ontogenetic moral development. Accordingly, the three developmental stages of moral consciousness – preconventional, conventional, and postconventional – lead, for Habermas, to different structures of actions, world views, and institutions in four levels of *social integration*: neolithic society, early civilization, developed civilization, and the modern-age society.[5] This description allows Habermas to draw a homology between individual and societal learning.

> The *learning mechanisms* have to be sought first on the psychological level. If that succeeds, with the help of cognitive developmental psychology, there is a need for additional empirical assumptions that might explain sociologically how individual learning processes find their way into society's collectively accessible store of knowledge. *Individually acquired learning abilities* and information must be latently available in worldviews before they can be used in a socially significant way, that is, before they can be transposed into *societal learning processes*.[6]

For Habermas evolution is a 'directed process' of accumulation of greater problem-solving capacities. That is to say, in the same way that individuals develop their cognitive competence and learn how to be moral agents capable of participating in a discursive situation, societies too evolve towards a greater rationality.

This theory of evolution is perhaps best understood in view of Habermas's Marxist belief in historical materialism, which he claims, in 'Toward a Reconstruction of Historical Materialism,' remains a constant feature of his philosophical orientation.[7] In this essay he argues that historical materialism is best suited to attempt the reconstruction of societal development. Against the widely held claim that 'the Marxist elements are more and more muted, and soften, in his work,'[8] I would like to emphasize Habermas's continued stress on Marxist themes such as the role and the importance of the critique of ideology, material conditions, social practices, and the ideal of liberation of society from domination. Still, given its root, Habermas's critical theory goes beyond the tradition of undogmatic Marxism by supplementing it with the insight of the social sciences and psychology, which provides him with a critical distance from orthodox Marxism.[9]

Criticizing the Marxist view of historical materialism for its one-sided emphasis on the role of work in human activity, however, Habermas argues that 'historical materialism does not need to assume a *species-subject* that undergoes evolution. The bearers of evolution are rather societies and acting subjects integrated into them.'[10] He contends that instead of classifying the social formations in terms of their modes of production he needs to 'search for highly abstract principles of social organization ... which institutionalize new levels of societal learning.'[11] Being rooted in the socially shared world views, *the principles of social organization* can define different social formations, their inner contradictions, and the types of crisis those contradictions entail.[12] The principles of organization 'determine the learning capacity, and thus the level of development, of a society.'[13] Crisis as coming to the fore of a contradiction latent in the organizational principle is what constitutes the development of society.

This concept of the organizational principles of society allows Habermas to describe the following social formations. In *primitive* society, the organizational principle is that of age and sex, which forms the kinship system as the core institution of society. 'Since no contradictory imperatives follow from this principle of organization, it is external changes that overload the narrowly limited steering capacity of societies.'[14] In the *traditional* social formation, the organizational principle is class domination, which displaces the kinship system and gives the role of the central institution to the state. Here, crisis arises as a result of internal contradiction: 'The contradiction exists between validity claims of systems of norms and justifications that cannot explicitly permit exploitation, and a class structure in which privileged appropriation of socially produced wealth is the rule.'[15] This crisis eventually leads to the *liberal-capitalist* formation, where the organizational principle is 'the relationship of wage labor and capital, which is anchored in the system of bourgeois civil law'[16] as free from the political-economic system: *civil society*. The capitalist principle of organization also uncouples the economic system from the political system, enabling it to 'make a contribution to social integration.' On the negative side, however, with the economic system thus freed, 'the susceptibility of the social system to crisis certainly grows, as steering problems can now become *directly* threatening to identity.'[17] To put it clearly, by 'crisis' Habermas means a situation 'when members of a society experience structural alterations as critical for continued existence and feel their social identity threatened.'[18]

While primitive and traditional formations find their legitimating power in myth and traditional authority, liberal-capitalist society 'finds its justification in the legitimate relations of production.'[19] In the nineteenth century the local struggles and internal contradiction of the liberal-capitalist formation are 'replaced by social confrontation of artisans, industrial workers, (and) the rural proletariat.'[20] According to Habermas, 'This dynamic produced new legitimation problems. The bourgeois state could not rely on the integrative power of national consciousness alone: it had to try to head off the conflicts inherent in the economic system and channel them into the political system as an institutionalized struggle over distribution. Where this succeeded, the modern state took on one of the forms of social welfare state – mass democracy.'[21]

Before turning to the possibility of democracy with respect to the crises of advanced capitalist society, we need to clarify what Habermas means by legitimation problems. Within the context of his theory of social evolution, Habermas is interested in uncovering the dynamic of changes in our modern society in two respects: first, to identify the possibilities of evolutionary development in the structure of society, and second, to identify the crisis tendencies of such structures. While his investigation includes earlier socio-economic formations, his focus is on modern capitalism and its potential to overcome its crises. In the structure of advanced capitalism, Habermas distinguishes three subsystems, the economic, the political-administrative, and the socio-cultural. He argues that as a consequence of the contradiction of the organizational principle of the capitalist system, crisis can arise in different subsystems. Crisis tendencies in each domain are followed up

Table 3 Crises in the subsystems of advanced capitalism

Point of origin (subsystems)	System crisis	Identity crisis
Economic	Economic crisis	—
Political	Rationality crisis	Legitimation crisis
Socio-cultural	—	Motivation crisis

Source: LC, 45.

in some detail (see table 3). For our purposes, however, it should suffice to reiterate Habermas's claim that in the final analysis the economic growth in capitalism, which 'takes shape as a function, not of generalizable interests of population, but of private goals of profit maximization,'[22] reveals a structural tension that is the source of legitimation deficit. But what exactly does he mean by *legitimation*?

According to Habermas a critical theory of society needs a concept of legitimation that allows for 'demarcation of the types of legitimate authority.'[23] In his view: 'Legitimacy means that there are good arguments for a political order's claim to be recognized as right and just, a legitimate order deserves recognition.'[24] This definition assumes an inherent connection between legitimacy and truth, and as such gives the concept of legitimacy a normative tenor. That is, '[t]he definition highlights the fact that legitimacy is a contestable validity claim.'[25] Furthermore, the concept of legitimacy only applies to political systems and is measured against the recognition of their claim to prevent social disintegration and to maintain 'society in its normatively determined identity.'[26] The recognition itself depends upon empirical motives, on 'what are accepted as reasons and have the power to produce consensus, and thereby to shape motives.'[27] The empirical motives, in their turn, depend on 'the level of justification required in a given situation.'[28]

With the Enlightenment's principle of reason replacing the material principle of justification of norms such as God and nature, the ultimate ground of justification is replaced by the formal conditions of justification. 'The procedure and presuppositions of rational agreement themselves become principles ... It is the formal conditions of possible consensus formation, rather than ultimate grounds, which possess legitimation force.'[29] Habermas calls these formal conditions for legitimacy *levels of justification*. He then contends that the shift from the traditional principles of justification to the formal principles of modernity is 'connected with social-evolutionary transitions to new learning levels,'[30] which for him means that the level of justification in modernity has become *reflexive*. By employing the insight of the last chapter as the procedural deliberation of discourse ethics, complemented by the reflexive character of modern levels of justification, Habermas believes that a definite step towards an emancipated society is to seek consensual ordering of political institutions based on the uncoerced agreement of all political participants as an independent learning process that does not rely on any ultimate ground. He writes:

> I can imagine the attempt to arrange a society democratically only as a self-controlled learning process. It is a question of finding arrangements which can ground the presupposition that the basic institutions of society and the basic political decisions would meet with the unforced agreement of all those involved, if they could participate, as free and equal, in discursive will-formation. Democratization cannot mean an *a priori* preference for a specific type of organization for example, for so called direct democracy.[31]

The achievement of this ideal, however, is forestalled by the internal crisis of advanced capitalism, which involves disturbances in the two fronts of social and system integration. Social integration refers to the socialization of acting subjects, who are socially related through '*lifeworlds* that are symbolically structured,'[32] while system integration refers to 'the specific steering performances of a self-regulating *system*.'[33] I will return to this distinction in the next section. The reason that this internal crisis hinders the goal of democratically arranged society is that societal evolution depends on the subject's learning processes, derived from communicative action, which belong to the domain of the lifeworld, while the ordering of the political system is not regulated by norms but governed by steering media. However, before moving on to a discussion of Habermas's system/lifeworld distinction, I need to consider whether the analogy between individual and societal learning that grounds his theory of social evolution is tenable or not. Such a critical examination is necessary because Habermas's account of evolution and the rational progress of society is built upon this alleged analogy between the individual's learning process, based on her cognitive competence, and the progress of post-conventional society. Therefore, to show whether this analogy stands or falls is an important component of a critical assessment of Habermas's project at this stage.

Locating the developmental logic at the base of the theory of social evolution implies the moralization of historical materialism. According to Habermas, '[d]evelopmental-logical connections for the ontogenesis of action competence, particularly of moral consciousness, have already been rendered plausible.'[34] Despite his own warning that 'we ought not to draw from ontogenesis over-hasty conclusions about the developmental levels of societies,' he insists that 'the evolutionary learning process of societies is dependent on the competences of the individuals that belong to them.'[35] His warning, however, serves as the ground for an immanent critique levelled against his theory of social evolution by other critical theorists, who charge that Habermas's analogy between individual and societal learning is an ontogenetic fallacy, arguing that the latter does not necessarily follow from the former.[36]

Anticipating this critique, first, Thomas McCarthy calls attention to 'questions concerning the applicability of ontogenetic models to social systems – the characterization of the infrastructure of society as a network of actions certainly does not suffice to justify this transposition.'[37] Perhaps more importantly, however, with reference to Kohlberg's theory of moral development, McCarthy in his 'Rationality and Relativism: Habermas' Overcoming of Hermeneutics' argues that in such models of the psychological development of moral agents there is an incongruity between the examination of the higher and lower stages of moral development. He contends that in the lower stages of cognitive development 'there is an asymmetry presupposed between the insufficiently decentered thought of the child, traditional culture, or whatever, and the differentiated, reflective thought of the investigator.'[38] In lower cases, then, 'we are dealing with the acquisition of unreflectively mastered know-hows.' Acquiring a higher level of cognitive ability, however, requires a break from the unreflective character of the lower stages and a move into a discursive and reflective cognitive level. But this means that a subject at this level has entered the moral psychologist's realm of argumentation. McCarthy concludes: 'Thus the asymmetry between the pre-reflective and reflective, between theories-in-action and explications, which underlies the model of reconstruction begins to break down. The subject is now in a position to argue with the moral theorists about questions of morality.'[39] Taking up McCarthy's criticism that both the lower and the higher level of cognitive development cannot be investigated with the same method, Seyla Benhabib draws upon the implication of this critique for Habermas's theory of communicative ethics in the following way:

> Even if evolutionary reconstructive arguments play a role in moral theory, they cannot serve to justify a specific kind of theory from among those

sharing a post-conventional stage of moral development. Developmental moral theory is *underdetermined* in this respect. Once we reach the stage of a universalist moral orientation in which individuals can generate normative principles of action through formal procedures satisfying criteria of impartiality, universalizability, reversibility, and prescriptivity, we can no longer arbitrate between competing moral theories on the basis of these criteria.[40]

The critique of the applicability of the ontogenetic model to social systems is further taken up and elaborated by Axel Honneth and Hans Joas, who argue that social formations can only be explained in terms of collective actions, and that Habermas's abstract logic of the development of society is historically too insensitive.[41] Klaus Eder's discussion of Habermas's ontogenetic fallacy is perhaps the most fruitful, since, as Piet Strydom has suggested, it not only spells out the problem, but also presents an outline of a solution. Eder states:

> On the one hand, the ontogenetic fallacy consists in drawing a conclusion from ontogenesis in respect of the change and development of culture or collective symbolic systems which can be accounted for only with reference to supra-individual learning process. At this level, therefore, the ontogenetic fallacy can be overcome by the introduction of the concept of social or collective learning process. On the other hand, the ontogenetic fallacy is committed when one transfers the ontogenetic model to the level of evolution. As suggested earlier, the solution of the ontogenetic fallacy at this level demands rather more drastic intervention. On the whole, it involves a radical break with the developmental logic conception of evolution as such.[42]

Finally, Michael Schmid argues along the same lines that 'the postulation of a developmental logic leads to questionable assumptions about the relation between ontogenesis and the development of worldviews,' and as such has to be abandoned since it burdens the empirical theory of evolution with normative ambiguities.[43] He contends that Habermas's hypothesis of optimization, latent in his theory of evolution, which interprets progress as higher problem-solving capacities, is quite misleading.[44] Other critical theorists such as M. Miller, J. Arenson, G. Frankenberg, and U. Rödel have contributed to this immanent critique of Habermas's theory of social evolution.[45]

Consequently, Habermas comes to fully accept the force of the above critique in his later writings to the extent that in *Eine Art Scha-densabwicklung* he writes: 'It would be a mistake to think of group identities as ego-identities in a large scale – the relationship between the two is not one of analogy but one of complementarity.'[46] As a result of the immanent critique of his evolution theory, Habermas abandons the analogy between a person-dependent ontogenetic learning process and the notion of social or collective learning. This move can best be seen in the second volume of *TCA*, where in discussing the subject's normative development in terms of her symbolic interaction, he criticizes G.H. Mead's theory as having an ontogenetic focus that causes him to ignore the phylogenetic aspect of the human lifeworld. Habermas concludes his discussion of Mead's theory of communication as follows:

> Thus Mead attributes normative validity directly to the sanction-free, that is, moral authority of the generalized other. The latter is supposed to have arisen by way of the internalization of group sanctions. However, this explanation can hold only for ontogenesis, for groups must have first been constituted as units capable of acting before sanctions could be imposed in their name.[47]

In taking up the genetic priority of society over the individual, Habermas finds Emile Durkheim's concept of 'collective consciousness' helpful. Appropriating this concept, he argues:

> Participants in symbolically mediated interaction can transform themselves, so to speak, from exemplars of an animal species with an inborn, species-specific environment into members of a collective with a lifeworld only to the degree that a generalized other – we might also say: a collective consciousness or a group identity – has taken shape.[48]

However, since Durkheim thought of collective consciousness as the expression of a wide range of cultural forms, the concept, according to Habermas, is too broad and undifferentiated. That is to say, Durkheim's notion of collective consciousness expresses both cognitive and moral aspects of group identity.[49] Habermas wants to distinguish the wider cultural values (e.g., religious, mythical) from more specific norms (e.g., ethics, law) to show the mediating function of communicative action, or what he calls the process of linguistification.[50] He wants to show that 'the socially integrative and expressive functions that were at first

fulfilled by ritual practice pass over to communicative action; the authority of the holy is gradually replaced by the authority of an achieved
consensus.'[51] Without going through Habermas's detailed discussion
of Mead and Durkheim and its validity, I would like to draw upon its
conclusion, which states that if we affirm the 'linguistification' of the
sacred, universalization of law and morality, and rationalization of the
lifeworld, we need to complement the theory of action with a system
theory. In other words, since the domains of social and system integration differ according to different actions, orientations, and crises, we
need to turn to a systemic theory that is 'accessible only to functionalist
analysis.'[52]

2. The System/Lifeworld Distinction

Before *TCA*, Habermas's critical position with regard to systems theory
was best formulated in his controversy with Niklas Luhmann,[53] and his
critique could be seen as a subtext to most of his writing. There, he
argued against the idea of a cybernetically self-regulated organization
of society as a 'negative utopia of technical control over history.'[54] Even
in *Legitimation Crisis* he criticizes systems theory from the standpoint of
the problems it poses for empirical analysis of social theory.[55] By the
time of *TCA*, however, he is convinced that society cannot be exclusively represented either as a domain of symbolic interaction or as a
systemic domain. Hence, he moves to combine the paradigm of lifeworld
with that of the system, hoping to obtain a more comprehensive account of modern societies. He argues: 'Since the collective subject of a
meaningfully constituted lifeworld, borrowed from transcendental philosophy, has been shown, at least in sociology, to be a misleading
fiction, the concept of system is proposed. Social systems are unities
that can solve objectively posed problems through supra-subjective
learning processes.[56] In discussing legitimation crises, Habermas distinguishes social integration, as the process of socialization of acting
subjects where integration is 'established by a normatively secured
or communicatively achieved consensus,' from system integration,
where a self-regulating system is maintained by way of a specific non-
normative steering mechanism. This distinction, Habermas contends,
'calls for a corresponding differentiation in the concept of society itself.'[57] So, he proposes '(1) that we conceive of societies *simultaneously*
as systems and lifeworlds. This concept proves itself in (2) a theory of
social evolution that separates the rationalization of the lifeworld from
the growing complexity of social systems.'[58]

For Habermas, the lifeworld is the context of meaningfulness against whose background human actions find their objective, subjective, and normative references. 'We can think of the lifeworld as represented by culturally transmitted and linguistically organized stock of interpretive patterns.'[59] The lifeworld is reproduced by different functions of communicative action that amount to renewal of knowledge, formation of personal identity, and social solidarity. In Habermas's words:

> Under the functional aspect of mutual understanding, communicative action serves to transmit and renew cultural knowledge; under the aspect of coordinating action, it serves social integration and the establishment of solidarity; finally, under the aspect of socialization, communicative action serves the formation of personal identities. The symbolic structures of the lifeworld are reproduced by way of the continuation of valid knowledge, stabilization of group solidarity, and socialization of responsible actors. The process of reproduction connects up new situations with existing conditions of the lifeworld ... Corresponding to these processes of cultural reproduction, social integration and socialization are structural components of the lifeworld: culture, society, person.[60]

It is, therefore, the medium of everyday communicative action that reproduces the culture, society, and person. Regarding this process, Habermas wants to make a further distinction between the symbolic structures of the lifeworld, which is covered by the reproductive processes, and the maintenance of the material substratum of the lifeworld.[61] The medium of material reproduction is that of purposive action, which is oriented towards attainment of objective goals and as such is not normatively regulated. When the symbolic reproduction of the lifeworld is interrupted or distorted by the norm-free medium of material reproduction (e.g., pressuring the city council to vote in favour of the ecologically unsound plan of a major corporation), the following failures, according to Habermas, will occur: problems of legitimation, orientation crises, and loss of meaning in the case of cultural reproduction; anomie and lack of solidarity in case of social integration; and crises of ego-identity and psychopathologies in the case of socialization.[62] These problems, Habermas contends, require increasing differentiation between the material reproduction of the lifeworld and the reproduction of its symbolic structure. He calls this process of differentiation *rationalization of the lifeworld*, which means that: '[t]he further the structural components of the lifeworld and the processes that contribute to maintaining them get differentiated, the more interaction contexts come under conditions of rationally motivated mutual understanding, that is, of consensus formation that rests *in the end* on the authority of the better argument.'[63] In other words, the process of rationalization keeps separate the different imperatives of the lifeworld and system, minimizing their interference. This idea helps to support Habermas's contention that society should be viewed neither solely as a system nor as the lifeworld alone, for as the hermeneutic sociology of *Verstehen* and pure systems theory have shown, both perspectives are too restrictive for an adequate social theory. The solution for him is to keep both perspectives: 'we [should] view society as an entity that, in the course of social evolution, gets differentiated both as a system and as a lifeworld.'[64] The theory of the evolution of society now has come to rest on the two processes of the growth of system complexity and communicative rationalization of life, where the first process, according to Habermas, has to be subordinated to the second one as a measure of progress.

The course of differentiation of the lifeworld and system in society also leads to their differentiation from each other, which Habermas calls 'the uncoupling of system and lifeworld.'[65] The evolution of society brings along new systemic mechanisms (e.g., administrative control, market economy) whose connection to the structural reproduction of society becomes increasingly weaker. From a systemic perspective, '[o]n this plane of analysis, the uncoupling of system and lifeworld is depicted in such a way that the lifeworld, which is at first coextensive with a scarcely differentiated social system, gets cut down more and more to one subsystem among others.'[66] From an internal perspective of the lifeworld, in the differentiated systems of capitalist society, which 'delinguistify' the media of communication into steering media of money and power, 'the lifeworld seems to shrink to a subsystem.'[67] One can see the Marxist distinction of base and superstructure in the background of Habermas's system and social integration and system/lifeworld distinction, which allows him to reiterate the Marxist claim that in the capitalist society the tension between social and system integration comes to the fore, and is made manifest, as oppression by the bourgeoisie.

> Under these conditions it is to be expected that the competition between forms of system and social integration would become more and more visible than previously. In the end, systemic mechanisms suppress forms of social integration even in those areas where a consensus-dependent

coordination of action cannot be replaced, that is, where the symbolic reproduction of the lifeworld is at stake. In these areas, the *materialization* of the lifeworld assumes the form of *colonization*.[68]

The colonization of the lifeworld takes place when the imperatives of systemic mechanisms penetrate the areas of action that are coordinated communicatively.[69] Habermas further explicates the process of colonization by stating that the media of *power* and *money* help differentiate the administrative and economic systems from the societal elements of the lifeworld, and the medium of law helps formal organization of the subsystems. As an example of this process, Habermas discusses the ever increasing legal regulation of societal life, which he terms the 'juridification of communicatively structured areas of action' (e.g., education, family life, mental and physical health, old-age life). The parallel process accompanying the process of juridification is *commodification*, where life experiences such as sexual relations, leisure activities, and personal development are influenced by the terms of the commodity economy and shaped by mass consumption.

Weber's theory of modernity attributes the fragmentation of the value spheres of art, morality, and the sciences to the increasing tendencies of bureaucratization and instrumentalization, which amount to 'loss of freedom' and 'loss of meaning.' Drawing on Weber, Habermas argues that the colonization of the lifeworld is not only the result of structural violence of purposive rationality but also the product of the uncoupling of system and lifeworld. The 'communicative infrastructure,' upon which the lifeworld is centred, 'is threatened by two interlocking, mutually reinforcing tendencies: *systematically induced reification* and *cultural impoverishment*.'[70] Against Weber, he argues that cultural improvishment is not the result merely of 'the differentiation and independent development of cultural value spheres that leads to the cultural impoverishment of everyday communicative practice,' but also of an 'elitist splitting off of expert cultures from the context of communicative action in daily life.'[71] As a result, individual actors are robbed of their ability to synthesize information and to produce a coherent interpretation of the world, which amounts to a fragmented consciousness that blocks enlightenment.[72]

At the end of the second volume of *TCA*, Habermas outlines the task of his critical theory of society based on his appropriation of systems theory and the introduction of the system/lifeworld distinction. Arguing that Marx's theory of value is too restrictive to account for the complexities of modern society, such as the uncoupling of the lifeworld and system and the colonization phenomenon, Habermas analyses the process of juridification in contemporary Germany[73] and the growth of the legal system in order to show how a critical social theory is a more adequate way of dealing with the crises of modern capitalism.[74] Despite their differences, he contends that '[t]he theory of communicative action does follow the Marxian model. It is critical both of contemporary social sciences and of the social reality they are supposed to grasp. It is critical of the reality of developed societies inasmuch as they do not make full use of the learning potential culturally available to them.'[75] Habermas contends that the three main lines of inquiry concerned with pathologies of modern society (i.e., theories of structural differentiation, the systems theoretical approach, and the action theoretical approach) miss each other's point and hence cannot even start a dialogue among themselves. The reason, he believes, is that 'the object domains of the competing approaches do not come into contact, for they are the result of one-sided abstractions that unconsciously cut the ties between system and lifeworld constitutive for modern society,'[76] In order to overcome this insufficiency, a critical theory of modern society needs to be sensitive to what Marx called 'real abstraction,' as deformations of the lifeworld or its reification. This can be achieved only as 'an analysis that at once traces the rationalization of lifeworlds *and* the growth in complexity of media-steered subsystems, and that keeps the paradoxical nature of their interference in sight.'[77] Habermas claims that his account of the processes of rationalization – which he calls 'the *genetic structuralism* of developmental psychology' – has provided such an analysis by incorporating and appropriating 'Weber's sociology of religion, Mead's theory of communication, and Durkheim's theory of social integration.'[78]

This theory, Habermas continues, also overcomes the one-sided emphasis of the Frankfurt School on the critique of instrumental reason and its entanglement in the Marxist philosophy of history, which could not support the normative foundation of its social theory and did 'not distinguish between problems of developmental logic and problems of developmental dynamics.'[79] Habermas believes that he has freed historical materialism from its philosophical ballast by way of two processes of abstraction: 'abstracting the development of cognitive structure from the historical dynamics of events, and abstracting the evolution of society from the historical concretion of forms of life.'[80] 'A theory developed in this way,' he continues, can no longer start by examining concrete ideals immanent in traditional forms of life. It must orient itself to the range of learning processes that is opened up at a given time by a historically attained level of learning. It must refrain from critically evaluating and normatively ordering totalities, forms of life and cultures, and life-contexts and epochs *as a whole*. And yet it can take up some of the intentions for which the interdisciplinary research program of earlier critical theory remains instructive.[81]

In constructing a critical social theory, Habermas has complemented his theory of communicative action with a systems theory that allows distinguishing between the developmental process in the norm-free domain of system and the norm-governed sphere of the lifeworld, thereby accounting for both reproduction and evolution of the symbolic interaction of society and deformation of the lifeworld.

Habermas may have hoped that the introduction of the system/ lifeworld distinction would allow his theory a higher degree of sensitivity and efficacy, but as critics have shown, it also creates as many problems as it supposedly solves. The reconstructive approach to the appropriation of systems theory is supposed to broaden the scope of the critical theory of society, while at the same time permitting a greater discrimination among different social formations based on their abstract principles of organization. Identifying the engine of the evolution of modern society as the uncoupling of the lifeworld and system, which amounts to colonization of the lifeworld when the system oversteps its boundary, gives Habermas's account a rigorist tenor that makes it suspicious of scientism. The scientism that was rejected in *Knowledge and Human Interest* seems to have reappeared, thanks to the seduction of systems theory. Thomas McCarthy is again first to detect and warn us about this scienticist tendency. In a paper entitled 'Complexity and Democracy, or the Seducements of System Theory,' he writes: 'Habermas once criticized Marx for succumbing to the illusion of rigorous science, and he traced a number of Marxism's historical problems with political analysis and political practice to this source. The question I have wanted to pose here is whether in flirting with systems theory he does not run the danger of being seduced by the same illusion in more modern dress.'[82] The reason for McCarthy's conjecture is that despite Habermas's earlier critique of systems theory, he has been attracted to its seemingly scientific stringency, which gives the appearance of grounding the theory on a firm scientific foundation. This move, according to McCarthy, undermines the utopian character of Habermas's critical theory that functions as a regulative idea. He argues that the analysis of systems theory regarding the social and system integrations is too restrictive because 'as they are defined by Habermas, [they] seem to be extremes rather than alternatives that exhaust the field of possibilities: the denial of one does not entail the other.'[83] Such a heavy borrowing from systems theory, McCarthy fears, means that Habermas 'runs the risk of not being able to formulate in these terms an answer'[84] to the question of the legitimate forms of representative democracy. For in representative democracy, systemic domains of politics, economy, administration, and so on are all taken to be governed by norm-free exchange media of money and power that constantly overstep their boundary and colonize the lifeworldly domains. Accordingly, Habermas's theory in its present form suffers from a serious weakness: *there is no guarantee that the lifeworld cannot be thoroughly dominated by the media of power and money.* As such, the theory cannot account for legitimate power in capitalist societies.

Axel Honneth has further elaborated the critique of the dualism of system/lifeworld. In an excellent study of the concept of power in Habermas, the Frankfurt School, and Foucault entitled *The Critique of Power,*[85] Honneth contends that Habermas's system/lifeworld distinction can be seen as a reaction to the post-structuralist charge against the Enlightenment that reason is the handmaiden of power. Habermas's distinction is supposed to make a theoretical point that an action system can function independently of normative constraints of discursive agreement and that a communicative action in the lifeworldly domain can occur independently of power relations. Honneth contends, however, that Habermas would not be able to maintain the system/lifeworld dualism while idealizing the latter as independent from power. This is important because it means that in Habermas's critical quest for the possibility of free society, his placing of the idea of critique within the lifeworld/system distinction undermines the goal of emancipation. If democracy is conditioned on freedom from the coercive and dominating influence of the steering media, while the same media are the functional principles of the material reproduction of society, then Habermas's theory leads to an *aporia.* These critiques of the system/lifeworld distinction, as we will see in next section, will motivate Habermas's later attempts to make room for a legitimate use of power within the lifeworldly domains.

3. How Is Legitimate Power Possible?

As discussed in the first section, Habermas's definition of legitimacy in

Communication and the Evolution of Society is normative since it assumes an internal connection between legitimacy and truth. In other words, the definition – that there are good arguments for the political system to be recognized – highlights the fact that legitimacy is a contestable validity claim.[86] Therefore, it is the formal conditions of a possible agreement among free and equal agents that possess the legitimating force. The justifying power of this political consensus is, however, thwarted by the crisis tendencies on the two fronts of social and systemic integration. In the course of colonization of the lifeworld, the steering media coordinate and influence actions in the political and administrative domains, depriving these systems of normative regulation based on an agreement around the more generalizable interest. While this process explains the cultural impoverishment and deformation of symbolic interaction, it also makes the account of consensus formation, and hence the legitimacy of political power, impossible. To be clear, the lifeworld/system distinction leads to two problems. First, as a result of the logic and the structure of lifeworld and system, which places power in the latter domain as a steering medium, the theory is unable to account for the legitimate use of power. Second, the consensus-driven discursive situation of the lifeworld has a homogenizing effect that arises out of the transcendental character of the universalizable interests. While the first problem, as a tension in the account of the lifeworld/system distinction, refers to an internal problem of the theory that persists even in homogeneous societies, the second problem is an external one that brings out the tension between the theory and the fact of pluralism. Thomas McCarthy discusses the resultant *aporia* in his insightful article 'Practical Discourse: On the Relation of Politics and Morality,'[87] where he contends that the model of practical discourse, which requires transcendence of both interest-based and value-based perspectives, is too restrictive to serve as 'a realistic normative ideal for democratic theory.'[88] That is to say, the theoretical problem of achieving a discursively justified agreement in the systemic domain (which makes accounting for political legitimacy impossible) is aggravated by a presupposed common culture in discourse ethics that allows the evaluation of needs and interests. To put it in McCarthy's words,

> If the evaluative expressions used to interpret needs have 'justificatory force' only within 'the framework of a common cultural heritage,' how can we reasonably expect to arrive at universal (i.e., transcultural) agreements on the acceptability of the consequences of a norm for the legitimate satisfaction of needs? Or to bring the argument closer to our present

concerns, how can we hope to achieve rational political consensus in a pluralistic society?[89]

Habermas's task is onerous since, in addition to the ideal of solidarity, as public will-formation, he also recognizes the facts of pluralism and individualism in our modern society. Under such conditions, he cannot appeal to the idea of rational compromise since it is too weak for the purposes of political consensus formation.[90] Thus, in McCarthy's words,

> The success of Habermas's universalization principle in getting from multifarious 'I want's to a unified 'we will' depends on finding 'universally accepted needs.' The argument just sketched suggests that this may not be possible when there are fundamental divergences in value orientations. The separation of formal procedure from substantive content is never absolute: we cannot agree on what is just without achieving some measure of agreement on what is good.[91]

The problems of diversity of world views and colonization of the lifeworld lead Habermas, in an article entitled 'On the Relationship of Politics, Law, and Morality,' to adopt the position that this 'whole web of overlapping forms of communication' needs to be institutionalized alongside of the institutionalization of practical discourse.[92] He accepts that administrative and market systems are inseparable parts of today's complex societies, but contends that they should be opened to the influence of the will of the public via informal procedures of deliberation, as formed outside governmental bodies. This is because, at this point, Habermas abandons the hope of democratization of governmental organizations in favour of the power arising out of the informal arena of the public sphere.[93] His hope is that opening the systemic domains to the regulatory influence of public deliberation will allow for both inclusion of differences and legitimate political power. In this context we need to consider Habermas's turn toward the concept of the institutionalization of discourse as a solution to the problem of system/lifeworld dualism that amounts to colonization.

4. Institutionalization of Discourse

As his critics have pointed out, Habermas's theory of evolution 'is not a theory of historical evolutionary processes but a normative theory, a utopian counter-model of modernity'[94] that, as such, remains separate from the actual development of society. The difference in value orientation of the political agents whose voluntary association constitutes the public sphere, once again, brings to the fore the tension between the democratic generalization of interests and the universalistic justification of norms. This gap between the normative and the actual mirrors Habermas's earlier difficulty when facing the gulf between the transcendental and the empirical, between the particular context of the good life and the universal claim of moral judgment, between justification and application that forced most of his theorizing into an abeyance. As we will later see in chapter 5, moreover, this diremption will reappear in the form of a gap between facticity and validity. Indeed, Habermas's normative theory has constantly attempted to provide an account of how the 'ought' and the 'is' are mediated. To bridge this gulf and to overcome the impasse of the dualism of lifeworld and system that threatens the emancipatory promise of his social theory, Habermas focuses on the idea of the institutionalization of the discursive procedure as the core of the lifeworldly interaction that would make the hypostasization of the moral insight possible. At the end of *MCCA* he writes, '[T]he disjunction between judgment and action ... has its counterpart: discourse cannot by itself insure that the conditions necessary for the actual participation of all concerned are met. Often lacking are crucial institutions that would facilitate discursive decision making.'[95] The normative character of Habermas's architectonic, despite its theoretical complexity and sophistication, always distances the theory from the actual history, society, interaction, conflict situation, and whatever else it is trying to address. In Benhabib's words, 'Critique and crisis remained disjointed in his social theory.'[96] As such, the theory always needs a mediating third term that connects the insight of the normative claim with the context of actual fact.

To recall our discussion at the end of the last chapter, Hegel's second objection to Kant aims to expose the insensitivity of the moral theory to the institutions and practices of society that cannot be judged solely only the basis of their relations to the moral law and to a totality of social relations that Hegel calls 'ethical substance.'[97] Habermas's normative theory of society is not open to this Hegelian critique. Institutionalization of discourse militates against the charges of empty formalism, since it allows the result of the norm-governed discourse to obtain objective validity by penetrating the institutions of society. Yet, as Benhabib has contended, 'the traditional Hegelian objection has a critical kernel which can be reformulated as a problem concerning the *plurality of norms*.'[98] Here 'the plurality of norms' refers to the bias of the Kantian moral theories that, in judging all norms of human action, privileges only the juridical norms and rules of law. In light of the awareness of this bias, then, the question for Habermas's theory becomes, '[I]s communicative ethics only relevant for the domain of juridical human relations? Does it suffer from the legalistic bias of Kantian moral theory in general?'[99] Given that the telos of communicative ethics is the discursive situation in the public space free from domination, then it is quite predictable that issues of justice are the primary concern of Habermas's theory, which means that discourse ethics too is vulnerable to the Hegelian charge of institutional deficiency. Benhabib's diagnosis of this problem is especially enlightening when she argues that despite Habermas's expressed focus on the relations of justice, 'there is a significant distinction between a legalistic or juridical conception of public life and a democratic-participatory *ethos*, and the theory of communicative ethics sits between these two stools uncomfortably.'[100]

This observation further testifies to Habermas's aforementioned ambivalence. In order to overcome this tension in his theory, Habermas becomes increasingly interested in delineating the institutionalization of the process of discursive decision-making as an effective form of democratization. However, such an outline is not fully developed until later in *Between Facts and Norms*, where he appeals to the medium of modern law in order for his critical theory to 'sit comfortably' between the two poles of facts and norms:

> A morality that depends on the accommodating substrate of propitious structures would have a limited effectiveness if it could not engage the actor's motives in another way besides internalization, that is, precisely by way of an institutionalized legal system that supplements postconventional morality in a manner effective for action.[101]

The examination of this attempt will be the topic of the next chapter, along with a consideration of what Habermas appropriates from the debate with his critics and an analysis of his ambitious attempt at theorizing deliberative democracy in *Between Facts and Norms*.

Chapter 5

The Imperilment of Critical Theory:
The Seductive Complacency of the 'Is'

It is true to say, provided it is rightly understood, that successful politics is always 'the art of the possible.' It is no less true, however, that the possible is very often achieved only by reaching out towards the impossible which lies beyond it.

Max Weber, from *Selections in Translation* (New York, 1978), 89

My foregoing discussion revealed that Habermas's pathology of modern society takes the form of translating the insight of his theory of communicative action and discourse ethics into a social and political theory of democracy whose critical thrust is to measure the distance between the 'is' of the political system and the 'ought' of the utopian free society.[1] In the reconstruction of such a critical theory of society, Habermas's appropriation of the lifeworld/system distinction and his theory of the evolution of society, while allowing for the recognition of the crisis tendencies in modern societies and for the diagnosis of the internal contradictions of 'the organizational principle' of the capitalist system, runs into the following problems: (1) the lifeworld/system distinction and the consequent idea of colonization of the lifeworld deprives Habermas's theory of the ability to account for a legitimate use of power in Western liberal-democratic states; (2) this inability in turn leads the ideal of emancipation into an aporia, since the theory places the idea of critique within the proposed distinction between the lifeworld and system;[2] and (3), as a result, critique and crisis remain disjointed in Habermas's theory,[3] which forces him to pursue the idea of legal institutionalization of discursive procedures as a device that mediates between the insight of the normative claim and the content of actual life. The recognition of these problems instigates a quest for an account of effective democratization as institutionalization of discur-sive decision-making processes that starts from Habermas's *Justification and Application* (1993) and finds a decisive form in *Between Facts and Norms* (1996). At the risk of sounding prosaic, I would like to state the connection between the aforementioned problems as clearly as I can so as to set the scene for what follows.

Habermas's original insistence on the separation of the just from the good deepened the gap between morality and ethics and was later treated in the framework of the problem of justification and applica-tion, which, in turn, was addressed by an appeal to the principle of appropriateness. At the same time and in order to recognize the social complexities of modern life, which required sufficient independence for the 'system imperatives' of the modern economy, Habermas adopted the lifeworld/system distinction, which allowed for a detailed account of how actions, in these two distinct domains, are coordinated and reproduced. But the distinction also rendered the theory unable to account for legitimate political power. The problem of formulating the general will as the legitimate political authority is intensified by the pluralism of world views. Appealing to legal theory, Habermas presents the notion of enacted law as a decisive solution in modern societies to operationalize the tension between facts and norms by adopting a mediating role – that is, maintaining the dualism of facticity and normativity without dissolving it in favour of one of the elements. Hence, these dichotomies (i.e., ought/is, norms/facts, justification/application, consensus/compromise, etc.) can be viewed as different binaries of Habermas's thought with respect to the original problem of morality/ethics at different stages of his elaboration of this theory. I do not mean, however, that these dualities are the same, but that they are different manifestations of an original tension arising from the Kantian separation of the right from the good.[4] The need to explicitly state this correlation arises out of the fact that in what follows these pairs are discussed in close connection to each other.

In this chapter, I will first show (section 1) that while Habermas's critical dialogue informs the need of his theory to account for legitimate power in the constitutional states, it also reveals an uncritical appro-priation of the liberal ideal of political justification that greatly influ-ences the direction of his work. Next (2), I will outline his monumental formulation of a theory of deliberative democracy as a response to the aforementioned difficulties, where the concept of modern enacted law is introduced to mediate between the informal influence of public opinion and the political power of the state. Finally (3), I will argue that by aligning so closely the concept of communicative power, legitimate law, and state power, Habermas robs us of our critical ability to reproach the system for its failings, thus compromising the critical heritage of his original theory.

1. *Justification and Application*: An Unassuming Haze of Forgetfulness

In his 'Practical Discourse: On the Relation of Morality to Politics,' McCarthy concludes his questioning of the priority of the right over the good by proposing that 'we have to modulate the idea of rationally motivated agreement beyond Habermas's basic distinction between strategically motivated compromise of interests and argumentatively achieved consensus on validity.'[5] To put it simply, he argues that the dichotomy of consensus/compromise is too restrictive for the purpose of formulating a political theory in and of our pluralist world. In order to move beyond this distinction, McCarthy proposes, we need to appeal to the theory of law.

Habermas takes up the challenge of resolving the difficulties highlighted by McCarthy in a major essay in his book *Justification and Application* (*JA*). As my earlier discussion indicated, the gist of the book's main chapter, 'Remarks on Discourse Ethics,' is Habermas's attempt to bridge the gap between the problem of justification and that of application via an appeal to Klaus Günther's[6] principle of appropriateness. Still, in my view, it is his attempt at formulating a response to McCarthy's criticism that proves the most significant in his later writings. This is where Habermas's reformulation and revision of some of his earlier ideas leads him to stray from the critical origin of his theory. I will begin illustrating my point by outlining his reply to McCarthy in 'Remarks on Discourse Ethics,' which essentially consists of two parts.

The Lure of 'Greater Abstraction'

First, while accepting McCarthy's claim that moral justification needs to be supplemented with the mediating character of law, Habermas contends that 'a discourse theory of law need not abandon the discursive model since it, too, can be *grounded in* discourse ethics.'[7] He recognizes the fact that a further move towards a multicultural society in today's world will shrink even more the number of questions that can be answered from the moral point of view. Nonetheless, he insists that 'finding a solution to these few more sharply focused questions becomes all the more critical to our coexistence, and even survival, in a more populous world.'[8] But, *pace* McCarthy, he insists that the dichotomy of the forced or rationally achieved agreement, in view of today's pluralism of reason, still does not allow any alternatives. Indeed, for him, the further differentiation of world views 'supports rather than undermines the universalistic approach of discourse ethics.' Habermas continues:

> The more that principles of equality gain a foothold in social practice, the more sharply do forms of life and life projects become differentiated from one another. And the greater this diversity is, the more abstract are the rules and the principles that protect the integrity and egalitarian coexistence of subjects who are becoming increasingly unfamiliar with one another in their difference and otherness.[9]

It is difficult to understand why one should read this passage the way Habermas intends it to be read; namely, that more differences lead to greater abstraction that produces consensus. A more unconstrained reading might be: more differences require more contextualization rather than abstraction, since agents' interests as the motivation of their interaction, even in homogeneous societies, are context-bound instead of being linked to an abstract and a priori moral law. This connection to a particular context would then make the consensus more difficult, once again putting in the foreground the problem of political legitimacy. Habermas, however, is adamant in his opposition to contextualism, and strongly dismisses the charge that because deontological approaches cannot operationalize the gap between one's duty and one's interest, we should question the approach itself. He rebuts: 'Only if it could be shown in principle that moral discourses must prove *unfruitful* despite the growing consensus concerning human rights and democracy – for example, because common interests *can no longer even* be identified in incommensurable languages – would the deontological endeavor to uncouple questions of justice from context-dependent questions of the good life have failed.'[10]

The lesson of this exchange for Habermas is that, in his attempt to overcome the gap between morality and ethics and the inability of his theory to account for the possibility of legitimate political power in complex and pluralist societies, his attention has turned toward more abstraction (via legal theory and appropriation of the concept of modern law). I will come back to this effort in section 2. But what gives this shift a decisive direction, which I will argue goes against the critical heritage of the theory, is the second part of his reply and his specific appropriation of liberal theory.

The Post-metaphysical Character of the Concept of Justice

The second part of Habermas's reply to McCarthy's criticism takes the form of an appeal to John Rawls's notion of 'overlapping consensus' in order to answer questions concerning the pluralism of world views. In warding off the communitarian charge of empty universalism and ineffective formalism, Habermas finds a great deal of affinity between his own project and that of John Rawls's theory of justice. Drawing on the Kantian tradition, both projects involve a deontological approach in respect to questions of freedom, morality, and law. Perhaps more importantly with respect to their dispute with communitarians, both authors give priority to the right over the good. Moreover, they both justify the legitimacy of norms based on the principle of rational consensus, which is to be defined procedurally.[11] I should like to point out that my brief discussion of Rawls and Habermas here is not an attempt to fully compare and contrast their views but simply to bring to the fore specific aspects of liberal theory borrowed by Habermas that, I will argue, influence his project.

Having faced the contextualist criticism and in an attempt to escape the charge of foundationalism, Rawls revises his claim to universally ground the concept of justice, in *Political Liberalism*, and instead limits the range of his claim to the formulation of the best concepts of normativity and justice in the tradition of Western political thought. Hence, instead of grounding the principles of justice on some ultimate foundations, Rawls suggests that they be justified on what reasonable persons, despite their different comprehensive world views, can agree upon in a liberal society. Since this view resembles his own principle of generalizability of interest, Habermas sees the virtue of such an overlapping consensus on principles of justice to be an abstraction 'from all comprehensive views of self and the world in which different conceptions of the good are articulated.'[12] Such a view, which Rawls calls 'political not metaphysical,' is also consonant with what Habermas calls the post-metaphysical character of our thinking in the modern world: 'A postmetaphysical concept of justice is not compatible with all comprehensive doctrines, only with non-fundamentalistic world-views.'[13] As for the non-foundationalist or reasonable doctrines, Rawls defines them as those which 'must recognize the burden of reason.'[14] The burden of reason or judgment refers to the sources of disagreement between reasonable persons who 'share a common human reason' and have 'similar powers of thought and judgment,'[15] and as such is 'of first significance for a democratic idea of toleration.'[16] This non-dogmatic character also emphasizes the self-reflexive mode of the modern concept of justice. Under such conditions of the post-conventional society, a reasonable person, according to Rawls, 'desires for its own sake a social world in which they, as free and equal, can cooperate with others on terms all can accept.'[17] Putting together the self-reflexivity and post-metaphysical character of the concept of justice and the reasonableness of the citizens of liberal states, Rawls's justification for the two principles of justice takes the form of what he calls a method of 'reflective equilibrium.'[18] Reflective equilibrium allows for an individual's concrete moral judgments to be brought into harmony with her higher-order moral principles,[19] hence, effectively connecting 'the real citizens of contemporary liberal societies who are flesh and blood'[20] in their different forms of life, with principles of justice. This connection, Rawls believes, allows for the principles of justice (instead of being ineffective and abstract) to be recognized and acted upon by citizens, hence providing legitimacy to the political order of the liberal state. Thus, Rawls describes this second aspect of reasonable persons as 'the willingness to recognize the burdens of judgment and to accept their consequences for the use of public reason in directing the legitimate exercise of political power in a constitutional regime.'[21] The fallibilistic and antifoundationalist characteristics of reasonable persons that allow for the recognition of burdens of judgment also yield the possibility of reasonable disagreement among them. This is because, as Rawls explains, it would be unreasonable to expect that 'conscientious persons with full powers of reason, even after free discussion, will all arrive at the same conclusions.'[22] This acknowledgment, however, as McCarthy contends in 'Kantian Constructivism and Reconstructivism,'[23] makes the tension between the pluralism of life forms and the universalistic and unifying character of principles of justice appear anew.

In the aforementioned essay, McCarthy further elaborates on the theoretical need to overcome the problems created by the lifeworld/system distinction. In demanding an account of legitimate power, and aside from the problem of colonization and the rigidity of the model of practical discourse, McCarthy states that, from the perspective of what Rawls calls reasonable pluralism, Habermas's ideal of democratic will-formation faces even further difficulties. Since, as Habermas himself acknowledges, the questions of justice and democracy have to be 'posed in terms of what is equally *good* for all, ethical disagreements may well give rise to disagreements about what is right or just. Under conditions of value pluralism, even ideally rational discourse need not lead to rational consensus.'[24] Following Rawls's lead, Habermas tries to address this problem by moving, in *Justification and Application*, towards a greater abstraction. This strategy has a double edge: while with respect to the problem of political legitimacy in pluralist societies the appeal to greater abstraction might prove fruitful, it takes Habermas so close to liberal theory that he loses sight of his critical distance. McCarthy explicates the move toward greater abstraction as follows:

> The idea is that when public discussion, rather than leading to rationally motivated consensus on general interests and shared values, instead sharpens disagreement by revealing particular interests to be ungeneralizable or particular values to be neither generally sharable nor consensually orderable, we can still reach a reasonable agreement by moving discussion to a higher level of abstraction ... This strategy gains some plausibility by reflecting the tendencies toward greater abstraction and generalization in modern legal and political systems. But that is not our concern at the moment. *What is of interest in the present context is that this move, if pushed far enough, lands Habermas closer to Rawls.*[25]

The concern, then, is that in appropriating Rawls's concept of overlapping consensus – which allows for a higher level of abstraction as a solution to the problem of legitimacy in the face of a plurality of world views – Habermas's borrowing ends up costing him more than he bargains for.

Motivated by the need to present a critique of modern society that aims at the emancipation of human subjects from domination (the task of critical theory as defined by Horkheimer), Habermas's endeavour to bridge the gulf between morality and ethics, the right and the good, leads him to warrant the abstraction from all comprehensive world views as justifiable only by recognizing the principles of justice potentially present in the existing political culture of liberal democracies. While it is correct that the reservoir of the emancipatory concepts that allow change and progress is always located within our tradition and our political culture, there is a difference between the actual concepts and practices of the status quo – let's call them *ideas* – and the potential concepts made possible by critique of the existing order – let's call them *ideals*. This idea/ideal distinction aims to accentuate the turn toward the legal theory and its significance. Justice is seen no longer as a guiding ideal, but as an idea actualized in legal institutions. The task of critical theory, as formulated by Horkheimer and Adorno, is threefold: (1) it is explanatory or descriptive of the pathology of society; (2) it is practical with respect to identifying the social actors capable of carrying out the critique; (3) and it is normative or utopian in terms of defining clear goals for the future.[26] Habermas's turn in extracting the critical criteria from the *ideas* of our actual existing conditions, and not from the utopian *ideals*, weakens the normative thrust of the critique in favour of its descriptive character, resulting in a political attitude that is critically deficient. This, however, is not to say that his theory has lost its critical thrust entirely, but to take note of the fact that, between the utopian norms and the present norms, the scale of theorization has moved in favour of the latter. This shift appears to have been inspired by 'the art of the possible.'

This conservative attitude comes to the fore when Habermas explains the need for the abstraction in Rawls: 'In a further step Rawls examines whether this abstraction is possible and whether it proves to be fruitful. The principles of justice justified in the original position should not be left hanging in the air but must also be capable of being acted upon, of falling under "the art of the possible."'[27] One may read Rawls's idea of 'the art of the possible' as the condition of feasibility for the resulting theory (i.e., once implemented, it should be capable of being self-sustaining by generating its own sources of support), which is an uncontroversial aspect of any coherent political theory; but it seems to me that since liberal theory's orientation is taken from the tradition of political culture in Western societies, 'the art of the possible' does not refer to a just political order that will arrive in the future (*the yet to come*) – an ideal – but rather to the status quo of the here and now. Evidence to support this interpretation of 'the art of the possible' is provided by the fact that neither Rawls's nor Habermas's formulation of their political theories has critically engaged the existing political systems; each instead has appeared as the systems' explication and justification. Indeed, in discussing what is relevant information for judging a constitution, Rawls admits to skipping over a difficult question of how the existing society contains grave injustices and to view such information as irrelevant.[28] Given the task of a theory of justice, in my view, such selectivity cannot be justifiably explained. Allowing the notion of 'the art of the possible' to function as the compass of the theory ultimately amounts to justifying the existing political order.

The fact of the matter is that, in Rawls, the ideal of justice is approached by way of the assumption of *stability*, which automatically imposes external constraints on the ideal of justice.[29] This is the case of the move from the utopian force of an ideal to the descriptive and explanatory character of an idea in Rawls. In contextualizing his theory in *Political Liberalism*, Rawls replaces the ideal of justice with the idea of stability.[30] Contestational claims are allowed only in so far as political stability is not compromised. But political contestations may well be concerned with issues of justice, which here take second seat to the assumption of stability.[31] But '[o]ur task as philosophers,' as Thomas Pogge in his critique of this complacent attitude of Rawls's *The Law of Peoples*[32] puts it, 'requires that we try to imagine new, better moral sentiments. Yes, we must be realistic, but not to the point of presenting to the parties in the original position the essentials of the status quo as unalterable facts.'[33]

The effect of this propinquity to liberalism, for Habermas's critical theory, is that the critical role of the emancipating utopia is exchanged for the feasibility of the principle of 'the art of the possible.' This is a distinction that perhaps can be best captured by a double, fulfilment/transfiguration, as introduced by Seyla Benhabib in her *Critique, Norm and Utopia*. Fulfilment and transfiguration represent two models of emancipatory critique of bourgeois democratic revolution. Here, fulfilment refers to a model of critique aimed at changes within the capitalist formation toward 'a better and more adequate form' of society. According to this model, 'emancipation is realizing the implicit but frustrated potential of the present' (*CNU*, 41). Transfiguration, by contrast, entails a utopian break with the status quo that enables a move beyond some aspects of the present. Fulfilment represents a substantive critique, while transfiguration empowers a normative critique. As a consequence, the distance between critique and reality shrinks in favour of accepting the existing political order as already legitimate. The focus of the theory shifts from exposing the forms of colonization, as the pathology of advanced capitalist societies, to the possibilities of democratization under the same conditions. The construction of such a process of democratization, which, I will argue, weakens some of our critical ability in reproaching the political system, is taken up in Habermas's monumental book *Between Facts and Norms*, which exemplifies the theoretical effect of his borrowing from liberal theory.

2. Power, Enacted Law, and Deliberative Democracy

Before turning to *Between Facts and Norms*, we should consider Habermas's view of the relation between morality and law in order to show the significance of his turn toward legal theory. Prior to *BFN*, Habermas argued that in order to uncouple lifeworld and system, law needed to institutionalize the separation and independence of the economic and the political systems from that of lifeworldly structures.[34] Such a separation of law and morality is achieved at the post-conventional level of social evolution, where moral and legal claims are judged, not on the basis of specific values of an ethical tradition, but rather according to abstract principles that can be criticized: 'It is here that there first emerges *the idea that legal norms are in principle open to criticism and in need of justification.*'[35] This is why Habermas still contends that modern law needs to be justified on the discursive criterion of normative rightness, even though the uncoupling of the lifeworld and system bestows a positivistic character upon modern law as an instrumentalistic system independent of discursive procedures of the lifeworld. This view of law in *Theory of Communicative Action* reveals Habermas's ambivalence toward the role of legal norms in modern society. On the one hand, law is conceived as being linked to morality and hence is a part of the lifeworld; on the other, law is considered as having an instrumental function, formally organizing the subsystems through legalization, and as such belongs to the systemic domain. The juridification theses refer both to this increasing intrusion of formal law, which Habermas calls 'deworlding,' in regulating more domains of modern society and to the colonization of the lifeworld. These theses do not entertain the possibility that law can be reconstructed in a way to regulate the function of the systemic media of power and money in order to protect the discursive procedures of the lifeworld from colonization. The subsequent result of such an approach is that Habermas's theory is unable to account for a legitimate political power in the democratic constitutional states. But in a few articles subsequent to *TCA*, Habermas revises his view concerning the role and the position of law.[36] Law, now, is envisioned as situated between the lifeworld and system, and as such it can be legitimated by moral and practical discourse. In *BFN* this revision takes the form of a further modification that pertains to the concept of power.

The treatment of the role and meaning of the concept of 'power' within Habermas's architectonic, as it was elaborated in the two volumes of *TCA* and later in *Moral Consciousness and Communicative Action*, undergoes some significant changes in *BFN*. Here he introduces the term *communicative power* in order to provide a more satisfactory solution to the problem of the legitimacy of the political power. With respect to this ongoing discussion, after attempting to clarify the original significance of the concept of power in Habermas's theory, I will examine the concept's later modification and extension in *BFN*. In the final section I will explore the implications of this revised concept, which gives Habermas's project a conservative tenor.

Rethinking the Concept of Power

In order to introduce the conceptual revisions in *Between Facts and Norms*, I would like to recall briefly some of the original features of Habermas's theory. Given his Marxist background, however weakened and revised,[37] it is not surprising that Habermas's notion of power is, in essence, a traditional view that conceptualizes power in terms of the language of contradiction: a conflictual view of power. In these terms, power is basically understood as the capacity of an agent, or an institution, to coerce or dominate others in societal interactions according to a hierarchical structure. Thus, the exercise of power is often seen as one-sided and top-to-bottom coercion by the state (i.e., a monarch, the church, etc.). *Knowledge and Human Interest* is captivated by this view of power as domination (*Herrschaft*) and coercive violence. In the later formulation of discourse ethics seen in the two volumes of *The Theory of Communicative Action*, under the influence of Parsons, Habermas comes to view power as a medium of coordinating action that presents an alternative to violence and, as such, is not necessarily negative; rather, it is not internally connected with discursive justification. Yet, as we have seen, if there is to be room for the notion of action coordination via understanding (*Verständigung*), discursive justification requires the neutralization of all claims to authority that draw on some external power. Hence, for Habermas, emancipation is possible only in a state of undistorted communication, free from power relations, where efforts are made not to achieve success over others but to understand (*Verstehen*) them. Again, as shown earlier, the difference in orientation towards either understanding or success pertains to Habermas's important distinction between communicative and strategic action. We learned that communicative interaction occurs 'when the participants co-ordinate their plans for action consensually, with the agreement reached at any point being evaluated in terms of intersubjective recognition of validity claims.'[38] Meanwhile in strategic action, actors try to influence the behaviour of others by forceful means (i.e., sanctions, threat of violence, etc.) to direct the interaction towards the satisfaction of their personal desire.

Regarding the proper domain of different interactions, we also learned that symbolic social interactions, such as communicative action, are produced in the realm of the *lifeworld*. As such, the lifeworld is the social and cultural context or horizon of meaningfulness. The domain of strategic action, as purposive action aimed at success, however, is that of *system*. In the systemic domain, interaction has the function of maintaining the system, and as such is steered by media of power and money; in the lifeworldly domain, interaction is oriented towards mutual understanding. To put it in Habermas's words, 'Whereas the aspect of social action most relevant to the symbolic reproduction of the lifeworld is that of *mutual understanding*, the aspect of *purposive activity* is important for material reproduction, which takes place through the medium of goal-directed interventions into the objective world.'[39] In this respect, Habermas sees *influence* and *agreement* as two mutually exclusive mechanisms that respectively distinguish the two action spheres of system and lifeworld. 'One can, therefore, define the lifeworld *negatively* as the totality of action domains which cannot be bent to conform to a description of media-steered subsystems.'[40]

The preceding discussion, then, suggests that the meaning and role of the notion of power is an intrinsic part of Habermas's theory of communicative action. Such a concept of power, understood either as violence or as coercive influence, has a negative connotation in the context of communicative theory, and in so far as this theory wants to guarantee fairness among rational agents it has to be avoided. However, as indicated earlier, there is in *TCA* a legitimate use of power as coercive influence. Indeed, in the systemic domains of politics and economy, which are concerned with the material substratum of society, power, as one steering medium, functions to maintain and reproduce systemic interaction. This functionality of the steering media manifests an instrumental character that aims at success in the objective world.

However, as we discovered in our discussion of the last chapter, a problem arises when the instrumental character of the systemic interaction, oriented towards efficient maintenance of the subsystems, invades

the understanding-oriented domain of the lifeworld. It is this illegitimate penetration of power into the communicative domain of the
lifeworld that Habermas calls the 'colonization of the *lifeworld*.' When
the system oversteps its boundary and power is imposed on the discursive situation, the result is the loss of freedom and meaning in the
lifeworldly domain. *This colonizing aspect of the concept of power in relation to the ideal of norm-governed communication needs to be traced in
Habermas's corpus.* As discussed at the end of the last chapter, this
juxtaposition of power as a steering medium and the idea of communicatively achieved understanding, which respectively account for system and social integration, has been perceived as problematic, provoking
important critical commentary in McCarthy, Honneth, and Benhabib to
name a few.[41] Taking the insight of these critiques, Habermas, in *Between Facts and Norms*, employs a paradoxical term, which appears to
combine the two poles of the opposition between communication and
power. Below I will show that as a result of closely tying communicative power to law, which is said to coordinate actions in both lifeworld
and system, Habermas's account ends up blurring the boundary between lifeworld and system in favour of the latter. This distortion, in
turn, intensifies the problem of legitimate power.

Modern Enacted Law and the Legitimizing Force of Communicative Power

Appropriating Hannah Arendt's concept of power,[42] Habermas introduces the term *communicative power*,[43] which has to be seen in the
context of theorizing deliberative democracy or, in his words, 'government by law.'[44] According to advocates of deliberative democracy,
citizens' participation in the democratic process possesses a rational
character. In a deliberative democracy the process of opinion and will
formation is explained as public discursive activity in which the citizens are engaged in argumentation that aimed at promoting more
generalizable interests by the force of a better argument. In this light,
we can see that Habermas's present project aims at responding to
criticisms of the original theory by drawing out its political, legal, and
institutional implications. This task can be better understood if we view
it in terms of the relationship between morality and law. In order to
connect the moral principle to ethical life, Habermas rethinks the role
he assigned to law and politics. *The legal system – now situated in his
thinking between lifeworld and system – can regulate political power by
absorbing the influence of political opinion and will-formation in the public*

sphere. But law as such is itself in need of justification, which entails Habermas's formulation of communicative power. To situate clearly the notion of communicative power within this project, we need to outline briefly the main thrust of the theory.

As discussed earlier, discourse ethics's narrow conception of morality focuses on questions of justification and, prior to *Justification and Application*, deliberately ignored the problem of application. The separation of justification from application in practical discourse ethics meant that programmatic and hypothetical reasoning for the justification of norms omits consideration of contextual institutions. As noted earlier, at the end of both *Moral Consciousness and Communicative Action* and *Theory of Communicative Action*, Habermas's solution is that discourse ethics needs to be complemented by a theory of socialization that accounts for the institutionalization of discourse ethics.[45] He believes that 'with the discourse ethics as a guiding thread, we can indeed develop the formal idea of a society in which all potentially important decision-making processes are linked to institutionalized forms of discursive will-formation.'[46] In *Between Facts and Norms*, Habermas presents a social theory that addresses the tension between moral norms and practical context, via legal institutionalization that is based on discursive procedures.

The tension between facticity and validity – as the German title of *BFN, Faktizität und Geltung*, suggests – appears at different levels. The *internal* aspect of this tension can be seen between law as demarcating the range of one's actions and choices, which are social facts, and law as associated with a universalizable principle of rights, which as the source of law's legitimacy is normative. The tradition of jurisprudence in Germany has been organized around the two conceptions of *Rechtsstaat* and *Sozialstaat*. According to the first concept, the formulation and implementation of law is done via abstraction from specific contexts. From a political point of view, such a formal approach proved too rigid to be effective in accommodating the legal authority of the state. Therefore, the competing concept *Sozialstaat* sought to overcome the abstractness and narrow the gap by operationalizing the tension between formal law and social facts. Of course, assigning such great import to the role of law begged the question, What is the source of legitimate lawmaking? Starting from the observation that law is at once a part of social reality (*Faktizität*) and a part of the normative order (*Geltung*), Habermas attempts to answer this question by appealing to a 'proceduralist conception' of 'reflexive law.'[47] He writes: 'A legal order is legitimate to the extent that it secures the equally fundamental private and civic autonomy of its citizens; but at the same time it owes its legitimacy to the forms of communication which are essential for this autonomy to express and preserve itself. That is a key to a proceduralist conception of law.'[48]

Such an account of the legitimacy of law is, at root, Kantian. For Kant, there is a hierarchical relation between the categorical imperative, as the principle of universalizability (U), and his principle of social contract, which, like Habermas's principle of democracy, describes a general procedure of law-making. Habermas, however, claims to abandon this hierarchy in favour of a more equivalent relation. In other words, while Kant subordinates law to morality, Habermas seeks to put them on a par. Of course, the claim that Kant subordinates law to morality – because the legitimacy of law is derived from the categorical imperative – can be contested, since one can argue that, for Kant, the categorical imperative underlies both law and morality.[49] For Habermas both morality and law draw their legitimacy from an underlying principle, which he calls the discourse principle (D). To ensure an impartial justification of norms, (D) states that 'just those action norms are valid to which all possibly affected persons could agree as participants in rational discourses.'[50] This principle is a norm that applies to a broader set of actions than moral actions. To establish an account of a legitimate legal system, or civil society, the discourse theory distinguishes between the principle of morality (U) and the principle of democracy. Adopting a Kantian perspective, Habermas takes (U) to refer to individual autonomy that functions as a normative basis for moral argumentation, whereas the principle of democracy[51] states that 'only those statutes may claim legitimacy that can meet with the assent (*Zustimmung*) *of all* citizens in a discursive process of legislation that in turn has been legally constituted.'[52] But unlike Kant, Habermas sees the relation between the legal and moral norms as *co-original*, that is to say, as primordially presupposing each other. 'The principle of discourse can assume the shape of a principle of democracy through the medium of law only insofar as the discourse principle and the legal medium interpenetrate and *develop* into a system of rights that brings private and public autonomy into a relation of mutual presupposition.'[53]

Hence, legitimate law-making is understood as resulting from institutionalized procedures that convert citizens' practice of self-determination, in the form of communicative and participatory rights, into the binding decision of political power. Habermas sees modern law as a system of norms that comprises a set of abstract rights recognized by all citizens in the form of a constitution or moral code. Viewed as a system of rights, modern law brings together popular sovereignty and individual rights, thus showing the co-originality of private and public autonomy.[54] 'By securing both private and public autonomy in a balanced manner, the system of rights operationalizes the tension between facticity and validity, which we first encountered as a tension between the positivity and the legitimacy of law.'[55]

It is important to note that by using the term 'operationalize' Habermas implies that, given the factual duality between formal moral norms and empirical facts, our attempt to translate the insight of the latter into the former should aim at maintaining the distinction without letting it be resolved in favour of one of the poles. To this end, Habermas believes that the guarantee that a system of rights provides by balancing public and private autonomy would avoid the mistake characteristic of both the liberal and civic republican tradition: each tends to emphasize one form of autonomy as the basis of legitimacy, while ignoring the other. His reconstruction of legitimate law, rather than reducing one aspect of autonomy to the other, juxtaposes basic rights and popular sovereignty equiprimordially. The medium of law, then, maintains the tension between the concrete context of claims of reason and their context-transcending idealization without allowing the tension to be resolved in favour of either pole. Once again, this is what Habermas means by 'operationalizing' the tension. The above formulation, however, should not amount to a confusion of the tension between popular sovereignty and individual rights, on the one hand, and the tension between context-dependent and context-transcendent norms, on the other. The two sets reflect the tension between facts and norms at different stages of theorization. In light of such a construct of modern law, the central claim of *BFN* with respect to the theory of deliberative democracy comes to the fore: there is an internal relation between the rule of law and democracy.[56]

According to Habermas, modern societies exhibit a tension between validity claims of legal order, which are expressed by constitutional and democratic institutions, and different forms of social and political power that intervene and interrupt the exercise of legitimate law-making.[57] This tension is what he calls the *external* tension between facticity and validity – which refers to the internal relation between law and politics. Confronting this tension, the theory's task is to provide an account of 'the legitimacy of a political order and legitimation of the exercise of political power.'[58] This new orientation of the theory illustrates a shift in its emphasis from the formal characterization of the ideal of justice (critique) towards the actual task of justifying the political government as legitimate. I will return to this point later.

Habermas warns that in order to ensure that an analysis of modern law is neither sociologically empty nor normatively indifferent, we need to conduct the analysis from a *dual perspective* that, at once, includes both the empirical and the normative aspects of law. In this context, state power is seen to reinforce the system of rights that governs the interaction of equal citizens. Habermas believes that an analysis of the relation between law and power will not bear fruit unless it is connected to an account of public reason. For him,

> [t]his latter account must ultimately refer to a democratic process of 'opinion and will formation' in the public sphere. As a formation of opinion and will, public discourse is not merely a cognitive exercise but mobilizes reasons and arguments that draw on citizens' actual source of motivation and volition. It thereby generates a 'communicative power' that has a real impact on the formal decision making and action that represents the final institutional expression of political 'will.'[59]

Therefore, in analysing the internal tension of the rule of law, Habermas supplements the account of state power and legal procedures with an account of public discourse. This account is designed to connect 'the informal discursive sources of democracy with the formal decision making institutions.'[60] Hence, there is a circular and reciprocal relation among communicatively generated power, legitimate law, and state power, which, Habermas believes, are co-originally juxtaposed. In his words, 'informal public opinion-formation generates "influence"; influence is transformed into "communicative power" through the channels of political elections; and communicative power is again transformed into "administrative power" through legislation.'[61]

The co-originality of legitimate law and political power suggests that there is a functional connection between the two. After they serve their intrinsic functions – for power, realization of collective goals or maintenance of the system, and for law, stabilization of behavioural expectations – power functions for law as the political institutionalization of law and law functions for power as the legal organization of the exercise of political power. This functionalist account of the connection between the codes of law and power, Habermas warns us, may be

Table 4 The functional connection between the codes of law and power

	Functions	
Codes	Intrinsic functions	Functions for each other
Power	Realization of goals	Political institutionalization of law
Law	Stabilization of behavioural expectations	Legal organization of exercise of political power

Source: BFN, 144.

misleading, because it suggests a self-stabilizing systemic relation between positive law and political power that can sustain itself. This account is problematic because it leaves out the source of law's legitimacy. (See table 4.)

Habermas insists that the early modern secularization of law has shown that such a legal form is not enough to give legitimacy to the exercise of political power. For 'law has a legitimating force only so long as it can function as a resource of justice ... But this source dries up if the law is made available for just any reason of state.'[62] The functionalist codes of both law and power, then, suggest that they have different perspectives: 'law requires a normative perspective, and power an instrumental one.'[63]

As for the constructed concept of communicative power, Habermas relies on Hannah Arendt's view of 'power as the potential of a *common will* formed in noncoercive communication.' In analysing Arendt's view, he writes:

> She opposes 'power' (*Macht*) to 'violence' (*Gewalt*); that is, she opposes consensus-achieving force of communication aimed at reaching understanding to the capacity for instrumentalizing another's will for one's own purpose: 'Power corresponds to human ability not just to act but to act in concert.' A communicative power of this kind can develop only in undeformed public spheres; it can issue only from structures of undamaged intersubjectivity found in nondistorted communication.[64]

In light of this description, it appears that what Habermas used to call 'power' is now labelled 'violence,' which is the imposition of one's will to manipulate or coerce another. What was previously known as a 'discursive situation' – which, freed from external constraints, amounted to intersubjective agreement – is now referred to as 'communicative power.' The latter, in turn, mobilizes public opinion and will-formation, thus influencing the process of institutionalization and, as a result, determining the legitimacy of law. The important consequence of this distinction is that it aligns power with legitimate law. Habermas draws the following implication: 'Here the law arising from renunciation of natural violence serves to channel a legitimate force identified with power. Arendt's distinction between power and violence negates this connection. Law joins forces *from the outset* with the communicative power that engenders legitimate law.'[65] The meaning of communicative power (*Macht*) has thus been separated from the negative connotation of the original concept of power (*Herrschaft*). As a legitimizing force behind administrative power, communicative power is positive, necessary, and co-original with administrative power and legitimate law. It is also exercised from bottom to top and generated horizontally among the participants of a communicative discourse.[66]

It should be apparent at this point that there has been a significant change from Habermas's original concept of power (i.e., domination) as a kind of *influence* that distorts the discursive situation – which was to be avoided – to the constructed notion of communicative power. Communicative power is again described as a sort of *influence*, but this time as a positive *influence* that, in turn, is the fruit of agents' consensual interaction rather than the result of their conflictual relations. I am aware that the contrast I am attempting to make between the original view and the later view may appear too stark. Still, even if we consider the finer move from the notion of power as domination or *Herrschaft* (in *KHI*) to the view of power as a medium of action coordination in the social organization whose systemic use can be legitimated (in *TCA*), to a further notion of power as communicative power, or *Macht*, that exerts informal influence on public deliberation (in *BFN*), the contrast remains between power as non-discursively redeemable forms of influence and power as discursively justifiable forms of influence. In this latest formulation, communicative power is this latter *influence* that gives law its legitimacy and, thereby, provides the political power of the state with its binding force. Now the question becomes, What is the significance of this change in terms of Habermas's project? More importantly, is this change of position consistent with his original architectonic?

The different perspectives between functionalist codes of law and of power (see the discussion on page 113 and table 4) lead Habermas to propose a distinction in the concept of the political itself that is consonant with the duality of normative and instrumental perspective. He thus distinguishes between *communicative power* and *administrative power.*[67] The introduction of this distinction, I believe, indicates a re-drawing of the boundary between lifeworld and system that favours the latter. In fact, the blurring of the lines begins as the result of the mediating function between lifeworld and system of the new construct of law, since modern law both incorporates post-conventional ideals and operationalizes systemic media. That is to say, for Habermas, the new construct of law includes both the normative character of discourse and the instrumental function of the system. As Bernhard Peters notes, 'This construct, however, sits somewhat uncomfortably between "system" and "lifeworld." If legal and political procedures can have this channeling and mediating function, what is left of the alleged uncoupling or separateness of the "systems," specially the state (or the political-administrative system), and of the alleged absence of normative integration in this domain? In this way, "systems" must at least be permeable by normative influences.'[68] Peters's question points to a possible consequence of Habermas's appeal to the medium of law that can prove costly, namely, the suggestion that the systemic domain is open to normative influence. The point, again, is not that system should not be submitted to the procedure of normative justification, but rather that, according to Habermas's account of the logic of integration and action orientation, the system remains inhospitable to discursive regulation. To suggest otherwise, as Habermas does now, amounts to collapsing the critical distance between utopia and reality, robbing critique of the judicious distance from its object. This is not to say that if, by some miracle, systemic interactions could be submitted to discursive evaluation, it would be a bad thing. Rather, the point is that despite Habermas's new elaboration, interactions in the economic and political systems remain instrumental, aiming at success and, sometimes, even at domination. Hence, to say merely that systemic actions are open to normative influence does not make them so. I contend that this attempt to assimilate the grey area of colonized lifeworld in favour of the systemic domains of administrative power compromises the critical heritage of the theory. Now, with respect to the possible implications of this new characterization of power, I would like to raise the following points.

3. Conceding Critique to the Complacency of the Real

The first question that needs to be asked is whether Habermas's theorizing has operationalized the tension between the normative and the empirical as he intended. At first glance, it seems that his distinction between power and violence, which allows for a legitimate use of power in the lifeworldly domain, remedies his original treatment of power. He believes that his differentiation, between power as generated communicatively and power as coercive *influence* or *violence*, is capable of discriminating between a power that deserves to be esteemed and a power that deserves to be disparaged.[69] The constructed concept of power will be also capable of interceding between moral norm and empirical context, since it generates legitimate law, which acts as a principle of appropriateness that translates the insight of moral principle into its content-minded application. Such an innovation allows the theory to overcome the charges of empty formalism, which rendered it incapable of accounting for a legitimate order of political power, by channelling the influence generated communicatively in the public sphere to the rank of laws and policies that are formally binding and effective. The communicative power of the informal arena of the political public sphere exerts a 'subjectless,' but intersubjective, influence on the formal power of enacted laws. It gives law legitimacy while enjoying protection against colonization by systemic media, that is to say, manipulation by coercive forces of money and power.

However, even on Habermas's own account of the functionalist codes of law and power, it is only the legitimate law-making engendered by communicative power that enjoys a normative perspective, while the perspective of the state's political power remains instrumental, steered by the media of money and repressive power. Hence, in the end, it still seems that, in so far as the question of normativity goes, it still pertains to the communicative domain of lifeworld separated from the economic and political (i.e., administrative state power) subsystems. And in so far as the question of the repressive, that is to say, non-discursive form of power goes, it is still the steering mechanism behind the systemic domain of political power, i.e., administrative and state power. In other words, the original gap remains unbridged. In this sense, one can say that despite the change of terms, the content of what Habermas meant by power remains the same, namely, in order for democracy and justice to prevail, the communicative process of public will and opinion-formation should not be guided by any *influence*, but by the force of a better argument. This ideal could be reached in the lifeworldly domain but not in the systemic domain, which still, in Benhabib's words, means that the insight of critique remains disjointed from crisis.[70]

From another angle, however, we can read the introduction of communicative power, and its close connection to administrative power via the medium of law, as indicating a significant change. As noted earlier, for the purpose of maintaining and reproducing systemic interaction, the role of power can be discursively regulated. In the market system, for instance, for the material reproduction of society the steering functions of money and power coordinate the instrumental actions that aim at success. In the systemic domains of economy and politics, however, there are also strategic actions that do not aim at rationally achieved agreement, but at obtaining mastery in the course of systemic competition or conflict. Hence, to propose, as Habermas does, that the mediating function of the law affirms that the political system of state administration, can be normatively regulated as well is to ignore the different logic of orientation and coordination of strategic actions. Such a proposal would suggest that the systemic domains of politics can also be oriented towards understanding, and not be influenced by the coercive force of money, power, and distorted reasoning. The point is not that this is an implausible assertion, but rather that it is inconsistent with Habermas's own account of social and system integration. For 'the creation of communicative power and the assertion and application of administrative power follow two different logics.'[71] Habermas's change of mind, suggesting that the political subsystem can be governed normatively, alludes to a rethinking of his original position with respect to the system/lifeworld distinction. The revision, as I mentioned earlier, pertains to redrawing the boundary between the lifeworld and system in favour of the latter.

Given Habermas's dedication and commitment to the issue of justice, however, it is obvious that he could not accept the above implication. As a response to charges against his theory, he would draw attention to the *reflexivity* of the discursive situation, which involves the self-critical character of communication. The reflexive nature of discourse draws attention to the ideal supposition that all validity claims in discourse are subject to critical evaluation. Habermas believes that the constitutional courts in liberal-democratic states are best suited to play this reflexive role.[72] Hence, according to the reflexive character of deliberative democracy, everyone is able to challenge and contest accepted norms and traditions in the public sphere. The problem, however, is that while discourse's reflexive mechanism allows one to critique the normalizing effect of the generalizable interest, it provides no guarantee that the less generalizable interests of the minorities generate any *influence* over legal and political institutions; for even in discursive terms, these kinds of interests cannot amount to an all-encompassing agreement.

Having realized, in his *Structural Transformation of the Public Sphere* (1989), that the derivation of the source of legitimacy for Western democracies from the specific characteristics of the political public sphere of late capitalism is too exclusionary and restricting, Habermas has moved towards grounding democratic legitimacy in the informal discursive procedures that feed the political will-formation and legitimate law-making.[73] To this end he constructs the concept of communicative power, as what possesses the best of both worlds (*lifeworld* and *system*): it is democratically generated and aims at reaching an agreement while exercising *influence* over the processes of political decision-making, thus giving them legitimacy. Consequently, in aligning communicative power with legitimate law, and state power, Habermas's approach seems to have legitimized political power as exercised in Western democracies. In doing so, however, he risks robbing us of our critical ability to reproach the system. For by theoretically tying the existing political and legal orders so closely to communicatively generated power – as their source of legitimacy – he seems to immunize political power to criticism. In seeing the principle of opinion- and will-formation as the underlying presupposition of both the political system and the lifeworldly communicative discourse, Habermas gets rid of the grey area where system previously colonized the lifeworld by overstepping its boundary. The implication of this change is severe, for it suggests that, in so far as we live in Western liberal-democratic states, there is no illegitimate use of power, since power is connected to communication – an assumption that ultimately disarms us of our critical ability to criticize the system.

Critical Theory as such seems to have lost its cohesion as an independent political trend, becoming a kind of left Rawlsian liberalism. This is why I venture to say that, in weakening the critical thrust of Habermas's theory, *Between Facts and Norms* marks a shift to a more conservative view, legitimizing the political system of the capitalist economy. This is a significant change if we recall that, according to *Theory of Communicative Action*, '[b]etween capitalism and democracy there is an *indissoluble* tension; in them two opposed principles of societal integration compete for primacy.'[74] Habermas's idea, in *BFN*, that the political system of state administration, too, is to be normatively governed and as such is legitimate dissolves the above-mentioned tension between capitalism and democracy in favour of the former.

This is a costly shift, for if the goal of political action in deliberative democracies is to reach consensus – around more generalizable interests – as its ultimate telos of political legitimacy, then the voices of difference in today's pluralist societies, which are less generalizable (or not generalizable at all), cannot be heard and, therefore, are excluded from the democratic process of opinion and will-formation. This is not, however, to say that discourse ethics does not allow a strong oppositional role to minority voices that can challenge the validity of decisions made according to the majority's interests; rather, that the actual acceptance of generalizable interests is open to the coercive influence of the non-discursive media. So, for example, in the United States, when it comes to gun-control laws, where a considerable public consensus exists to restrict the production and sale of guns, the public's interest does not have the same influence on legislators as the power of the NRA lobby group.

We can sum up by saying that to bring the insight of the moral norm to bear on the context of ethical life, to resolve the problem of colonization of the lifeworld by the system, and to account for the possibility of legitimate political order in pluralist societies, Habermas's appeal to the concept of modern law – as what mediates between norms and facts, between lifeworld and system, and connects communicative power to political power – remains unavailing. For according to Habermas's own account, the different nature of moral claims and ethical claims, and the different logic of social and systemic reproduction and integration, do not allow for the mediation of the third term (law) unless the rigid way in which the original dichotomies of morality/ethics, justification/application, and norm/fact were defined is reformulated.[75] Habermas cannot remain faithful to the Kantian separation of *Moralität* and *Sittlichkeit*, which bestows an either/or character on his inquiry, while looking for a third term to break away from the tight boundary of this dichotomy. From such a standpoint, with such rigid dualisms, no immanent theory of moral action is possible.[76]

In the real world of politics, where normative constraints are either absent or loosened, or stretched too thin, it is naive to think that in the process of opinion- and will-formation the communicative power of lobby groups *and* that of minority groups exercise the same *influence*. The 'dual perspective' that Habermas suggested[77] as a solution to the external tension between facticity and validity falls short of effectively addressing the challenges of social and political powers that disrupt the process of legitimate law-making. We don't need to look far to see how major legislation involving issues like gun control, tobacco regulation, term limits, and campaign finance reform are, in effect, decided not by people's interest and their communicative power, but rather by the coercive and sometimes violent influence of big lobby groups. Therefore, existing political and legal orders are not, per se, 'communicatively governed.' Law that arises purely through power politics, pressure-group influence, or systemic workings, as much existing law does, does not bear the stamp of discursive validation. In his otherwise sympathetic review of BFN, Peter Dews reminds us that

> [t]here is no critique here of law as such. Yet ten years ago, in *The Theory of Communicative Action*, Habermas described the increasing intrusion of law into the lifeworld as 'de-worlding,' or as isolating and antagonizing individuals, and disrupting a social integration essentially grounded in values, norms, and processes of understanding. He now renounces this conception of an unavoidable dilemma whereby a simultaneous process of emancipation and colonization is the result of encroaching 'juridification' [*Verrechtlichung*]. *Yet it is fair to ask whether his earlier insights may not have been suppressed by his current, more positive evaluation of law.*[78]

These considerations, then, suggest that Habermas has not succeeded in narrowing the gap between the moral norm and the ethical context by operationalizing the original tension. The new orientation of Habermas's theory towards justifying how the existing political order is legitimate (the 'is'), at the expense of de-emphasizing the formal constraints of the ideal of justice (the 'ought'), drastically reduces its critical and normative thrust. The normative aspect of the task of Critical Theory, instead of being oriented toward a utopian future, has been made to serve the theory's explanatory aspect in justifying the existing order. This imperilment of the critical tenor of the theory implies that deliberative democracy is not the project of bringing about a more just order to come, but simply a possible order that exists. Arriving at this conclusion is obviously the furthest thing from Habermas's set goals. Our dissatisfaction with this conclusion, then, demands that we search for a way to rejoin the idea of democracy with critique and utopia. In the next chapter, I will attempt to show that the ideal of radical democracy can be further pursued by complementing Habermas's theory with some of the insights of postmodern political theory so as to recover the critical thrust of Habermas's project.

Chapter 6

Recovering the Critical Impulse of Habermas's Theory of Democracy

But, then, what is philosophy today – philosophical activity, I mean – if it is not the critical work that thought brings to bear on itself? In what does it consists if not in the endeavor to know how and to what extent it might be possible to think differently, instead of legitimating what is already known?

Michel Foucault, *History of Sexuality Volume 2* (1990), 9

To provide a remedy for the problem of modernity – as the critical account of human beings' self-constitution as moral subjects – Habermas abandoned the philosophy of consciousness in favour of a philosophy of language that allowed him to highlight the emancipatory character of communication as the underlying principle of human interaction. His formulation of this project focused on how such a symbolic reproduction of the lifeworld was disrupted by the media of material reproduction. The expression 'colonization of the lifeworld' captured his diagnosis of the ills of modernity. The task of critical theory with respect to this problem was to delineate the conditions of possibility for preventing the subordination of the symbolic reproduction of the lifeworld to the material reproduction of the system, and hence to outline the conditions of undistorted communication as a form of emancipation. His analysis, however, proved too restrictive since it did not differentiate between different forms of power and resistance. As a result, Habermas turned towards legal theory in order to be able to account for different forms of power and different modes, levels, and sites of resisting them. Before this turn the problem was, to put it crudely, that the colonization was everywhere and all powers were bad. With the medium of law now between the system and the lifeworld, the danger now becomes that there is no colonization and every power is good.

William Scheuerman's insightful assessment of *Between Facts and Norms*, in 'Between Radicalism and Resignation,' illustrates the unfortunate by-product of Habermas's uncritical drawing upon the actually existing political order. He contends that 'Habermas's justified acknowledgment of the *intellectual* virtues of liberal and democratic thought *à la* Mill or Rawls, and his justified attempt to correct the theoretical failings of his earlier forays into democratic theory, seems to have generated a troubling side-effect: an inadequately critical assessment of "real-existing" capitalist democracy.'[1]

My preceding discussion sought to illustrate that the shift towards legal theory in Habermas's later works entailed a significant change in the tradition of Critical Theory: a theoretical move toward liberalism that amounted to weakening the connection between critique and the utopian ideal in favour of a justificatory explanation of the real, existing political order, along with an appeal to more abstractions as a way of overcoming the problem of the plurality of world views (see chapter 5, section 1). This change in direction imperilled the critical impulse of Habermas's theory of democracy. An appropriate question, then, is how to revive the critical impulse of Habermas's theory along the lines of the tradition of Critical Theory. This is a crucial question, since his conservative shift risks assimilating Critical Theory into mainstream political theory as a kind of radical or left liberalism. In an interview with Simon Critchley, Axel Honneth, a close colleague, sympathizer, and interlocutor of Habermas, is even more critical of this turn towards liberalism, arguing that it entails the end of Critical Theory: 'It [Habermas's theory] no longer really presents the broader aims of that philosophical culture or school, because [the shift] would mean that Critical Theory is introduced into mainstream political theory or political philosophy and then would give up its own identity.'[2] The object domain of discourse ethics is no longer a theory of justice or morality, but rather a theory of political legitimacy. Indeed, the terminology employed by the theory – such as 'social norm,' 'public discourse,' 'valid consensus,' 'general interest,' and 'all affected actors' – invokes the categories of political philosophy. Without intending to characterize Habermas's approximation to liberal theory as completely negative, I would like to consider two theoretical insights that can help revitalize the critical thrust of his theory. First, I believe that revisiting Michel Foucault's concept of critique as a local socio-political diagnosis of our present – that is, genealogical historiography – will make available a model of power relations more comprehensive than Habermas's restrictive view. Second, appropriating Jacques Derrida's analysis of the deconstructability of law reveals justice as the experience of the undecidable – that is, an open-ended and contestational procedure that is always to come, *à-venir* – will reclaim the utopian ideal of democracy as a political compass that always remains outside and beyond the real.

I will begin my discussion by analysing Habermas's attempt to reexamine John Rawls's *Political Liberalism* that began with an exchange in the *Journal of Philosophy*[3] and continued in *The Inclusion of the Other*.[4] I contend, in section 1, that with respect to recovering the critical thrust of his theory this attempt, via his exchange with Rawls, falls short of its goal. Next, by recalling Habermas's critical exchange with Foucault in the early 1980s, I will contend (section 2) that his concept of power needs to be enhanced by the Foucauldean analysis of power as a network of contestational relations. I will argue that Foucault's theory of power is more conducive to providing a diagnosis of the present as the task of a critical political theory. Appropriating the Foucauldean strategy of genealogical historiography, I will contend, would boost the critical tenor of the Habermas's theory of deliberative democracy. It would also allow for non-ideal features of the cultural context such as biases regarding race, sexuality, and gender to be counted as contestational relations involving force that, as such, belong to the category of political power. Finally, in section 3, I will argue that in order to reclaim the utopian aspect of the theory of deliberative democracy we need to shift our focus from the goal of rational consensus, as the ultimate telos of our social life, to the goal of the institutionalization of procedural contestation, which views democratic politics as the experience of absolute alterity and democracy as what Derrida calls 'the yet to come' (*à-venir*), which can only be approximated but never completely attained.

1. Revisiting Rawls's Political Liberalism in *The Inclusion of the Other*

With respect to the problem of political legitimacy, Habermas believes, along with John Rawls, that in today's pluralist societies social norms are valid only if the subjects they govern see themselves also as the authors of the norms. Yet in his exchange with Rawls, Habermas distinguishes his response to the challenges posed by the plurality of world views in modern societies from that of Rawls. Indeed, his approach in the two chapters of *The Inclusion of the Other* that reflect this exchange is in sharp contrast to his more receptive analysis in *Justification and Application*. Given that in my preceding chapter the main charge of a conservative shift in Habermas was partially attributed to his uncritical reception of Rawls's *Political Liberalism*, it is important to see whether, and to what extent, his new engagement allows him to resuscitate the utopian aspect of his critical theory.

In the first essay, 'Reconciliation through the Use of Public Reason,' Habermas's main objection to Rawls is that he collapses the distinction between the justification of norms and their acceptability. For Rawls, recognition of the fact of pluralism bestows a political – not a meta-physical – character on *PL*'s conception of justice as fairness. To ensure that such a political concept of justice falls under the 'art of the possible' – that it is 'practicable' – Rawls makes his concept of person sufficiently neutral that it can be acceptable to different world views. Thus, an 'overlapping consensus' can be formed around the concept of justice as fairness. What bothers Habermas is 'Rawls's working assumption that such a test of acceptability is of the same kind as the test of consistency he previously undertook with reference to well-ordered society's po-tential for self-stabilization.'[5] The test of acceptability is concerned with whether justice as fairness can form the basis of an overlapping consen-sus, while the test of consistency is concerned with the congruence of justice as fairness and the individual's idea of the good in a well-ordered society. There are two levels of theory formation: first, where the principles are justified, and second, where those principles are brought forth to public discussion. Habermas suspects that Rawls's methodological parallel is problematic. He questions whether the test of the acceptability of the conception of justice as fairness can take place 'in an immanent manner' from within the theory, since 'it is different from a hypothetical examination of the capacity of a society, already organized in accordance with principles of justice, to reproduce itself.'[6] The test of acceptability should, rather, take place at the second stage of theory formation by 'real citizens of flesh and blood' in a public discus-sion. Such a test of the legitimacy of a just political order is not the result of its *actual*, but *contingent, acceptance* by citizens, but rather of a *justified acceptability* of the order by the *actual public* regardless of their indi-vidual world views.

Hence, he argues, 'Rawls must make a sharper distinction between acceptability and acceptance.'[7] Habermas further argues that the way the notion of overlapping consensus is juxtaposed with the principle of stability in Rawls deprives the former of acceptability in the sense of validity and correctness of the theory, and instead treats it as 'an index of utility,' bestowing a functionalist character upon the question of acceptability. To put it simply, instead of *justified* acceptability Rawls has settled for an *actual* acceptance of the theory. If Rawls is to rule out this functionalist reading of his theory, he must allow for an epistemic sense of the validity (i.e., justification) of his theory so as to preserve the normative weight of the concept of justice as fairness. In this respect, however, his use of the predicate 'reasonable' in place of the predicate 'true' suggests that in view of the pluralism of world views he does not want to claim a cognitive status for his theory. Habermas continues:

> The problem is not Rawls's rejection of moral realism or the consequent rejection of a semantic truth predicate for normative statements, but the fact that he does attach such a truth predicate to worldviews (comprehensive doctrines). He thereby denies himself the possibility of exploiting the epistemic connotations of the expression 'reasonable,' connotations that he must nevertheless attribute to his own conception of justice if it is to be able to claim some sort of normative binding force.[8]

Habermas believes that viewing the test of justified acceptability of the theory as an actual acceptance entails that Rawls's account of the constitutional state 'accords liberal basic rights primacy over the democratic principle of legitimation.'[9] This priority in turn suggests that Rawls fails to bring the liberties of the moderns, that is, private rights, into harmony with the liberties of the ancients as political rights of participation.

In response to Habermas's essay, Rawls elaborates a detailed reply at the end of *PL*. At the core of his response, Rawls describes Habermas's theory as being a metaphysical view whose misgivings about the limitation of the liberal theory of justice as fairness stem from its demanding philosophical logic.[10] He argues that, given his move from the philosophical justification of the theory of justice to a political justification, objections such as Habermas's simply overburden his theory with questions of philosophical ideas of truth, justification, person, and so on that his theory is not designed to answer.[11] While this account of Rawls's reply is brief and oversimplified, it should suffice for my purpose of showing the significance of what Habermas takes from liberal theory in his turn towards legal theory. With this in mind, I will proceed to Habermas's second essay on Rawls, entitled '"Reasonable" versus "True," or the Morality of Worldviews.'

Habermas begins with a discussion of the 'political' and 'freestanding' status of Rawls's theory whose self-referential character can be understood as a political claim within that domain. In developing such a theory, Rawls wants to 'leave philosophy as it is.'[12] Habermas, however, doubts whether a free-standing theory in the political domain can also be free-standing in the philosophical domain. He writes: '[I]t is hard to see how Rawls can explain the epistemic status of a freestanding political conception, without taking a position on philosophical questions which, while not falling under the category of the metaphysical, nevertheless reach well beyond the domain of the political.'[13] Habermas simply rejects the claim that from the fact of pluralism, which requires a political approach rather than metaphysical one, it follows that political theory can itself move entirely within the domain of the political.[14] In his view, the political/metaphysical division rests on the dependence of 'reasonable' on 'true' in Rawls, since it would not be 'obvious why publicly defensible and actor-independent reasons should only support the 'reasonableness' of a political conception.'[15] He contends that since Rawls abandons the straightforward Kantian strategy of explicating the moral point of view in terms of the original position and informing 'justice as fairness' by a conception of practical reason in *A Theory of Justice*, his *Political Liberalism*

> [r]epresents a shift to an entirely new framework within which reason loses its central position. Practical reason is robbed of its moral core and is deflated to a reasonableness that becomes dependent on moral truths justified otherwise. The moral validity of conceptions of justice is now no longer grounded in a universally binding practical reason but in the lucky convergence of reasonable worldviews whose moral components overlap to a sufficient degree. However, the remnants of the original conception cannot be seamlessly integrated into the current theory.[16]

The reason for Habermas's claim in the last sentence of the quoted passage is that he sees a conflict between Rawls's new division of the burdens of justification and 'the reasonableness' of political justice and the 'truth' of world views in *PL*. He holds that the reasonableness required by the idea of overlapping consensus is based on the division of labour between the political, as what all citizens can agree upon, and the metaphysical, as a citizen's reason for individually accepting it as true. He agrees with Rawls that in leaving it 'up to each comprehensive doctrine to say how its idea of the reasonable connects with its concept of truth,'[17] the idea of overlapping consensus preserves an internal connection between political justice and the moral components of world views.[18] With respect to the issue of justification, however, we are left with an uneasy asymmetry: the public conception of justice raises a weak claim to reasonableness, while the non-public doctrines raise strong claims to truth. Habermas argues that the participant/observer perspective implied by the idea of overlapping consensus entails a conception of justice based on a 'non-public' use of reason – an individual's use of reason only from within her own interpretive framework. For Habermas, such an 'idea of overlapping consensus involves a decisive weakening of the rational claim of the Kantian conception of justice,'[19] since it rests on what Rainer Forst calls a 'private use of reason with public-political intent.'[20]

For a Kantian like Habermas this result is unacceptable: 'That a public conception of justice should ultimately derive its moral authority from nonpublic reasons is counterintuitive. Anything valid should also be capable of public justification. Valid statements deserve the acceptance of everyone for the same reasons.'[21] He attributes this problem to the lack of an explicit recognition of a third standpoint beside that of a participant and observer, as in a 'We,' the citizens. 'Because such a perspective is lacking, the conception that emerges as "reasonable" must fit into the context of the different worldviews in each case taken to be true by the corresponding parties.'[22] Habermas believes that in accounting for the possibility of an overlapping consensus Rawls must at least tacitly assume the third perspective of a 'We' as the citizens.[23] To acquire such a perspective, and thus to submit comprehensive doctrines to a requirement of practical reason, would mean that an overlapping consensus is possible based on an appeal to an epistemic authority that itself is independent of world views.[24] The epistemological underpinning of a conception of justice shows that Rawls cannot completely steer clear of philosophical controversies. For Habermas, by contrast, moral perspective is not the same as the perspective of comprehensive doctrines, since the latter relies on ethical reasons that are context-dependent while the reasons for the former are context-independent and cognitive; which is to say, 'like the truth of descriptive statements, the rightness of moral statements can be explained in terms of the discursive redemption of validity claims.'[25] Hence, 'a political justice that stands on its own moral feet no longer needs the support of the truth of religious or metaphysical comprehensive doctrines.'[26] Consequently, he argues, 'the concept of practical reason cannot be drained of moral substance and morality cannot be relegated to the black box of comprehensive doctrines.' Habermas concludes: 'I cannot see any plausible alternative to the straightforward Kantian strategy.'[27]

The above criticism appears in sharp contrast with what we learned from Habermas's discussion of Rawls in *Justification and Application*. There, Habermas approved and appropriated Rawls's appeal to the ideas of overlapping consensus and reflective equilibrium, since they seemed to resolve the problem of a plurality of world views based on a move toward a greater abstraction. What can explain such different reactions to Rawls? Habermas's explanation is that at the time of *JA* (1989 for the German text) he had only known to Rawls's ideas through two of his earlier sketches of *PL*, in 'Justice as Fairness: Political not Metaphysical'[28] and 'Justice as Fairness: A Brief Restatement,'[29] which seemed consistent with Habermas's own post-metaphysical approach. However, when *Political Liberalism* came out, Habermas realized that, in his rush to satisfy the critics, Rawls had given up too much. In providing a response to the challenge posed by the fact of pluralism, Rawls's new constructs place the burden of public consensus – as the ground of legitimacy of the political system – on the mere felicitous overlapping of their non-public truth instead of the moral point of view of practical reason. From Habermas's point of view such a shift of accent from the Kantian concept of practical reason to the ethico-existential stand of comprehensive doctrines would be an unacceptable move.

Does this criticism allow Habermas a more critical stance than Rawls? The answer is both yes and no. Yes, in that it distinguishes his discourse theory as a proceduralist theory that leaves the substantive agreement on principles of justice open to the procedure of public deliberation.[30] Thus, for example, the substantive formulation of a moral principle, such as that of distributive justice, is left to the discursive deliberation of law-making within a concrete context of constitutional states that materialize it in the form of 'to everyone according to their need,' or 'to everyone according to their ability,' or 'the same for everyone,' and so on. In this respect, Habermas's approach is at the same time both more rigorous and more flexible than Rawls's: it is more rigorous because his account of the legitimacy of political system rests on the context-independent, and hence universally binding, practical reason, and avoids the relativism of a lucky convergence of comprehensive doctrines' concept of truth. And it is more flexible in leaving 'more questions open because it entrusts more to the process of rational opinion- and will-formation.'[31]

Habermas's theory does not sufficiently recover its critical force, since its normative formulation explains and justifies the real, existing political order via an appeal to legal theory and the concept of modern law, bending toward an uncritical affirmation of the status quo. Thus, the 'ought' of the normative ideal tends to coincide with the general description of the way things really are. Such consonance bestows an ideological function upon the normative ideals with respect to the discussion of empirical (non-ideal) questions. Thomas McCarthy once again is one of the first critical theorists to warn us about the danger of such a double role for normative ideals. In his unpublished paper 'Liberal Theory and Racial Injustice,' and on the point of the ideological function concealed within normative theory, he writes: 'The result is, on the one hand, a euphemized account of the normative ideas, past and present, actually at work in political society, and on the other hand, *a failure to scrutinize critically the background understandings of society that do, despite the abstraction and idealization, always enter into the formulations of ideal theory.*[32] Giving such a prominent role to political reality renders normative theory blind[33] – a point that McCarthy drives home when, with respect to the relation between Habermas's recent writings, and such blind spots, he writes:

> On this last score, what Habermas argued in *Between Facts and Norms* to be true of legal theory applies *Ceteris paribus* to political theory – namely, that it relies upon implicit background assumptions drawn from some preunderstanding of contemporary society's structures, dynamics, problems, potentials, and dangers. *These implicit 'images' or 'models' of society tacitly enter into normative-theoretical constructions and often play a covert role in what appear to be purely normative disagreements. Deep disagreements in normative theory ... often turn on disagreements about the 'facts' being assumed, implicitly as well as explicitly, about markets, classes, genders, roles, global formations, and the like.*[34]

As a result, Habermas's normative theory makes too many concessions to the 'real-existing' political order of Western democracies, for it takes the existing institutions of liberal-democratic states as the starting point for its normative theorization. Habermas's theory (and Rawls's for that matter) treats the goal of a democratic project – that is, free society – as a concrete end that can be achieved once and for all.[35] On this account, justice and democracy are the same as the institutions designed to bring them about, which is why both Habermas and Rawls assert that liberal-democratic societies have a self-corrective capacity through their existing institutions sufficient for their reform. This, of course, is the result of the new orientation of the theory towards 'the art of the possible,' which consequently shrinks the critical distance between the real and the ideal in favour of the former. The fact of the matter is that, while one can find much of the institutionalization of discursive ideals *à la* Habermas in liberal-democratic states, the little democracy that we get is often accompanied by a great deal of injustice. Inadequate critical assessment of the political order not only has the unfortunate effect of weakening the voices of protest and dissent, but also amounts to political complacency and happy presentism.

Hence, I hold that in order to save political theory from becoming ineffective with respect to political reality, we have to examine critically the genealogy of accepted ideas and principles of reason used to construct a political conception of justice. Such a genealogy would reveal how these ideas, usually in connection to questions of power and interest, have been and still are deeply contested.[36] It also becomes a distinguishing mark between a more effective critical theory and the complacency seen in both Habermas's and Rawls's later writings. I would propose that in order to resuscitate the critical spirit of Habermas's political theory we need to find a way to annex to it the idea of critical genealogy and the disciplinary analysis of power. To this end, I will draw on Habermas's exchange with Foucault in order to extract a concept of power that is more adequate to the task of critically analysing the pathology of modernity. In adopting this strategy of correcting the weakening of Habermas's critical theory, I am aware that at first glance postmodern political theory would appear to be at variance with his idea of rationality. I will begin by stating that the easy charge of 'irrationalism' made against postmodernism can be rejected if we pay sufficient attention to the distinction between 'progressive rationalities' and rationality as such. Progressive rationalities constitute globalizing theories in search of what is absolute, necessary, universal, and ahistorical in our experience in order to draw a continuous and progressive line of knowledge accumulation over our history. The globalizing tendency of such rationality is, indeed, inconsistent with the post-metaphysical character of modern life. To question progressive rationality is not to reject reason. Equating the two arises out of one of humanism's binary oppositions, namely, reason/non-reason, which necessitates that questioning any rationality be viewed as an act of non-reason, or madness. Indeed, to remain faithful to the role of reason and the idea of critique, even the truth of progressive rationality should be submitted to critique.[37] From this standpoint one can say that modernist and postmodernist theories are not mutually exclusive, but rather both belong to what Richard Bernstein calls 'the new constellation'[38] of modernity/postmodernity, and thus we can draw on the strength of one to correct the weakness of the other.[39]

2. Incorporating the Insight of Foucault's Theory of Power

In presenting the pathology of modernity, Habermas characterized the main problem of advanced capitalist society as the colonization of the lifeworld, and hence defined the chief task of critical political theory as exposing and resisting this colonization. To resist systemically induced reification and cultural impoverishment entailed a political concept of the positive elimination of power that would allow for the possibility of a free society, that is, democracy. Habermas's earlier concept of power – that is, domination (*Herrschaft*) – as what was to be eliminated in the conflictual dichotomy of lifeworld and system proved too restrictive, since it could not allow for recognition of positive instances of power that needed to be supported. His later revision, which views power as communicative influence (*Macht*) on legislative and judicial institutions, is also restrictive, for it overlooks different power relations that have varied cultural underpinnings.

The consideration of this inadequacy of Habermas's concept of power is important with respect to the task of critique, since it reveals blind spots in his normative theory. As discussed earlier, these blind spots arise where norms, based on idealization of the real, marginalize what falls outside the defined boundary of the 'normal' and treat the difference as an anomaly. Accordingly, Habermas's and Rawls's normative theories of justice fall short of voicing the legitimate demands of racial, gender, and cultural groups, since the design of the theory favours as its norm a notion of the human subject that excludes the norm's different variants. As critics have pointed out, in both theories the rationality (which is at root Kantian) that defines a competent rational and moral subject is primarily reflective of a white, affluent European male.[40] Critical race theorists and feminists, for example, have pointed out the tension between the universalist feature of such Kantian theories and their exclusionary practices in political policy-making. Idealized normative models of political theory, such as those of Habermas and

Rawls, do not have any place for the non-ideal elements of race, gender, sexuality, culture, and so on in their form, and only apply to the non-ideal world as a result. Thomas McCarthy explains the ambivalence of normative theory as follows:

> Thus non-ideal theory pulls normative political theory back in the direction of the empirical social reality it began by abstracting and idealizing itself away from. But there are no theoretical means at hand for bridging the gap between a color-blind ideal theory and a color-coded political reality, for the approach of the ideal theory provides no theoretical mediation between the ideal and the real – or rather, what mediation it does provide is often only tacit and always drastically restricted.[41]

Hence, the recovery of the critical character of the theory would depend on whether we are able to find an idea that makes our theory sensitive to diverse forms of non-ideal elements. In this respect, I believe Michel Foucault's concept of power can compensate for the deficiency of Habermas's 'domination-juridical' model of power.

This appropriation of Foucault for Habermas's critical theory may appear counterintuitive, since Habermas's detailed and repeated criticism of Foucault is well known. In *Philosophical Discourse of Modernity*, Habermas severely attacks Foucault's genealogical historiography, accusing him of cryptonormativism and anti-modernism.[42] He argues that Foucault's genealogical analysis appears in 'an irritating double role,'[43] empirical and transcendental, that reveals a functionalist self-referentiality, and that his attack on the humanist values of modernity is by no means value-free but contains a decisive value judgment that, given the lack of a normative criterion in his theory, cannot be justified.[44] This tone was later modified thanks to what Habermas saw in Foucault's 'What Is Enlightenment?' and to their long discussion in Paris before Foucault's death.[45] Foucault describes himself as belonging to the critical tradition of Kant and calls his project a 'Critical History of Thought.'[46] In their meeting Foucault put Habermas's concern about the lack of a normative criterion in his theory at ease by inviting Habermas to wait for the last volume of his *History of Sexuality*.[47] He outlined an ethics of aesthetic existence that contained an immanent criterion of normativity. This model forms the basis of a response to Habermas and other rationalist critics of Foucault who ask, 'If genealogy is only a tactic why fight at all?'[48] It presents a philosophical ethos with a positive attitude toward life, one based on an ethics of care for the self, and as such stands in opposition to indifference, acquiescence, and surrender. An attitude based on acquiescence suggests that the end of humanism is the end of everything; it is nihilism. Habermas would be right to ask, 'Why fight at all?' if such nihilism were the ground of Foucault's thinking. But Foucault's concept of agonism (i.e., combat, to which I will return) suggests an active affirmation of life that proposes a new ethics. Such an ethics of aesthetic existence requires that we treat our lives as works of art, a task that demands transvaluation based on a search for a more productive power relation, better struggle, and a fuller life. Such an immanent criterion works as a normative yardstick that is capable of justifying one's ethico-political preferences.

Moreover, in his 'What Is Enlightenment?' Foucault showed that he did not take modernity as an entry on the calendar, but rather as an ethos, a critical attitude that aims to find out, in the distance between the relevant past and our present, how we have come to be, think, and act the way we are and do. Habermas shares Foucault's interest in writing the critical histories of our present, and 'they both hold that such histories are to be written with what Habermas once called "a practical intent," the intent to alter our self-understanding in ways that have consequences for practice.'[49]

For Foucault, to connect critical analysis to one's present is to give a genealogical historiography. He believes that genealogy is the design, the proper tactic of the philosophical ethos that ensures constant critique of the relation of our present to our self-constitution as moral subjects. For Foucault, '[t]he critical ontology of ourselves has to be considered not, certainly, as a theory, a doctrine, nor even as a permanent body of knowledge that is accumulating; it has to be convinced as an attitude, an *ethos*, a philosophical life in which the critique of what we are is at one and the same time the historical analysis of the limits that are imposed on us and an experiment with the possibility of going beyond them.'[50] A critical ontology of our present, according to Foucault, has to find responses to the following questions: 'How are we constituted as subjects of our knowledge? How are we constituted as subjects who exercise or submit to power relations? How are we constituted as moral subjects of our action?'[51] The aim of his analysis of power relations, therefore, is to expose their mechanism and show their effect on subject formation. In this respect, it is useful to delineate how Foucault's notions of emancipation and power differ from Habermas's earlier thinking on the same issues. As discussed earlier, for Habermas power *previously* meant domination, and as such it was always coercive and manipulative. It was a view of Power (with a capital P) based on a model of conflictual hierarchy (*Pouvoir*). Hence emancipation, for Habermas, meant a state of undistorted communication, free from power relations, where efforts were made towards understanding and not towards success. Foucault's notion of power, by contrast, is based on a model of horizontally criss-crossing power relations that create a network of reciprocally affective relations. By his account, we can never completely free ourselves from power relations – power in the sense of *puissance*,[52] something that is always exercised, at all levels and in all directions. He believes not only that we are captive in the network of power relations, but also that these relations are constitutive of our identity and our truths. So, for Foucault, emancipation does not mean liberation from power relations, or to put it in Habermas's terms, 'undistorted communication.' Rather, it means being able to analyse critically the power relations that surround us and identify the most productive ones in order to engage in them through critical genealogy and agonism. This critical ethos constitutes what Foucault calls *a practice of the self*. He is suspicious of the terms liberation and emancipation[53] because they presume an alienated human nature that can be brought to a final reconciliation, and instead talks about practices of freedom in order to target its practical forms. For example: '[W]ith regard to sexuality, it is obvious that it is by liberating our desire that we will learn to conduct ourselves ethically in pleasure relationships with others.'[54] This, for Foucault, entails a freedom that must be practised ethically, 'for what is ethics, if not the practice of freedom, the conscious [*réfléchie*] practice of freedom?'[55] Ethics as care for the self is thus the attitude informed by reflection and manifested through practices of freedom that constitute one's relations of power.

In *Between Facts and Norms*, Habermas comes a long way toward modifying his rigid concept of power, and now tends to emphasize the democratic exercise of power.[56] From a Foucauldean perspective, however, despite Habermas's recent addition of the 'juridical' aspect to the earlier 'domination' scheme, his model of the analysis of power relations in general remains inadequate. It is inadequate because the juridical model at best gives us another dichotomy: legitimate use of power (i.e., power by consent) versus illegitimate use of power by the state (i.e., power by coercion).[57] Foucault explains the limitation of this view as follows:

> I don't want to say that the State is not important; what I want to say is that relations of power, and hence the analysis that must be made of them, necessarily extend beyond the limits of the State. In two senses: first of all

because the State, for all the omnipotence of its apparatuses, is far from being able to occupy the whole field of actual power relations, and further because the State can only operate on the basis of other, already existing power relations. The State is superstructural in relation to a whole series of power networks that invest the body, sexuality, the family, kinship, knowledge, technology and so forth.[58]

Habermas's view of power as the dichotomy of legitimate/illegitimate state force is, therefore, ill equipped to deal with complex ailments of modernity such as caste, segregation, gender inequality, and discrimination. In order to analyse these ills critically, Foucault begins by pointing out that our legal and political relations are not a reflection of some natural law, but are institutionalized relations of force that sustain and preserve a historically contingent disequilibrium of power. Such a disequilibrium imposes a sense of struggle or conflict upon power relations, which gets expanded beyond legal and political institution and re-inscribed 'in social institutions, in economic inequalities, in language, of bodies themselves of each and everyone of us.'[59]

This view of power surpasses the limitations of Habermas's model, which is based on the binary opposition of consent and coercion, and shows that power does not flow in one direction from top to bottom as a right that one *has*, but flows everywhere in all directions as a force that one exercises only in action. Given that the focus of Foucault's approach is to study the *how* of the exercise of power, its effect, and the discourses of truth it produces, the practical and analytic advantages of this approach for the purpose of overcoming the blind spots of normative theories become apparent. He writes:

> The course of study that I have been following until now – roughly since 1970/71 – has been concerned with the *how* of power. I have tried, that is, to relate its mechanisms to two points of reference, two limits: on the one hand, to the rules of right that provide a formal delimitation of power; on the other, to the effects of truth that this power produces and transmits, and which in their turn reproduce this power. Hence we have a triangle: power, right, truth.[60]

With respect to this triangle, then, the question that traditional political philosophy has asked, Foucault tells us, is 'How is philosophy as the discourse of truth able to fix limits on the rights of power?' He poses instead a different question that aims at finding '[w]hat rules of rights

are implemented by the relations of power in the production of discourse of truth?'[61] Foucault points out a mutual dependency between
the exercise of power and the production of truth. This should make it
plain that for Foucault truth is not simply masked power: 'when I talk
about power relations and games of truth, I am absolutely not saying
that games of truth are just concealed power relations – that would be a
horrible exaggeration.'[62] His problem, rather, is to understand 'how
truth games are set up and how they are connected with power relations.' He reiterates this commitment in one of his last interviews, in
May 1984, when he says, 'What I have tried to do is the history of the
relation which thought maintains with truth; the history of thought in
so far as it is the thought of truth. All those who say that for me truth
does not exist are simple-minded.'[63] Here, Foucault gives one of his
clearest explanations on the relation of truth to political power, which
as we will see later is consistent with the Derridean ideal of democracy
as a 'yet-to-come.' He states:

> Nothing is more inconsistent than a political regime that is indifferent
> towards truth, but nothing is more dangerous than a political system that
> claims to prescribe the truth. The function of 'truth-telling' is not to take
> the form of law, just like it is useless to believe that it entirely resides in the
> spontaneous games of communication. The task of truth-telling is an
> infinite task: to respect its complexity is an obligation that no power can
> refrain from, except by imposing the silence of servitude.[64]

In regard to his study of the relation between right and power,
Foucault believes that since medieval times royal power has been the
centre around which legal thought has been elaborated. 'It is in response to the demands of royal power, for its profit and to serve as its
instrument or justification, that the juridical edifice of our society has
been developed. Right in the West is the King's right.'[65] The crucial
function of the discourse of royal right has been 'to efface the domination intrinsic to power' of the monarch so as to provide the latter with
legitimacy and legality as the effective embodiment of sovereignty.
Foucault attempts to change the mode of analysis of the discourse of
right in order to pay sufficient attention to the fact of domination – not
the domination of the King, but 'the manifold forms of domination that
can be exercised within society.'[66] Foucault thus sees systems of right
and law as instruments of relations of domination. He writes: 'Right
should be viewed, I believe, not in terms of a legitimacy to be estab-

lished, but in terms of the method of subjugation that it instigates.'[67] Foucault warns us that in order to conduct an analysis of power as relations of domination a certain number of methodological precautions are necessary. First, this analysis must not concern itself with regulated and legitimate forms of power, but rather with 'power at its extremities, in its ultimate destinations, with those points where it becomes capillary, that is, in its more regional and local forms and institutions.'[68] For it is in these instances that power overrides the rules of right that control it and 'extends itself beyond them, invests itself in institutions, becomes embodied in techniques, and equips itself with instruments and eventually even violent means of material intervention.'[69] Second, the analysis should not be concerned with power from the internal point of view, at the level of conscious intention, so as to provoke the unanswerable question 'Who has power and what will he do with it?'[70] Instead, our analysis should aim to discover how it is that subjects are constituted as subjects. Foucault urges us to stay away from the model of juridical sovereignty, which is limited to the relationship between the sovereign and subject, and to focus our analysis on the 'techniques and tactics of domination,' for then we will recognize a new mechanism of power – non-sovereign power – invented by bourgeois society, which Foucault calls disciplinary power. The model of disciplinary power goes beyond the power of state institutions; it provides effective instruments for the production and accumulation of knowledge. Analysis of disciplinary power as relations of domination surpasses the Leviatanean model of power by showing how phenomena of repression, discrimination, and exclusion take place as a result of the function of the power mechanism. The explanatory power of this model, hence, goes beyond Habermas's consensus/coercion model of legitimate/illegitimate power. The point of introducing Foucault's analysis of power is not to jettison the legal model of the analysis of power, but to expand the dimensions of its definition of power to include disciplinary power. On the complementary relation of these two models, he writes:

> Hence, these two limits, a right of sovereignty and a mechanism of discipline, define, I believe, the arena in which power is exercised. But these two limits are so heterogeneous that they cannot possibly be reduced to each other. The powers of modern society are exercised through, on the basis of, and by virtue of, this very heterogeneity between a public right of sovereignty and a polymorphous disciplinary mechanism.[71]

The juridical model recognizes social injustices either as economic domination or illegitimate use of the sovereign right. The need to expand this model arises out of its limited capacity to include and account for other forms of social inequalities. Thus, 'the symbolic force that structures the formation and hierarchization of social identities fails to be understood as a type of political power.'[72] The insight of Foucault's analysis that relations of power have a constitutive effect – that is, they make individuals subjects[73] – is irreducible to the analysis of the juridical model.

> This constitutive dimension of discursive power, denoted by the term *épistème*, brings to light a cultural logic imbricated in the production of social hierarchies that are marked by conflict rather than by solidarity. This logic is not reducible to a ruling economic class or political elite, or to the types of power specific to the economy (exchange) and the state (law). Foucault's theory of power offers an alternative approach to the critique of cultural domination.[74]

Such a theory allows for other fields of power that do not fit under the rubrics of the power of a sovereign or of economic power to be recognized as political power, a realization that needs to be taken into account for the formulation of a critical theory of democracy. I believe that from this strategic standpoint we can scrutinize the theoretical justification of normative theory with an eye to the biases that have roots in the pre-theoretical depth of their cultural background. A Foucauldean theory of power exposes these biases as a mutually reproducing function of the power/knowledge relations of our modern practices. It brings into the light social injustices involving the non-ideal categories of cultural politics such as biases concerning the politics of race, gender, ethnicity, and sexuality. Along the same lines, Axel Honneth in 'The Social Dynamics of Disrespect,'[75] argues that Habermas's emphasis on the rationality of economic and administrative systems tends to overlook the results of continuing struggle between different social groups. He contends that the social groups' experience of the constriction of their 'moral point of view' is not, *pace* Habermas, the result of a restriction of their linguistic competence but a violation of their identity claims, which they acquire through socialization. Foucault's model of power is better suited to analyse the recognition or lack of recognition of different social groups' identity claims, which are usually connected to their socio-economic status.

Perhaps an example will better show the greater usefulness of Foucault's analysis of power.

Despite its diversity, feminist theory offers a clear case where postmodern political theory has proven more fruitful than Habermas's normative theory.[76] Foucault's analysis of power allows for a more differentiated account of the subject's self-constitution with respect to gender identity, whereas the Habermasian model, which postulates the concept of 'Man' as the paradigm of humanity, is inadequately gender-sensitive. Indeed, Foucault's theorization has lent itself much more easily to the discourses of gays, women, ethnic groups, and racial minorities than have most normative theories. A comparative account, with respect to the critical ability of Habermas's and Foucault's analyses, shows that while Habermas's juridical model of power can give a critical account of social injustices such as economic domination and the illegitimate use of sovereign power, it fails to criticize injustices that fall beyond the realm of juridical power, such as issues involving the constitution of the subject. I believe that this restricted view of power has become even further constrained by the formulation of the concepts of communicative power and enacted law, and their relation in *BFN*. For while on the juridical model such cases as the undue influence of lobby groups and unregulated campaign funds could be criticized in terms of the domination of discursive space by norm-free steering media, after *BFN* the connection between communicative power, legitimate law-making, and political power blurs the boundary between the norm-governed and norm-free domains of political interaction. This inadequacy, however, should not be taken to mean that Habermas's account of deliberative democracy could not provide any critique of the actual practices of liberal democracy. Indeed, as my present discussion of his model of power shows, his theory can critique certain kinds of injustices in existing democracies. For example, Habermas's theory can still provide critical analysis of some aspects of the problem of gender inequality, such as unequal pay or the lack of daycare, as instances of economic injustices, but it cannot give a critical account of a problem such as the normalization of heterosexuality, which affects the formation of individual subjects' social identity but falls outside the scope of either economic domination or the illegitimate use of political power.

While the range of my discussion does not allow me to develop this line of argument further here, I hope to have shown that a synthesis of Foucault's critical theory of power with Habermas's critical theory of politics is required for a more thorough approach to studying the pathologies of modernity and the possibility of democracy. Interestingly enough, Orville Lee, a fellow critical theorist, has recently proposed the same synthesis: 'A synthesis of a cultural theory of power [Foucault and Bourdieu] with the reconstructive efforts of critical democratic theory [Habermas] is necessary if a more comprehensive framework is to be developed for analyzing the underlying source of, and the remedies for, the compound forms of economic, political, and symbolic inequalities.'[77] While Lee and McCarthy's articles bestow a certain validity to my intuition with respect to bringing the insight of Foucault's theory to bear on Habermas's critical theory,[78] I now propose – without enjoying the same theoretical support in the literature – to take on the additional task of considering the insight of Derrida's recent writings in political theory for the purpose of further recovering the critical thrust of Habermas's position.

3. Democracy and the Inclusion of Difference: Derrida's Insight

Habermas also charges Jacques Derrida, as a 'young conservative,'[79] with 'performative contradiction' (see chapter 3, section 3). In *Philosophical Discourse of Modernity* he argues that Derrida's total critique of reason deprives the post-structuralist view of a normative standard he otherwise needs in order to justify his ethico-political preferences.[80] Derrida's method of deconstruction is charged with eliminating 'the genre distinction between philosophy and literature,' robbing them both of their substance.[81] In terms of my discussion here, the problem can be framed in the form of the following question: What does/can deconstruction contribute to the task of reconstructing a normative theory of democracy?

Answering this question will also reveal what can be borrowed from Derrida in order to enrich Habermas's theory of deliberative democracy. In so far as the question asks about the postmodernist contribution to addressing our contemporary socio-political problems, an answer can be formulated along the following general lines. The postmodernist critique has exposed the exclusionary and totalizing aspects of every system and the normalizing effect of their discourse/practices, thus allowing for the voices of *difference*, of the *other*, and of the *margin* to be heard through a demeanour of destabilization, of resisting abstract totalities and universalism. If the above question, however, is demanding a systematic political theory in place of a local critique, then it has missed the very point of postmodern analysis, which aims at exposing the authoritarianism of theoretical systems. Stephen White concisely describes the point of such demands and questions as follows:

> We thereby would become engaged in an imperialistic project of forcing poststructuralism to speak our traditional language, to accommodate itself to our standard, foundational distinctions: rational/irrational, legitimate/illegitimate, and so forth. The cognitive machinery of traditional ethical-political reflection would thus be allowed to operate upon poststructuralism in such away that the latter would likely appear to be rather incoherent.[82]

The postmodernist strategy, therefore, is to engage in a struggle against the totalizing tendencies of abstract systems via regional resistance. Such analyses deliberately resist turning into new theoretical systems, hence rendering the above question, at best, misguided and uncharitable. For, if the aim of deconstructive strategy, for instance, is to destabilize theory by showing what lies beyond its boundary, then to ask why deconstruction does not provide us with a political theory is already to have missed the point – to have not listened well.[83] Thomas McCarthy seems to accept as much when he writes, 'Deconstructive activities seem here to be necessarily complementary to activities of building, repairing, and improving the norms, principles, laws, and institutions by which we live.'[84] Yet he argues that since the political-practical import of deconstruction is essentially negative, it is 'parasitic on construction and reconstruction, and that he has had very little to offer in the way of positive ethico-political proposals.'[85] In my judgment, however, it is misleading to conclude that a destabilizing strategy of deconstruction is necessarily negative, if negative denotes an evaluative judgment. In so far as deconstruction contributes to the critique of our present in the effort to find out who we are as human subjects, in distinction from our past, its contribution is as positive as any other form of critique. As for the adjective 'parasitic': since we always find ourselves within a deconstructable context to describe the relation between deconstruction and this context, as 'parasitic' is tautological at best. I agree that further clarification along the lines of Derrida's more recent writings can prove deconstruction to be even more helpful to our socio-political concerns. But to admit that Derrida's approach is in need of further clarification should not amount to underestimating its critical value.

Derrida is aware of the scepticism surrounding the fruitfulness of deconstruction for a theory of justice and democratic politics, but believes this scepticism is laden with the assumption that, because of its lack of normative criteria, deconstruction cannot accommodate any discourse on justice. He writes: 'The "sufferance" of deconstruction, what makes it suffer and what makes those it torments suffer, is perhaps the absence of rules, norms, and definitive criteria that would allow one to distinguish unequivocally between *droit* and justice.'[86] This opening to his important paper 'Force of Law: Mystical Foundation of Authority' is indicative of a new direction that his work has taken during the past decade. He begins here his analysis that separates justice from law by stating that enforceability is implied in the concept of justice as law. Such an element of applicability of justice as it becomes law gives rise to the question of the legitimacy of law. 'How are we to distinguish between this force of the law, this "force of law," ... and the violence one always deems unjust?'[87] Subsequently, he notes that the English and French have essentially translated the German word *Gewalt* as violence and have one-sidedly ignored 'the fact that *Gewalt* also signifies, for Germans, legitimate power, authority, public force.' Hence, for Derrida too, there exists a legitimate power, a public force that needs to be esteemed. Still, he wants to do something more. In his attempt to distinguish between justice and law he turns his attention to the origin of law and its claim to legitimacy, asking, 'How are we to distinguish between the force of law of a legitimate power and the supposedly originary violence that must have established this authority and that could not itself have been authorized by any anterior legitimacy, so that, in this initial moment, it is neither legal nor illegal – or others would quickly say, neither just nor unjust?'[89]

In his analysis of the American Declaration of Independence[90] Derrida poses a question with respect to the founding authority of the declaration: [W]*ho signs, and with what so-called proper name, the declarative act which founds an institution?*'[91] There is, therefore, a signature at the heart of the founding act. He further asks, 'But just whose signature exactly?'[92] to which he answers, 'By right, the signer is thus the people.'[93] This is where the moment of *undecidability* comes to the fore: 'Is it that the good people have already freed themselves in fact and are only stating the fact of this emancipation in [*par*] the declaration? Or is it rather that they free themselves at the instant of and by [*par*] the signature of this Declaration?'[94] Derrida characterizes this moment of undecidability as entailing an obscurity between the performative and constative act. This obscurity brings to the fore the moment in which we are faced with the task of deciding the ground of the authority of the founding moment, which, according to Derrida, is resolved by the force of performative's effect as birth-giving, a founding act. This moment is similar to Arendt's concept of 'new beginning' and to what Habermas has called the act of 'constitution giving.' Comparing Arendt and Derrida on the originary moment of law-giving, Seyla Benhabib writes, 'I want to suggest that ultimately at a formal level of analysis there is indeed *no solution* to the paradox of the constitution of revolutionary authority.'[95] I read this as reaffirming what Derrida calls the moment of undecidability, where we have to declare an authority by way of a performative act.

The act of declaration constitutes the American people by the sheer force of signing: 'the signature gives itself a name.'[96] The paradox of republican founding, that is to say, the authority and the legitimacy of the originary law, is, therefore, addressed not arbitrarily, as Derrida's critics charge, but along the same lines as Habermas's and Arendt's proposal of viewing the revolutionary moment as the moment of constitution-giving, namely, as a new beginning, a new birth, of name-giving, an ability or force of signing. According to Derrida the act of making law consists of a *coup de force*: 'The coup of force makes right, founds right or the law, gives right, *brings the law to the light of day, gives both birth and day to the law* [donne le jour à la loi].'[97] But the justice of law or justice as law is not justice; it is a legitimate authority that as such is enforceable. But 'law is not justice,'[98] for justice is not reducible to law. Law can be deconstructed, calculated, and exercised; it allows us to move towards justice, to approximate it, to be more just. But justice itself can never be fully achieved because it is incalculable, it is undeconstructable, it exists beyond or outside law. In this connection, Derrida could agree with Habermas that liberal-democratic institutions can approximate justice through law, but he would not agree that the presence of law means the attainment of justice. To put it in Derrida's words, 'Justice is the experience of the aporia, of an impossible.'[99] This is why to have law, in the same way that Habermas's theory appeals to legal theory and law, or in the same way that liberal theory has law, is never a guarantee of justice.[100] Social consensus is not the result of shared world views but a temporary balance of power and interest, which warrants Foucault's sense that '[h]umanity does not gradually progress from combat to combat until it arrives at universal reciprocity, where the rule of law finally replaces warfare; humanity installs each of its violences in a system of rules and thus proceeds from domination to domination.'[101] Habermas weakens the utopian and hence the critical dimension of his theory when he puts all the eggs of his deliberative democracy into one basket of legal theory. To mistake the presence of law for the achievement of justice and democracy is to fall prey to political complacency that dulls one's critical ability. The form of critique may vary, but its thrust should not.

One way of presenting a critique is through a Habermasian method of reconstructive sciences; another way is through a Derridean deconstructive strategy. This is what Thomas McCarthy means when he writes, 'Whatever has been constructed can be deconstructed, destabilized and recontextualized and so on. By the same token it can also be reconstructed, improved, restablized, and so forth.' But he goes on to protest that 'Derrida rarely mentions this side (reconstructivist) of the ledger.'[102] However, one could ask whether Habermas has ever employed deconstructive analysis in his work – not in the Marxian sense of ideology critique that reveals the interests of a particular social group behind their strategic actions, but in the Derridean sense of deconstruction of an entire system. In my view, in the same way that it would be insensitive and, perhaps, even violent to ask Habermas to incorporate deconstructive practices in his critical theory, it would be beside the point to ask Derrida to provide us with a universalistic political theory. Against such misplaced demands, Foucault, in a combative mode, writes:

> Under no circumstances, should one pay attention to those who tell one: 'don't criticize, since you are not capable of carrying out a reform.' That is ministerial cabinet talk. Critique doesn't have to be the premise of a deduction, which concludes: this then is what needs to be done. It should be an instrument for those who fight, those who resist and refuse *what is*. Its use should be in processes of conflict and confrontation, essays in refusal. It doesn't have to lay down the law. It isn't a stage in a programming. It is a challenge directed to *what is*.[103]

The provocative and polemical tone of the quote aside, the point is clear: there are different forms of critique and they may have different tasks as well. A deconstructive critique, then, simply performs a different task than that of a reconstructive one. For a deconstructive strategy to resist the temptation of presenting a theoretical system, however, is not to say that it is indifferent to, or unproductive for, the treatment of such concepts as justice, ethics, law, freedom, etc. Indeed, these concepts have taken centre stage in some of Derrida's more recent writings.[104] Therefore, the vulgar criticism that deconstructive critique amounts to political aloofness ignores, or counts as insignificant, one strategy of postmodernist criticism that Seyla Benhabib, another critical theorist, calls 'crucial for the ethos of contemporary democratic communities.'[105]

To sum up the insight of deconstructive strategy for a critical theory of politics, I would state that Derrida defends the political aspect of the project of modernity, that is, the ideal of democracy.[106] The emancipatory project in his work is approached, by way of deconstruction as a mode of political intervention, with the goal of showing that no power is absolute and that no plurality of meaning can be fixed in language.[107]

Habermas and other critical theorists strive towards devising a theory of critical analysis of modern institutional arrangements that would grant human subjects emancipation from different forms of domination. The compatibility of these two projects can further be noted with respect to the goal of their political theorization, namely, that of justice. Derrida concludes his discussion in 'Force of Law' by describing the ideal of political justice or democracy, not as a definite and fixed ideal that can be completed once and for all, but as an ideal that

> [m]ay have an *avenir*, a 'to come,' which I rigorously distinguish from the future that can always reproduce the present. Justice remains, is yet, to come, à *venir*, it has an, it is à-*venir*, the very dimension of events irreducibility to come. It will always have it, this à-*venir*, and always has. Perhaps it is for this reason that justice, insofar as it is not only a juridical or political concept, opens up for l'*avenir* the transformation, the recasting or refounding of law and politics. 'Perhaps,' one must always say perhaps for justice.[108]

To view the value of justice and democracy as à-*venir* is not to say that they will arrive in a future, but that they will never arrive, they are unachievable, and they only can be approximated. To say that they are unachievable is not to say that they are false hopes, but to say that they are ideals, utopian conceptions that guide our political endeavours, always remaining beyond our reality as its compass. 'For democracy remains to come; this is its essence in so far as it remains: not only will it remain indefinitely perfectible, hence always insufficient and future, but, belonging to the time of the promise, it will always remain, in each of its future times, to come: even when there is democracy, it never exists, it is never present, it is never present, it remains the theme of a non-presentable concept.'[109]

What is the value of this view for the purpose of resuscitating Habermas's weakened theory? His theory (and Rawls's for that matter) treats the goal of a democratic project, that is, democracy and social justice, as a concrete end that can be achieved once and for all. For them justice and democracy are the same as the institutions that aim to bring them about, which is why both authors assert that liberal-democratic societies have a self-corrective capacity through the existing institutions that are necessary for their reform. As discussed earlier, this emphasis on actually existing democracy breeds political complacency. The value of Derrida's view of democracy as *à-venir* is that it does not allow the complacency of the real to debilitate the pursuit of the ideal.

Derrida picks up the theme of political responsibility in his *Politics of Friendship*.[110] He constructs his analysis around a short phrase that Montaigne quotes from Aristotle, 'O my friends, there is no friend.' At the heart of this seemingly paradoxical call, he tells us – this performative contradiction, to use Habermas's phrase – lays an appeal to an ethical disposition that is not yet present, but needs to be established. The call

> [r]esembles an appeal, because it makes a sign toward the future: be my friends, for I love or will love you (friendship, as Aristotle also said, consists rather in loving than being loved [VIII 9, 25–30], a proposition on which we have not yet finished mediating) listen to me, be sensitive to my cry, understand and be compassionate; I am asking for sympathy and consensus, become the friend to whom I aspire.[111]

This call is a prayer, Derrida tells us, in the Aristotlean sense: as *eukhē* it is a discourse that, like a performative, is neither true nor false. Like an ethical 'ought,' this prayer aims to approximate an ideal that is lacking, a yet to come:

> There are no friends, that we know, but I beg you make it so that there will be friends from now on. What is more, how could I be your friend, and declare my friendship for you ... if friendship did not remain something yet to happen, to be desired, to be promised? How could I give you my friendship where friendship would not be lacking, that is, if it already existed ... Perhaps this is because we have an idea of friendship and what it should be, in the ideality of its essence or telos, and thus *in the name of*

friendship we must conclude, alas, that, if there is friendship, 'there is no friend.'[112]

According to this view, friendship is not what we have at present, but rather what belongs to an ethos of promise, of commitment, of responsibility that remains open to the future. This call to friendship invokes an ethical *response to the Other*: the question of responsibility. 'One says "answer for," "answer to," "answer before" [répondre de, répondre à, répondre devant]. These three modalities are not juxtaposable; they envelop and imply each other.'[113] At the heart of friendship Derrida notes the co-implication of responsibility and respect, which 'calls for a rigorous rereading of the Kantian analysis of respect in friendship. There is no friendship without "respect for the Other" ...'[114] This rereading brings to the fore a tension between two dimensions of friendship: the absolute singularity of the Other and the universality of moral law. On the one hand, such a tension renders friendship

> foreign or unamenable to the *res publica* and thus could not found a politics. But, on the other hand, as one knows, from Plato to Montaigne, from Aristotle to Kant, from Cicero to Hegel, the *great philosophical and canonical discourses* on friendship ... will have linked friendship explicitly to virtue and to justice, to moral reason and to political reason. These discourses will have even set the moral and political conditions for an authentic friendship – and vice-versa.[115]

Critics have expressed doubts about whether the deconstructionist strategy is the most effective way to disrupt metaphysics and think post-metaphysically about ethics, law, and politics. For example, Thomas McCarthy, in an assessment of Derrida's paper, asks 'whether "friendship" is the best place to start thinking about ethics, law, and politics.'[116] At the same time, however, he concedes the critical and emancipatory function of Derrida's strategy:

> Treating friendship as 'a privileged place for reflecting' on law, morality, and politics does provide an instructive antidote to the leveling, difference-denying tendencies of much moral and legal theory, of the Kantian sort as well. It helps make us attentive to what gets left out of generalizing schemes, of what is ignored, excluded, or assimilated by them. And it can serve to remind us that universalizing theories of justice do not exhaust the domain of the ethical.[117]

Finally, with respect to the issue of difference and pluralism, I believe that Derrida's view of justice and democracy as an ongoing procedure that is open to new interpretation and new contestation, and is never complete, is more appropriate to the description of the ideal of deliberative democracy as a procedural argumentation among free and equal citizens with different world views than is Habermas's model. Of course, Habermas repeatedly emphasizes the open-ended and fallibilistic character of his model of discourse theory. But these expressions are in tension with the architectonic of his theory of communicative action, which emphasizes the role of consensus as the ultimate telos of communication,[118] and re-emphasize it in the principle of democracy as the *assent of all* citizens to legitimate law.[119] Thus, given the place of consensus in Habermas's political theory, dissent and conflict come to be seen in a negative light as anomalies that need to be eschewed. Albrecht Wellmer, in his critique of the conception of consensus in Habermas, put the same point in the following way: 'The ideal communication community would be beyond error, dissent, non-understanding and conflict, but only at the cost of bringing language to a halt, ... and this means at the cost of a cancellation of [the] linguistic-historical life-form of human beings.'[120] This demeanour prevents Habermas from fully recognizing that the conflicts between fundamental values can never be resolved. Without this recognition one cannot claim to recognize the value of a pluralism of world views, as Habermas does. Because in order for a deliberative democracy to be a pluralist democracy, it cannot view the diversity that it governs as something to be overcome, as Habermas's principle of democracy demands, but as a source of strength that should be esteemed. Derrida sums this point up when he declares, 'No politics without *différance*.'[121] Chantal Mouffe explicates the recognition of difference as a democratic value as follows:

> This requires the presence of institutions that establish a specific dynamic between consensus and dissent. Consensus, of course, is necessary, but it should be limited to the institutions that are constitutive of the democratic order. A pluralist democracy needs also to make room for the expression of dissent and for conflicting interests and values. And those should not be seen as temporary obstacles on the road to consensus since in their absence democracy would cease to be pluralistic.[122]

Thus, to understand the task of democratic politics entails the recognition of the agonistic aspect of social relations as one of its definitive elements, which in turn reveals the goals of harmony and reconciliation as misplaced hopes. The engagement of differences constitutes the political, which takes consensus as a regulative idea of organization rather than a constitutive idea of harmony and reconciliation. To view the role of consensus as regulative does not mean that it governs political discourse; rather it functions as a critical idea that aims to promote the productivity of the outcome. Such a regulatory and critical character is also, for consensus, more consistent with post-metaphysical thinking than is its constitutive role. Therefore, the telos of pluralist democracy cannot be consensus, because the very moment of its realization would also be the moment of its destruction. Indeed, what makes democratic politics persist is the irreducibility of difference and the ongoing political engagements that keep its promise open. The institutions of a democratic society that view justice as the experience of irreducible alterity, therefore, enact a sensitive dynamic between consensus and dissent. At the end, if we are to take the insight of postmodern political theory seriously and view democracy as embodying the irreducible conflicts among different groups, and see justice as the compass meant to guide and govern this struggle, then we have to pose the question of political legitimacy anew. How can solidarity, which is needed for the legitimacy of political power, be attained in diverse societies? The next chapter will explore a possible answer to this question.

Chapter 7

Constitutional Patriotism as an Answer to the Problems of Diversity and Solidarity

Our task is to find a language for our need for belonging which is not just a way of expressing nostalgia, fear and estrangement from modernity. Our political images of civic belonging remain haunted by the classical polis, *by Athens, Rome, and Florence. Is there a language of belonging adequate to Los Angeles?*

Michael Ignatieff[1]

German nationalist intellectuals still reject the lessons of the Enlightenment, the French Revolution, and Ernest Renan: that the 'nation' in democratic states – if it is anything at all – cannot be the protection of the particularity of the volk *against outside forces. It must, rather, be the symbol of a 'daily plebiscite' within society itself on democratic participation in political self-organization.*

Reinhard Merkel[2]

So far in my assessment of Habermas's pursuit of the ideals of justice and democracy I have shown that while his theory's discursive method and its communicative aims foster a critical character and give it an open-ended approach consistent with our post-metaphysical condition, this character and this approach are compromised as a result of a shift in *Between Facts and Norms* that marks the theory's new orientation towards the 'real, existing democracy' as opposed to the one that is *yet to come.* The modern life of liberal states is marked by a multiplicity of world views and rapid changes in the composition of their political communities that are brought about by speed, technology, and globalization. Indeed, recognition of the facts of diversity and pluralism as conditions of our modern democracies demands that the justification of political decisions no longer be made with reference to conflicting

moral values, but rather be left open to procedures of public deliberation among differences that are governed by law. The presence of law in
the legal and institutional apparatus of liberal democracies, however,
should not be taken as the achievement of justice. For law is a means to
the end that is justice; justice itself is never completely realized. In *The
Inclusion of the Other* Habermas's theorization goes some distance in
reviving the pursuit of the ideal of democracy as a *yet to come*. For
instance, his rearticulation of the principle of U points to 'a moral
universalism sensitive to difference,' which as such 'takes the form of a
nonleveling and *nonappropriating* inclusion of the other in *his otherness*.'[3]
Such a move enables Habermas to respond to some of the foregoing
criticisms and reform his critical theory so to frame the problems of
power and legitimacy in terms of the possibility of social cohesion and
solidarity – which gives stability to the political regime – in the face of
growing diversity – which enhances political contestation and conflicts.

In *The Inclusion of the Other* Habermas's response to this problem is
presented in the form of the doctrine of 'constitutional patriotism,' a
principle of political association whose role it is to 'sharpen sensitivity
to the diversity and integrity of the different forms of life coexisting
within a multicultural society.'[4] In this sense, the idea of constitutional
patriotism is presented in order to reconcile the goal of solidarity, which
requires recognition of a shared identity, with the fact of cultural diversity in today's liberal democracies so as to accommodate greater inclusion. The problem of diversity in multicultural societies requires us to
rethink the notions of identity, citizenship, nation, state, and solidarity
and their relation to each other. To this end, Habermas's effort here is
concerned with the following question: How is the solidarity that
grounds the legitimacy of a political order achieved in a free but diverse
society?

In this chapter, I will first outline (section 1) Habermas's answer to
the above question in the form of his doctrine of constitutional patriotism. Motivated by the aspiration to leave behind the politics of ethnic
nationalism, Habermas claims that, given the internal relation between
the rule of law and democracy, the conditions of membership in, and
unity of, a liberal democracy should be the object of law. In a post-
national society the loyalty of the citizens of a democratic state to law
replaces the traditional bonds of belonging, fostering a sense of solidarity and political unity, which he calls constitutional patriotism
(*Verfassungspatriotismus*).

In section 2 I will consider some criticisms levelled against constitutional patriotism by both liberal and republican theorists such as Canovan, Yack, Taylor, and Viroli. They charge that even when citizens of a democratic state see themselves as authors/subjects of the law, neither the legitimacy of the political order nor citizens' identification with it is guaranteed, which in turn puts the issue of solidarity on shaky ground. These theorists dispute the claim that allegiance to a set of abstract laws can promote a strong enough sense of identity and belonging necessary for political legitimacy. The key point of divergence in this debate, I believe, is between the *empirical* thrust of the critique of liberal nationalists and republican patriots – which argues that, historically, the bond of membership *has been* decided according to 'natural' ties of a pre-political group – and the *normative* thrust of the project of constitutional patriotism, which focuses on how political association *should* be decided. Having made this distinction, my elaboration on the concept of constitutional patriotism (section 3) is normatively informed. Finally, in section 4 I will argue that in order to remain true to the spirit of critical theory, the Habermasian account of constitutional patriotism should be seen, not merely as replacing one fixed identity (traditional) with another (post-conventional), but as an open-ended process of political identity-formation that allows for a more flexible and transient identity; one that is consistent with the diversity, hybridity, and pluralism of our modern world.

1. Constitutional Patriotism

From the theoretical perspective of political philosophy it is intriguing that two opposing tendencies, of ever-growing globalization and revived nationalism, open the debate on constitutional patriotism. For constitutional patriotism is seen both as consistent with the cosmopolitan tendency of globalization and as an answer to the rise of nationalism. While the term has been coined recently,[5] its roots go back to the Enlightenment and to the question of whether the problem of identification should be decided according to an ethnic or a civic sense of belonging. As such, constitutional patriotism presents itself as an answer to the diremption of the binding force of belonging and the universal norms of modernity. Whatever else nationalism may imply, it is a powerful indication of a desire and need to belong to a politico-cultural entity that determines one's identity. Such a need used to be satisfied by identification with a historically pre-existing *ethnos*. However, the increasing social and racial intercourse among different nations has resulted in the facts of pluralism and diversity, thus rendering the appeals to ethnic and national ties more and more problematic. It is in such a context that Habermas speaks of the ideal of constitutional patriotism, which pledges, as an alternative to the national sense of belonging, to unite citizens under a civic contract aimed at ideals of human rights, justice, and democracy.

On Habermas's account of deliberative democracy, legitimate law-making is understood to result from institutionalized procedures that convert citizens' practice of self-determination, in the form of communicative and participatory rights, into the binding decision of political power.

> This understanding of democracy leads to the normative demand for a new balance between the three resources of money, administrative power, and solidarity from which modern societies meet their need for integration and regulation. The normative implications are obvious: the integrative force of solidarity, which can no longer be drawn solely from sources of communicative action, should develop through widely expanded autonomous public spheres as well as through legally institutionalized procedures of democratic deliberation and decision making and gain sufficient strength to hold its own against the other two social forces – money and administrative power.[6]

But how do we develop solidarity? Habermas's strategy is to approach the problem of social cohesion and unity in relation to the role of legal institutions and enacted law, for he believes that solidarity can be the object of law.

As discussed earlier, for Habermas there is an internal relation between the rule of law and democracy. A complementarity is envisioned, on the one hand, between morality and law and, on the other, between law and politics. Given this complementarity he writes, 'As positively valid, legitimately enacted, and actionable, law can relieve the morally judging and acting person of the considerable cognitive, motivational, and organizational demands of a morality based entirely on individual conscience.'[7] Modern law is viewed as a system of norms that comprises a set of abstract rights recognized by all citizens in the form of a constitution. Such a construct of law, while it is produced through the procedures of democratic will-formation – as the only source of post-metaphysical legitimacy – itself generates solidarity as a form of social integration. Accordingly, for Habermas, through the process of discursive deliberation citizens of liberal-democratic states who come to see themselves simultaneously as both the authors and the subjects of the law will accept the legitimacy of the political order. In recognizing the legitimacy of this order, citizens will also identify with it and feel a sense of loyalty to it, fostering a sense of solidarity. 'Solidarity ... arises out of law only indirectly, of course: by stabilizing behavioral expectations, law simultaneously secures symmetrical relationships of reciprocal recognition between abstract bearers of individual rights.'[8] To say that such a sense of solidarity and togetherness is needed for sustaining deliberative democracy does not entail that the shared identity must stem from a common language, common ethnicity, or common religion. The commonality necessary for the practice of deliberative democracy is a shared political culture of participation, communication, and contestation within the framework of constitutional law. 'The political integration of citizens ensures loyalty to the common political culture. The latter is rooted in an interpretation of constitutional principles from the perspective of the nation's historical experience.'[9] What allows the fostering of constitutional patriotism, then, is the promotion of the procedures of public deliberation through which free and equal citizens come to recognize one another as compatriots with their differences intact, bonding together by way of exercising their participatory and communicative rights in a joined effort. Fostering such a political culture is not merely based on good persuasion and better argument, but also draws upon 'more or less fortunate patterns of traditions, civilized forms of intercourse, socialization patterns, school systems, and so on.'[10]

The abstract laws are not envisioned in order to homogenize differences and violate their autonomy. Rather they are formulated in order to facilitate the coexistence of differences within a political community. These abstract rights then get filled in according to the particularities of a concrete political association. 'Each national culture develops a distinctive interpretation of those constitutional principles that are equally embodied in other republican constitutions – such as popular sovereignty and human rights – in light of its own national history. A "constitutional patriotism" based on these interpretations can take the place originally occupied by nationalism.'[11]

For Habermas, a move toward a greater abstraction that become hypostasized – *vis-à-vis* the pressures of multiculturalism, on the one hand, and globalization, on the other – in a constitution is the expression of a country's political culture, which 'must be uncoupled from the level of subcultures and their political identities.'[12] This uncoupling takes the form of an unending process of discursive procedures that is filled in by the political actors according to their concrete history. The result is a civic patriotism whereby political values such as stability and political legitimacy emerge from citizens' communicative understanding of a shared polity, as opposed to a shared national identity.

Constitutional patriotism as such promises to replace nationalism by providing the civic bond of citizenship necessary for one's sense of belonging and identity while avoiding nationalism's damaging features. Such an understanding of the concept, however, has also given rise to worries that mere principles are too weak to produce and maintain a deep sense of identification and belonging.[13] In the following section I will critically assess some of these unfavourable views of constitutional patriotism.

2. Questioning the Civic Bond of Citizenship

The Pre-political 'We'

For most political theorists the problem of belonging or identity, as the source of unity in the body politic, is framed within the idea of the modern state. On this account, the idea of the modern state is anchored on a political principle of unity. Liberal nationalists such as Yael Tamir,[14] David Miller,[15] and Margaret Canovan,[16] explain the principle of unity in terms of *nationalism*, where nation and state coincide through a series of political movements and public policies. For them, nationalism serves to provide solidarity among members by constituting a collective political subject – a 'we.'[17] From this perspective, liberal nationalists look with suspicion upon the civic bond of constitutional patriotism. For example, Margaret Canovan, in her recent paper 'Patriotism Is Not Enough'[18] has eloquently voiced the objection that constitutional patriotism ignores the basic matrix against whose background political associations are constituted. Critics of constitutional patriotism like Canovan worry that the cosmopolitan spirit of the concept in its all-encompassing coverage of human community ends up disregarding particular loyalties and concrete identities of human subjects that bind them together as 'fellow-countrymen.'[19] Their opposition to the idea of constitutional patriotism stems from the concern that it discounts and disregards the diversity of particular identities that are prior to it. But perhaps their chief question with respect to constitutional patriotism is whether the connecting civic bond among citizens is strong enough to create and maintain a sense of socio-political identity necessary for the democratic exercise of political authority. As we will see below, the critical edge of Canovan's paper, especially her idea of the priority of a pre-political entity that grounds any political association and contract, aims at making any affirmative answer to this question impossible.

Advocates of constitutional patriotism have argued that the concept is capable of accommodating difference and plurality in so far as citizens are socialized into a common political culture of liberal-democratic values.[20] Canovan's first argument is that 'the project of avoiding the illiberal effects of nationalism by basing the state upon shared liberal values is self-defeating,'[21] since to instil the political culture of patriotism based on liberal principles requires an authoritative and coercive socialization of citizens. That is because, she explains, in our increasingly multi-ethnic and multicultural world, achieving consensus on liberal-democratic principles cannot be taken for granted. The prima facie plausibility of this claim, however, should not blind us to the fact that the binding force of a constitution arises precisely out of the *necessity* of finding an associative political norm that is abstracted from the concrete differences of pluralist society, an abstraction which is made possible in so far as the diverse groups are brought together as citizens by virtue of being subject to the same law, that is, the constitution. The universalistic content of the abstract laws are to be complemented with an ethical substance of constitutional patriotism that 'has to sharpen sensitivity to the diversity and integrity of different forms of life coexisting within a multicultural society.'[22] This requires that cultural majorities only promote a constitutional patriotism that separates political culture from all non-political matters of their particular forms of life, while cultural minorities are given 'extensive guarantees of status, rights to self-administration, infrastructural benefits, subsidies, and so on.'[23]

Moreover, to put different groups' demands for recognition in the Kantian language of *The Metaphysics of Morals*, one can argue that their rights only find meaning within 'a rightful condition under a will uniting them, *a constitution* (*constitutio*), so that they may enjoy what it is laid down as rights.'[24] In other words, the very possibility of dissent with respect to democratic principles requires a prior civic condition in which the individual members of a people are related to each other via a constitution in a state.[25] It is only within such a political community of patriots that the diverse claims of particular identities, which demand certain group rights and recognition, find meaning. This recognition of, and subscription to, a set of rights crystallized in a constitution bestows a reciprocal character on the political parties' competition and contestation, connecting them as free and equal partners within the same political entity. For, while the absence of such a connection as the *idea* of a constitutional bond may still accommodate the political struggle of different ethnic, religious, and cultural groups, it is only its reality that can reciprocally bound their actions and satisfy their expectations. For any good Kantian like Habermas the form and the content of political membership are matters of justice: hence the proper form of political identity and union is produced where citizens are willing to grant one another certain rights, and abide by certain rules that can be universally agreed upon. That is why, for example, the aboriginal peoples or francophones in Canada demand greater autonomy and protection for their cultural identity not just from anyone in the world but precisely from Canadians, and within the context and against the background of the Canadian constitution, their reservations notwithstanding. Therefore, from the possibility of disagreement and contestation within constitutional states it does not follow that the maintenance of the civic bond of patriotism requires illiberal coercion by law.

The claim that citizens can share loyalty to such a polity centred on law, for Canovan, 'begs vital questions about the state.'[26] The gist of her criticism is that the advocates of constitutional patriotism take the underpinning character of liberal democratic states, namely a 'people,' for granted, where a 'people' is defined as 'a trans-generational political community, members of which recognize the state as "our" state and thereby confer upon it the legitimacy and power it needs.'[27] What this definition reveals, however, is a conflation of a 'people' and the 'state.' For while it is true that a population, a 'people' precedes any political contract, it is not true that such an entity is politically significant in the sense that a 'state' is. Again, it should suffice to recall *The Metaphysics of Morals*, where Kant argues that from the perspective of right,

[t]he act by which a people form itself into a state is the *original contract*. Properly speaking, the original contract is only the Idea of this act, in terms of which alone we can think of the legitimacy of a state. In accordance with the original contract, everyone (*omnes et singuli*) within a people gives up his eternal freedom in order to take it up again immediately as a member of a commonwealth, that is, of a people considered as a state (*universi*).[28]

The aspiration of constitutional patriots is at root Kantian,[29] in that they want to construct democratic institutions that protect the rights of all citizens whether they share the same pre-political ancestry or not. Indeed, where Dieter Grimm argues that 'as long as there is not a European people that is sufficiently "homogeneous" to form a democratic will, there should be no [European] constitution,' Habermas reiterates that the solidarity that is to take form in constitutional states is one of 'abstract, legally mediating, solidarity among strangers' and not an ethnic one.[30] Critics such as Canovan still argue that the reason the institutions of the European Union are famously weak is that Europe does not possess a specific, historic nation-state.

Habermas, however, believes that the political culture of a country, embodied in its constitution, is capable of providing its citizens with a double identity of belonging simultaneously to a constitutional agreement and to a specific concept of the good life, which makes one 'be both a member and a stranger in her own land.'[31] On this view, constitutional patriotism starts with a thin concept of solidarity as membership according to abstract and universal principles in a political community, then grows thicker as the abstract principles get filled in by the concrete content of a particular community in its constitution. Such a legally mediated sense of solidarity, then, can in turn foster a 'national consciousness.' Whether a national consciousness of a modern community allows its population to understand themselves 'as a nation based on ethnic membership or as a nation of citizens'[32] is an ancillary question that requires empirical treatment.

To continue with Canovan's argument: she insists that the claim that the constitutional state can provide an impartial coverage of all diverse national or ethnic groups that commands their loyalty naively overlooks the more fundamental political glue holding the state together, namely, the 'people.' She asks, Where does the state draw its power from?[33] Habermas's answer to this question is straightforward: 'What unites a nation of citizens, as opposed to a *volksnation*, is not some primordial substrate but rather an intersubjectively shared context of possible mutual understanding.'[34] Countries such as the United States, Switzerland, and Germany have provided strong empirical support for such claims of the advocates of constitutional patriotism. In a bold move, however, Canovan adopts a strategy of reinterpreting these cases in order to draw the opposite conclusion, namely, that these instances in fact show how membership ties and loyalties are rooted in identities defined by 'birth and blood.'[35] Putting aside for the moment the question of the connection between such identity and a citizen's sense of belonging, and the superficial plausibility of this claim for Germany,[35] such a criterion certainly will not hold for the United States, Switzerland,[37] and other multi-ethnic and multicultural states such as Canada and Belgium.[38]

Canovan's attempt to explicate her strategy of reinterpretation amounts to highly controversial and ambiguous claims such as the followings: '[T]he component parts of Switzerland are deeply rooted communities defined by *birth and blood* as well as geography. These have grown together in the course of a shared history, producing a strong sense of pride in distinctive *Swiss-ness*'; or 'Americans are defined and united primarily by *birth* and *inheritance*'; or '[A] polity is "ours" because it was our parents' before us.'[39] Knowing that Switzerland is a multi-ethnic nation and the United States a country comprising recent and old immigrants from all over the globe, it is hard to make sense of 'Swiss-ness,' or of the decisive role of 'blood and inheritance' in defining Americans.[40] Indeed, Abraham Lincoln's position on what defines Americans strongly contradicts such definitions:

> We have besides these men – descended by blood from our ancestors – among us perhaps half our people who are not descendants at all of these men ... finding themselves our equals in all things. If they look back through this history to trace their connection with those days by blood, they find they have none ... but when they look through that old Declaration of Independence ... [they feel] ... that it is the father of all moral principle in them, and that they have a right to claim it as though they were and that they have a right to claim it as though they were blood of the blood, and flesh of the flesh of the men who wrote that Declaration, and so they are.[41]

Therefore, to assume that Americans are Americans solely on the basis of 'blood and inheritance' is simply not correct. Consequently, ethnic, linguistic, or religious belonging should not be considered the chief characteristic for political association in diverse communities; rather, it should be civic competence. While Canovan would rightly point out that such a civic competence itself arises out of the historical context of a certain community, it is its normative bearing that makes all the difference between a traditional society and an ideal state, that is, constitutional patriotism.

Hence, with respect to the similar example of Canada and its rich cultural composition of different cultural groups, one can ask what it might mean to say that they relate to the Canadian polity as theirs because it was their parents' before them. Except for aboriginal people, it is simply not the case that as Canadians we relate to our 'Canadianness' because it was our parents' before us. They didn't live here and there was no Canada until 135 years ago. Settler groups came here – and are still coming[42] – and founded Canada when, despite their diverse ethnic and cultural backgrounds, they expressed their will to live together in a set of laws that reciprocally bound them. In the words of Attracta Ingram, another advocate of constitutional patriotism: 'In the normative reconstruction of the modern state, political histories began with a founding act,'[43] the act of constitution giving (see section 3 in chapter 6). She further argues that '[t]he significance of the founding myth is that it denies the relevance of any historical identity for claims on the state apart from the identity it constructs itself.' Accordingly, 'the state itself is the source of its own unity, the same idea we are now calling constitutional patriotism.'[44] Thus, with respect to the ideal of solidarity and a sense of belonging, to keep referring to a pre-political entity, a 'people,' simply misses the mark of political association. Indeed, what now binds people together more than ever before in Canada is their allegiance to the same constitution – the reservation of the most francophone Quebecers notwithstanding – which recognizes all people as free citizens, equally subject to its laws. I will return later to the Canadian example to explain the tension between the ideal constitutionalism and the problem of Quebec.

This, of course, is not to deny that such features as one's ethnicity, culture, and religion are important parts of one's identity, but to distinguish between one's identity as a citizen and particular identities as members of a family, a clan, an ethnic group, and so on. For these all involve different associations. Indeed, particular loyalties are identity-builders, and as such, *pace* Martha Nussbaum,[45] their consideration is both morally and politically relevant. Yet for such loyalties to be so considered in the face of increasing diversity, there must be something that allows them to negotiate their moral and political claims upon each other, an overarching principle that brings them together and pays them their due: universal principles of human rights. As citizens we have good reasons to impose limits decided by political principles of human rights on particular associations within the political union. The alternative view, which is to subordinate overarching universal principles to concrete identities, would imply that everyone should be divided into different groups of a certain background and claim state-hood,[46] which, as the critique of liberal-nationalism has shown, is absurd.

With respect to the viability of this alternative, it should suffice to consider the existence of *national minorities* within nation-states, which confronts liberal nationalism with an internal problem: are nation-states 'nation building or nation destroying?'[47] In Will Kymlicka and Christine Straehle's survey article this dilemma is summed up as follows:

> Liberal nationalists have typically argued that because national identity is important to people's freedom and self-respect, and because a common national identity serves many legitimate liberal-democratic values, there-fore it is morally desirable for nations and states to coincide. However, this position now seems self-defeating. To promote a common national iden-tity by destroying minority nationality seems hypocritical (and often unre-alistic). Yet we cannot hope to grant all national minorities their own state.[48]

Indeed, the disintegrating effect of the belief that the boundaries of the state should coincide with the borders of the nation has been ren-dered most devastatingly evident in the Balkans during the past dec-ade. Therefore, the liberal nationalists' claim that there exists an entity, a 'people,' a 'we,' that precedes the constitutional state and as such should be given a normative role in unifying the members of the state is theoretically naive and increasingly unrealistic. It is naive because the pre-political 'we' it describes is qualitatively different from the political association of the same people after they give themselves a constitu-tion, and it is unrealistic because it is inconsistent with the heterogene-ous and diverse reality of today's democratic states.

Friendship and Love of 'Patria'

Like liberal-nationalism, republican patriotism too is suspicious as to whether the bond of citizenship based merely on universal principles is sufficient to foster and uphold one's identity. In the influential paper 'Cross-Purposes: The Liberal-Communitarian Debate,'[49] Charles Taylor makes several clarifying distinctions between ontological issues and advocacy issues. As the ultimate ground of explanation, ontological issues have divided atomists from holists, while advocacy issues that concern matters of policy divide individualists from collectivists.[50] From the perspective of a holist-individualist he brings issues of identity and community to bear on universal principles such as justice. This perspective allows him to identify a difference between 'matters which are for me and are for you, on the one hand, and those which are for us, on the other.'[51] He distinguishes between a mediately common good (e.g., sharing a joyful experience with a lover) and an immediately common good (e.g., friendship or the act of sharing as an intrinsic good). Taylor then claims that in order for a feeling of patriotism to exist in a republic, citizens need to identify with one another based on 'a sense of a shared immediate common good.'[52] In such a situation 'laws' are viewed as reflecting the dignity of citizens' identities. This view, while it has a certain prima-facie plausibility because of its intimate notion of identity and patriotism, seems to be unnecessarily thick. In other words, the answer to Taylor's question 'Who am I?'[53] need not exclusively be answered in terms of one's nationality, since, first, there are many more values, practices, and allegiances that constitute one's identity, and second, all these variables should be run through a filter of what is relevant to the task of political association. Furthermore, political association and membership are not just about my identity but also about the identity of those others, strangers, who live in the same political community as I do. Indeed, the fact of pluralism has made Taylor's idea of an intimately close tie held publicly among different participants impossible in modern society, which is why Taylor's suggestion seems to describe a pre-political identity that as such overburdens the ties of political association. Clearly, it is not necessary for me, in order to feel politically connected to another citizen, that she has to be my lover or my best friend. Michael Ignatieff is right when he writes, 'Words like fraternity, belonging and community' – and I would add intimacy, love, friendship – 'are so soaked with nostalgia and utopianism that they are nearly useless as guides to the real possibilities of solidarity in modern society.'[54] Indeed, in order to meet the conditions of fair and workable social cooperation and political association we need not taint the liberal virtues of tolerance, reasonableness, civility, and a sense of fairness with the overburdening language of love, fraternity, friendship, and other unhelpful words.[55]

From the same perspective of civic republicanism, Maurizio Viroli's objection that mere shared universal principles and values are not enough for citizens to identify with their institutions because they would be 'too distant and too general,'[56] should be rejected. For citizens recognize themselves as the authors of universal principles and values in the form of laws that apply to them. They would feel closely and concretely linked together by virtue of such an association. For Viroli, as for Taylor and other republican theorists, 'the republic is a political ordering and a way of life; that is, a culture.'[57] While Viroli describes republican patriotism as a political allegiance based on the principles of justice and reason, the cultural dimension that he attributes to this political creed injects the concept with a concrete content that commands citizens' passion and love for their country.[58] Again, I would contest Viroli's use of such loaded words as 'love' and 'passion' for one's 'patria,' which unnecessarily overburdens the task of describing what is needed for political association in today's world. Indeed, a brief overview of the literature reveals that concepts such as community and patria are not unanimously esteemed, but sometimes viewed with scepticism and understood as catachresis – that is, the words have no literal referents, and trigger the self-destruction of their definition as soon as they are articulated.[59] Contrary to Taylor's and Viroli's romanticized ideals of identity and patria, the political intimacy needed to foster a feeling of civic republicanism – that is trust – merely requires that citizens recognize themselves in the laws and institutions of the state in which they live – a condition made possible through the procedures of public deliberation and participation.

Habermas is aware of the deep-rootedness of such a traditional concept of identity when he asks, 'Can we, and do we want to, give up the comforts and the dangers of a conventional identity that is incompatible with a *critical* appropriation of tradition?'[60] *Pace* Taylor and Canovan, constitutional patriots are neither unaware of the link between the 'political' and 'pre-political' nor do they want to downplay its significance; rather, they are interested in the critical assessment of this connection that will enable them to go beyond it. There is no escape from the context in which one finds oneself, and that being the case, one always is situated within a community. Given the heritage of the Enlightenment, the insight of constitutional patriots is that one must be able to assess critically and choose one's political association.

Bernard Yack makes a similar criticism of constitutional patriotism based on the priority of the cultural context, charging that any chosen set of political principles in the end is a culturally inherited identity.[61] His critique, however, has a double edge, for he claims that the accounts of both ethnic nation and civic nation are incomplete in so far as they one-sidedly emphasize the element of either rational choice or cultural inheritance. This position is close to Habermas's in terms of the complementarity of tradition and critique. Still, Yack sees Habermas as stressing rational choice at the expense of ignoring the tradition that grounds choice. Confronting Habermas's account, he argues that consent to any contract such as a constitution always happens against the background of a pre-political community of shared memory and history, which is why East Germany's transition from communism to liberal democracy took place by reunification with West Germany, and not just any liberal-democratic state.[62] He charges that the contractarians and neo-Kantian political theorists who advocate constitutional patriotism, while tacitly relying on the existence of the historical community, fail to account for this assumption. For Yack, 'the idea of the civic nation, with its portrayal of community as a shared and rational choice of universally valid principles, is itself a cultural inheritance in nations like France and the United States.'[63]

In response to Yack, it is worth remembering our discussion in the last chapter according to which a nation, as the result of an originary act of constitution giving, is qualitatively different from the community that precedes it. Moreover, it appears that, in Yack's sense, everything we do is a 'cultural inheritance,' since everything we do is located within the historico-cultural context of our life. Such a broad sense of 'cultural inheritance' gives Yack's critique a tautological tenor, for as Hillary Putnam has put it, where else can we start but from our historical and cultural context. Still, 'the cultures, practices, procedures we inherit are not an algorithm to be slavishly followed.'[64] Thus Putnam insists, in connection to the relation between *tradition* and *reason*, we must *balance* two points: '(1) talk of what is "right" and "wrong" in any area only makes sense against the background of an *inherited tradition*; but (2) traditions themselves can be *criticized*.'[65] To reiterate, the mere fact that something is inherited does not mean that we cannot go beyond it, and to want to surpass it also does not mean ignoring it; rather, one can believe in the continuous renewal of the critique of one's present and past. 'Reason is, in this sense, both immanent (not to be found outside of concrete language games and institutions) and transcendent (a regulative idea that we use to criticize the conduct of *all* activities and institutions).'[66] Along the same lines, if the Habermas-Gadamer debate has taught us anything, it is that our situatedness within a certain critical tradition does not mean historical determinism. Rather, it would mean that our critical ability, coupled with innovative interpretations of the tradition, allow for new ideals and norms, which in their turn can inspire change. Whatever the inherited traditions are, therefore, members are both entitled to, and capable of, assessing their merit in regard to continuing, discontinuing, or reforming them. Hence, in order to achieve constitutional patriotism, the universal principles of liberal political culture must be critically interpreted and appropriated from the perspective of specific national or cultural traditions.

3. On the Normative Aspect of Constitutional Patriotism

Being aware of the dangers of ethnocentrism and nationalism, neither Canovan nor Yack is unsympathetic to constitutional patriotism. They rather seem to be insisting on a sort of explicit recognition of a communally inherited background against which any discussion of civic association is based. Such a critique, however, ignores the normative aspect of the concept of constitutional patriotism. That is to say, while constitutional patriotism starts from the given contingencies of Western democracies, it aims at a new political mode of association that is both consistent with the diversity of our modern societies and in line with the ideal of free society, that is, democracy. As a normative project, constitutional patriotism starts with disillusionment with all traditional bonds of political association that are based on ethnicity, religion, language, race, and so forth. By acknowledging the fact of pluralism in post-conventional societies – where actions are oriented toward universal and ethical principles – this project recognizes the need for a new bond that includes all these particularities. None of these factors is a 'necessary or permanent precondition of a democratic process'; they merely form a transitional and historical constellation.[67] Accordingly, Habermas proposes to 'decouple' political integration from cultural integration in multicultural democratic states. In order for this idea of decoupling to work, however, Thomas McCarthy argues, Habermas 'has to understand "decoupling" in process terms – as an ongoing accomplishment of something that is never fully realized.'[68]

The post-conventional identity of the modern subject as a rational agent ('reasonable' in Rawls's terminology) makes the normative proposition of constitutional patriotism possible. A post-conventional level of interaction among a group of *people* – who come together as free and equal subjects and want to be politically associated through a constitution – entails their action having a legalistic orientation and being capable of appealing to universal and ethical principles.[69] For such a bond to hold, their allegiance to the universal principles need not be equally strong; ideally speaking, however, it must be sufficient. The number and the composition of the people taking part in such a contract are decided according to the practical feasibilities of a specific context, by which I understand a set of actual conditions that determine the limits of political experience. Accordingly, when both Yack and Canovan speak of German unification as an instance of the binding force of a pre-political community, not of a liberal-democratic constitution, one can contend that with respect to the goal of East Germany's transition from communism to constitutional democracy, its unification with West Germany can be explained in terms of the practical feasibility of the event that hypostasized the normative project. In the German context, national history and tradition is confronted with the citizens' post-conventional critical attitude. In such a context, 'where national traditions are questioned and historical discontinuities are most strongly felt,' the post-national identities of citizens 'who critically reflect upon and then transcend their particular traditions in favor of universal values' are most likely to emerge.[70]

Thus, with respect to the idea of practical feasibility I would make a distinction between constitutional patriotism and cosmopolitan citizenship, as advocated by such political theorists as Joseph Carens and Martha Nussbaum.[71] For while constitutional patriotism can provide political legitimacy for a liberal-democratic state (which can be a nation-state, multination state, or supranational state), cosmopolitan citizenship is simply beyond the reach of our practical possibilities. It is doubtful we can find many people in liberal democracies who are in favour of a cosmopolitan system where people can move freely in the world, settle anywhere, work, and vote. This is not to say that such an idea (which is an aspect of the Enlightenment's ideal of perpetual peace as expressed by Kant) is inconsistent with the idea of civic citizenship, but simply to point to our practical limitations with respect to the pursuit of a utopian ideal. Indeed, while Kant regards the idea of the 'international state' [Völkerstat] as unachievable, he advocates the idea of 'a federation of nations' [Völkerbund].[72] He dismissed the former idea as 'practically unattainable' and, according to Kenneth Baynes, claimed that, 'such a conception would likely give rise to a "soulless despotism" in which citizens no longer felt bound to laws of their state.'[73] Therefore, I believe that to speak of constitutional patriotism and cosmopolitan citizenship interchangeably, as cosmopolitans like to do, gives way to easy refutation of the former based on the absurd practical consequences of the latter.

Some critics, however, may still insist that even when citizens see themselves as authors and subjects of the law, the legitimacy of the political order is not guaranteed, nor is a practical sense of social solidarity. If, however, we view the constitutional state as composed of 'reasonable' people who have to live together despite their differences, it is hard to understand why their recognition that they are the authors of the system of laws that applies to them all equally is not enough psychologically to make them identify with each other as fellow compatriots. Such psychological knowledge, grounded on the citizens' communicative understanding, is sufficient to legitimize political association and gives it a necessary cohesion. Here, a sense of belonging arises out of identifying with a set of institutions and practices that express the polity of the original law of which all members recognize themselves as authors. Such recognition prevents citizens from feeling alienated, allowing them to feel at home even if they are recent immigrants from a different culture, and hence promotes political unity. In this sense, as Michael Ignatieff states, 'The legitimacy of institutions is not a matter of tradition, but a matter of function.'[74]

When one feels that one is recognized as an equal member in a political community, one develops a sense of belonging, which in turn results in a sense of solidarity among compatriots. Thus, while one might be a black, Muslim woman of a North African culture living in Montreal, one still can feel Canadian in so far as one feels loyalty to the Canadian constitution and its fundamental Charter of Rights and Freedoms. The outpourings of grief in response to the passing of Pierre Elliott Trudeau in the fall of 2000 made this point plain. The feeling of a 'we' that brought a Cameroonian man, who lives in Quebec City, to stand behind me in a line-up to say good-bye to Trudeau, along with the Chinese woman from Vancouver in front of me, *pace* Canovan and Yack, is the result not of a common inheritance of blood or culture by birth, but of a feeling of unity that is based on the recognition of a civic bond that Trudeau symbolized. Therefore, to say that the constitutional tie is too weak to keep us together politically is simply not true.

Here, I would like to discuss the Canadian situation in light of my discussion of constitutional patriotism as a normative ideal that should be brought to bear on the reality of specific cultural traditions. To this end, my account will admittedly be brief and simplistic. In earlier times – in so far as the pre-political 'we' that both Canovan and Yack are concerned with is concerned – the dominant identity of English-speaking Canada was British, and entailed a strong identification with the British Crown and imperial institutions. French Canadians, meanwhile, were an oppressed minority living the legacy of colonialism under the tutelage of Anglo economic interests and the Catholic church. As for the critical interpretation of this cultural tradition, since the 1960s, modern civic patriotism has emerged clearly in both English and French Canada. In English Canada this was strongly articulated and framed by Trudeau's vision of a modern, liberal, centralized, bilingual nation-state living under a Charter of Rights. For many French Canadians, this civic patriotism was embodied in the vision of a modern, liberal, centralized Quebec nation-state. Now to bring the point of my argument to bear upon this example, in such a post-conventional context the ideal of constitutional patriotism *can*, and *should*, guide the political negotiation and contestation of anglophone, francophone, and Aboriginal people to create a fair regime of political association. Hence, while there is a historical context that grounds the Canadian political identity, the diversity and the developmental maturity of its political forces both enables and requires us to surpass particularistic criteria of membership in favour of a universal criterion of rights.

4. Transient Identities and Hybrid Belongings

In this final section, I would like to advance a more radical reading of Habermas's doctrine of constitutional patriotism. Habermas speaks of the tension between facticity and validity as constitutive of the legal and political system. On the basis of the foregoing discussion, a radical reading of this insight would emphasize two elements of the political: (1) the open-endedness of the process and (2) the permanence of difference. Thus, the political can be described as an ongoing process of contestation, negotiation, and conflict among differences governed by law. According to such an understanding of the political, the idea of constitutional patriotism cannot consist merely of replacing national identity with a post-national identity. For the very motives that cause the evolution of citizen identity from a national to a civic one will keep affecting citizens' political identity-formation and moulding it anew. Thus, Habermas writes, '[t]he identity of a nation of enfranchised citizens is not something fixed.'[75] I believe there is a strong enough strand in Habermas to make the above reading plausible. Consider this: 'The ethico-political self-understanding of citizens in a democratic community must not be taken as a historical-cultural a priori that makes democratic will-formation possible, but rather as the fluid content of a circulatory process that is generated through the legal institutionalization of citizens' communication.'[76] I would like to suggest, therefore, that the sense of identity or belonging produced by procedures of public deliberation is essentially different from the traditional sense of identity, since public deliberation is an enduring process that is constantly renewed. The traditional sense of belonging constitutes a fixed concept of identity that is centred on a national, ethnic, linguistic, or religious feature or other pre-political given as the common denominator of political association, while the very point of continuous deliberation is to revise and renew the political bond of unity as new challenges arise. From this perspective, therefore, constitutional patriotism need not be seen merely as something that replaces conventional identity with post-conventional identity, but as what, in fact, in continuity with the diversity and pluralism of our time, resists the creation of another fixed kind of identity altogether. Patchen Markell, a fellow critical theorist, along the same lines writes: 'On this reading, constitutional patriotism is not a kind of affectively charged *identification* with a set of universal principles; instead, in keeping with the risks and dangers that come to inhabit the reproduction of all sorts of identity (even in postconventional situations), constitutional patriotism is a habit or practice that *refuses* or *resists* the very identifications on which citizens also depend.'[77]

The problem with the traditional view of the political as the community of friends, defined against a common enemy and with a shared identity, is that it tends to draw its members into a circle, excluding the Other who falls outside the circle. On this view, citizens are friends who have a certain natural affinity based on native ties and national identities, which closes the border of the political on those who lack the natural place of birth. In contrast to this view, a radical reading of constitutional patriotism would advocate the sort of political ties that can be framed in terms of a Derridean language of friendship. Unlike Taylor's and Viroli's concept of friendship, however, this friendship is not based on affinity, natural sameness, analogy, or native resemblance. It is, rather, a 'friendship without memory itself, by fidelity, by the gentleness and rigor of fidelity, bondless friendship.'[78] Derrida explains this idea of friendship by way of the logic of the 'without' (*sans*), of the 'X without X,' where something is effected without being assimilated, homogenized, and annulled. Therefore, the political relationship among friends, compatriots, is one without relation, that is, classical ties, and out of it arises a community without community. Overcoming the natural bonds of a native soil allows for such a community to become more hospitable to the displaced, the exiled, and immigrants. To extend the protection of 'citizenship' to these people, who accept the principles of human rights and democracy, requires that we rethink our concept of belonging and membership in the political community: belonging is understood not as an already given but as a contract deliberated in the present and a constantly renewed allegiance.

The reason this may seem like a strange concept of belonging at first glance is because political theory lags behind the radical and rapid changes that are taking place in the world. Today's subject is not a homogeneous citizen of a unilingual, uninational, and unireligious community of modernity, but a heterogeneous citizen of a multicultural world. Today's urban communities, too, are no longer small, homogeneous cities where everyone knows everyone else; rather, they are huge multicultural cosmopolitan centres with their Chinatown, little Italy, Indian quarter, etc. In such transient places, where hybridity has dissolved the cohesion of any conventional permanence, solidarity cannot be envisaged in terms of fixed identity as a political glue that holds us all together. If it feels awkward to think in terms of hybrid identity, '[i]t is because our language has not caught up with modernity. We think of belonging as permanence, yet all our homes are transient. Who still lives in the house of their childhood? Who still lives in the neighborhood where they grow up?'[79] Of course, '[h]ome is where one starts from,'[80] but it is also '[t]he place we have to leave in order to grow up, to become ourselves. We think of belonging as rootedness in a small familiar place, yet home for most of us is the conclusive arteries of a great city. Our belonging is no longer to something fixed, known and familiar, but to an electric and heartless creature eternally in motion.'[81] Such a fluid conception of identity and citizenship is bound to frighten those who would like to have a permanent and unchanging criterion that measures and protects their identity, in the same way that Salman Rushdie's *Satanic Verses* frightened the Ayatollah and his followers. For this work too 'celebrates hybridity, impurity, intermingling, the transformation that comes of new and unexpected combinations of human beings, cultures, ideas, politics, movies, songs. It rejoices in mongrelization and fears the absolutism of the pure. *Mélange*, hotchpotch, a bit of this and a bit of that is *how newness enters the world.*'[82]

The newness that has entered our world with force is that of ever-growing pluralism, diversity, and hybridity, which have increasingly made an appeal to traditional measures of identity problematic: na-

tional homogeneity is no longer an adequate assumption for a conception of citizenship. It should be noted, however, that these new facts are
not celebrated here for their own sake but for what their recognition
can do to fine-tune a critical political theory that is focused on the ideals
of justice and democracy in a diverse society. The effort to recognize
differences should not paralyse the execution of public policies by a
legitimate government, nor should it lead to anarchy and resignation.
Instead, a politics of difference should serve the end of what justice
demands by paying differences their dues. Thus, a practical test for a
politics of difference is to see whether it can accommodate the effective
exercise of policy-making. For any radicalized and exaggerated account
of difference and change would become self-defeating if it makes the
exercise of policy-making impossible.

Indeed, the recognition of the post-metaphysical conditions of our
world along with its globalizing tendencies require that we conceive of
the ideal of solidarity as political membership that involves a project of
appropriating a set of universal laws based on deliberation and negotiation among concrete subjects within a concrete culture. Such a project,
which must allow for the greatest degree of inclusion, is never complete
and remains open to the demands of future contestation. In such a
political community we may not be as intimately connected to each
other as we were in the ancient polis, city-state, or nation-state, but at
least our association envelops all those who, despite their differences,
live in the same political community.

4. Conclusion

The philosophical efforts of Jürgen Habermas have centred on the
pursuit of modernity's ideals of free society and justice. Appropriating
the linguistic turn in philosophy, he has overcome the pessimism of the
early Frankfurt School philosophers through his theory of communicative action, which reveals an emancipatory character in the human
subject's communicative interaction. On this model, the pathologies of
modern society are understood in terms of the lifeworld's colonization
by the system; emancipation is understood as preventing this colonization. But the thesis of colonization makes an account of legitimate
political power impossible; that is, the theory is unable to explain how
citizens can convert their communicative understanding, developed in
the lifeworld, into government policies. This shortcoming led Habermas
to redefine the possibility of free society in terms of legitimate law-

making. His turn to legal theory in *Between Facts and Norms* is anchored in the concept of modern law, which is situated between lifeworld and system and as such is said to mediate between the two. Legitimate law-making is understood as the result of institutionalized procedures of public deliberation, which convert citizens' practices of self-determination, in the form of communicative and participatory rights, into the binding decisions of political power.

However, the constructed concept of law, as what brings the insight of moral norms to bear upon the context of practical life, sits uncomfortably between lifeworld and system. Indeed, by aligning so closely the concepts of legitimate law, communicative power, and political system, Habermas's new approach fails to ensure emancipation, for it legitimizes political power as exercised in liberal-democratic states. The weakening of the theory's critical tenor in his recent writing is also due to his restrictive view of power, which is fashioned after the juridical model and its by-product, the consensus/coercion distinction. This view one-sidedly emphasizes the ideal of consensus as the goal of democratic politics, making it blind to legitimate dissent and differences.

However, an outline of a possible way of recovering the critical thrust of Habermas's theory, by borrowing from postmodernist political theory, has emerged here. I have argued that by appropriating Foucault's analysis of power we can enhance Habermas's narrow model of juridical power, and allow for other forms of power relations – in the non-ideal domains of culture, race, sex, gender, and so on – to be considered as types of political power. Such an enhanced model allows the exposure of the possible, yet latent, biases of normative theories, and deepens our analyses of social injustices and inequalities. Furthermore, Derrida's deconstruction of law has radicalized our understanding of the ideals of justice and democracy by characterizing them as *à-venir*. The advantage of postmodern political theory is that it warns us against the complacency of normative theories, with their emphasis on the institutionalization of law. By separating the exercise of law from the goal of arriving at a just state, and by expanding Habermas's theory of power, postmodern political theory can provide an antidote to the happy presentism that arises from an uncritical adoption of real-existing democracy into normative theory. Such sensitivity will allow for recovering the utopian dimension of our critical theory of politics. This model of politics assigns a critical role to the concept of consensus, allowing for the inclusion of dissent and difference in democratic politics.

The recognition of the fact of pluralism and its enduring impact on the political require that traditional questions regarding the pursuit of the ideals of free society and of justice be posed anew. Habermas has met this challenge by theorizing constitutional patriotism as a form of solidarity within diverse political communities. To keep the critical spirit of his effort sharp, however, his account of political legitimacy needs to be based not on yet another form of fixed identity (replacing the national identity of traditional forms of belonging), but on a sense of identity that remains open to the multiplicity of cultural forms of life and to constant changes in the composition of their political association. I acknowledge that this sketch of a way to complement Habermas's critical theory with some insights of postmodernist political theory and my proposed interpretation of constitutional patriotism can be elaborated in greater detail. Still, I believe they suffice for the purpose of reclaiming Habermas's account of deliberative democracy within the tradition of a Critical Theory that resolutely pursues the ideals of modernity. In my view, it is from this perspective still that we are best equipped to approximate the ideals of justice and a free society.

Abbreviations

Benhabib

CNU   *Critique, Norm, and Utopia*

Derrida

FL   'Force of Law'
DI   'Declaration of Independence'

Foucault

PK   *Power/Knowledge*

Habermas

AS   *Autonomy and Solidarity*
BFN   *Between Facts and Norms*
CES   *Communication and the Evolution of Society*
IO   *The Inclusion of the Other*
JA   *Justification and Application*
KHI   *Knowledge and Human Interest*
LC   *Legitimation Crisis*
MCCA   *Moral Consciousness and Communicative Action*
NC   *New Conservatism*
PDM   *Philosophical Discourse of Modernity*
PT   *Postmetaphysical Thinking*
TCA 1   *Theory of Communicative Action*, vol. 1
TCA 2   *Theory of Communicative Action*, vol. 2
TP   *Theory and Practice*

McCarthy

II   *Ideals and Illusions*

Rawls

PL   *Political Liberalism*
TJ   *A Theory of Justice*

Notes

Introduction

1 This introduction was written in early 2000, when most political changes around the world were toward democracy and peace. Since then a lot has changed, including major setbacks in the Middle East peace process. The most influential among these changes, of course, stemmed from the terrorist attacks in the U.S. on September 11, 2001, which introduced a new chapter in the world's political history. However, even with the rise of extremism, Habermas has redoubled his effort to engage different sides of the conflict in a rational dialogue. In May 2002 he made a ten-day trip to Iran, where he gave lectures in several universities and talked to artists, politicians, and intellectuals. The aim of his engagement was to demythologize the discourse of 'Axes of Evil' and keep the channels of discussion open (see *Frankfurter Allgemeine Zeitung*, interview by Christiane Hoffmann, 18 June 2002).

2 '[M]oral theories which develop a cognitivist approach are essentially theories of Justice.' Habermas, *Autonomy and Solidarity*, ed. Peter Dews (London: Verso, 1986), 249 (hereafter *AS*).

3 'Under the modern condition of life, none of the competing traditions can claim *prima facie* general validity any longer. Therefore, even in practically relevant questions, we can no longer back up convincing grounds with the authority of unquestioned traditions ... We should not expect a generally valid answer when we ask what is good for me, or good for us, or good for them; we must rather ask: what is *equally good for all*? This "moral point of view" constitutes a sharp but narrow spotlight, which selects from the mass of evaluative questions those action-related conflicts which can be resolved with reference to a generalizable interest; these are questions of justice.' *AS*, 248–9.

4 'Political power is not a characterless medium; its use and organization must themselves be submitted to moral limitations. The idea of the constitutional state [*Rechtstaat*] is intended to answer this difficulty.' *AS*, 253.

5 J. Bohman, 'Habermas, Marxism, and Social Theory: The Case of Pluralism in Critical Social Science,' in P. Dews, ed., *Habermas: A Critical Reader* (Oxford: Blackwell, 1999), 55.

6 J. Shklar, 'Giving Injustice Its Due,' *Yale Law Journal* 98 (1989): 1135–51.

7 See Axel Honneth's 'The Social Dynamic of Disrespect: Situating Critical Theory Today,' in *Habermas: A Critical Reader*, 320–37. He argues that the original research program of the Frankfurt School does not merit further development unchanged, and proposes that Habermas's communication paradigm, which is conceived in terms of a theory of language, needs to be complemented by a theory of relations of recognition and their violation. The need to replace the comprehensive approach of Critical Theory with an eclectic approach that synthesizes the results of the best contemporary social-science theories is also recognized by James Bohman's contribution to the same collection (see note 5 above), and also by recent writings of younger critical theorists such as Thomas McCarthy ('Liberal Theory and Radical Injustice: Toward a Critical Theory of Race,' unpublished manuscript) and Orville Lee ('Culture and Democratic Theory: Toward a Theory of Symbolic Democracy,' *Constellations* 5, no. 4 [1999]: 433–55).

1: The Unfinished Project of Modernity and the Heritage of Critical Theory

1 The first use of the word 'modern' occurs around the end of the fifth and the beginning of the sixth century. In 476 a Teuton named Odovakar seized the imperial throne, marking the fall of the Roman Empire. But the German assailants did not do the greatest damage. It was Pope Gregory the Great (540–604) who ordered the destruction of the greatest remaining public library in Rome to ensure the triumph of the Church. And it is here that, for the first time, we see the use of the word modern. Derived from the Latin adverb *modo*, which means 're-cently' or 'of present time,' the word modern (*modernus*) was used to distinguish the break between the officially Christian present and the Roman and Pagan past (*antiqus*).

2 Robert B. Pippin, *Modernism as a Philosophical Problem* (Cambridge: Basil Blackwell, 1991), 23.

3 Pippin explains the source of this discontent as follows: 'Modernism in art, again a descendant of the romantic movement, eventually came to reflect bourgeois culture's growing dissatisfaction with itself, a sense that moder-

nity's official self-understanding – enlightened, liberal, progressive, humanist – had been a misunderstanding, a far too smug and unwarranted self-satisfaction, a subject matter naturally suited for irony and satire' (*Modernism as a Philosophical Problem*, 32). By emphasizing the modern character of the human subject as independent from the tradition, aesthetic modernity proclaimed that artistic creativity did not lend itself to any outside authority (morality, religion, etc.) as a mere medium, for it was a self-defining and autonomous activity. The self-making aspect of artistic imagination made the problems of individuals' autonomy and autochthony central to aesthetic modernity, which still was in need of self-grounding.

4 Jürgen Habermas, *Philosophical Discourse of Modernity* (Cambridge: MIT Press, 1987), 8 (hereafter *PDM*).

5 Immanuel Kant, 'An Answer to the Question: What Is Enlightenment,' in *Foundation of the Metaphysics of Morals*, trans. L.W. Beck (Indianapolis: Bobbs-Merrill, 1959), 85–92.

6 Michel Foucault, 'The Subject and Power,' in H.L. Dreyfus and P. Rabinow, eds, *Michel Foucault: Beyond Structuralism and Hermeneutics* (Chicago: University of Chicago Press, 1982), 216.

7 Kant, 'What Is Enlightenment,' 85.

8 Foucault, 'What Is Enlightenment?' in Paul Rabinow, ed., *The Foucault Reader* (New York: Pantheon Books, 1984), 38. In this insightful essay on Kant, Foucault states that modern philosophy can be understood in terms of the attempts to respond to the question *Was ist Aufklärung?*

9 Kant, 'What Is Enlightenment?' 86.

10 See Johann G. Fichte, *Sciences of Knowledge*, trans. P. Heath and J. Lachs (New York: Meredith Corporation, 1970).

11 Georg Wilhelm Friedrich Hegel, 'Whence Came the Positive Element?' in *On Christianity*, trans. T.M. Knox and R. Kroner (New York: Harper & Brothers, 1961), 71.

12 Hegel, *Faith and Knowledge*, trans. W. Cerf and H.S. Harris (Albany: State University of New York Press, 1977), 55.

13 Ibid., 56. Hegel, in *The Difference between Fichte's and Schelling's System of Philosophy* (see note 17, below) argues that the basic principle of Fichte's thought was that of identity, I = I. While Fichte begins by positing (*Setzen*) the 'I,' his account of thinking includes the positing of an object of thought that stands in opposition to the Self. Hegel's critique of Fichte is that, in viewing thought as equivalent to understanding, thinking appears as a self-alienating activity. This failure is the result of not realizing that thinking always involves the unifying ability of reason. Habermas draws on

Hegel's critique when he writes, 'Hegel was convinced that the age of the Enlightenment culminating in Kant and Fichte had erected merely an idol in reason. It had falsely put understanding [*Verstand*] or reflection in place of reason [*Vernunft*] and thus elevated something finite to the status of an absolute' (*PDM*, 23–4).

14 Hegel, *Philosophy of Right* (Oxford: Oxford University Press, 1952), 286.

15 Habermas, *PDM*, 17.

16 *PDM*, 7.

17 Hegel, *The Difference between Fichte's and Schelling's System of Philosophy*, trans. and ed. H.S. Harris and W. Cerf (Albany: State University of New York Press, 1977), 130.

18 *PDM*, 42.

19 Habermas, *On Society and Politics: A Reader*, ed. Steven Seidman (Boston: Beacon Press, 1989), 32.

20 Karl Marx, 'Contribution to the Critique of Hegel's Philosophy of Right,' in E. Kamenka, ed., *The Portable Karl Marx* (New York: Viking Penguin, 1983), 121.

21 Marx, *A Contribution to the Critique of Political Economy*, ed. Maurice Dobb (New York: International Publishers, 1970), 20–1.

22 Marx, 'Theses on Feuerbach, in C.J. Arthur, ed., *The German Ideology*, Part One, thesis XI (New York: International Publishers, 1970), 123.

23 Martin Jay, *The Dialectical Imagination* (Berkeley: University of California Press, 1973), 4.

24 Ibid., 44

25 Martin Ludtke in his 'The Utopian Motif Is Suspended: Conversation with Leo Lowenthal' (*New German Critique* 38 [Spring/Summer, 1986]: 109) cites Lowenthal's rejection of the term 'interdisciplinary' in favour of a more appropriate 'supradisciplinary,' which indicates a critical attitude toward the use of the basic validity claims of the separate disciplines as opposed to an uncritical gathering of them.

26 Max Horkheimer, *Kritische Theorie: Eine Dokumentation*, vol. 1 (Frankfurt: S. Fischer Verlag, 1968), 375.

27 Jay, *Dialectical Imagination*, 47.

28 Herbert Marcuse, *Negation: Essays in Critical Theory*, trans. J.J. Shapiro (Boston: Beacon Press, 1968), 39.

29 This is not to ignore Weber's severe critique of capitalism, but rather to highlight its self-defeatist character, which nonetheless maintains that capitalism is the highest form of rationality.

30 Horkheimer, *Critical Theory*, trans. M.J. O'Connell (New York: Herder & Herder, 1972), 207.

31 *Negation*, 19
32 Horkheimer, *Eclipse of Reason* (New York: Continuum Publishing, 1947), vi.
33 Theodor Adorno, *Minima Moralia: Reflections from Damaged Life*, trans. E.F.N. Jephcott (London: NLB, 1974), 50.
34 Horkheimer, *Eclipse of Reason*, 93.
35 Horkheimer and Theodor W. Adorno, *Dialectic of Enlightenment*, trans. J. Cumming (New York: Continuum Publishing, 1987), 224.
36 Ibid., 225.
37 Habermas, *Autonomy and Solidarity*, ed. Peter Dews (London: Verso, 1986), 98.

2: Communicative Action Theory and Linguistic Interaction

1 Habermas, *Knowledge and Human Interest*, trans. J.J. Shapiro (London: Heinemann, 1968; hereafter *KHI*).
2 *KHI*, 4.
3 *KHI*, 308.
4 'The Postscript to Knowledge and Human Interests,' in *KHI*, 354; 'A Reply to My Critics,' in A. Honneth and H. Joas, eds, *Communicative Action* (Cambridge: MIT Press, 1991), 234.
5 Postcript to *KHI*, 314.
6 Habermas, 'A Review of Gadamer's Truth and Method' in F. Dallmayr and T. McCarthy, eds, *Understanding Social Inquiry* (Notre Dame, Ind.: The University Press 1977), 361.
7 Habermas, in preface to *Zur Logik der Sozialwissenschaften* (Frankfurt am Main: Suhrkamp Verlag, 1970).
8 Habermas, *Theory and Practice* (Boston: Beacon Press, 1973; hereafter *TP*), 168–9.
9 Anthony Giddens, 'Labour and Interaction,' in J. Thompson and D. Held, eds, *Habermas' Critical Debates* (Cambridge: MIT Press, 1982); also see Goran Therborn, 'Jürgen Habermas: A New Eclecticism,' *New Left Review* 67 (1971): 69–83.
10 Hans Joas, 'The Unhappy Marriage of Hermeneutics and Foundationalism,' in Honneth and Joas, eds, *Communicative Action*, 99; Thomas McCarthy, *The Critical Theory of Jürgen Habermas* (Cambridge: MIT Press, 1981), 24–6.
11 Axel Honneth, 'Work and Instrumental Action,' *New German Critique* 26, (1982): 31–54.
12 Ibid., 54.
13 *KHI*, 62.

14 *KHI*, 45.

15 Habermas, 'Technology and Science as "Ideology,"' in *Toward a Rational Society* (Boston: Beacon Press, 1973; hereafter *TRS*), 91.

16 Here a curious thing happens. After he recovered what was neglected by Marx and the Frankfurt School, namely, communicative action, Habermas's enthusiasm in *Theory and Practice* takes him so far as to suggest that purposive-rational action is embedded in communicative action and hence in language. Discussing the concept of language in 'Hegel's Jena Philosophy of Mind,' Habermas writes, 'Instrumental action, as soon as it comes under the category of actual spirit, as social labour, is also embedded within a network of interactions, and therefore dependent on communicative boundary conditions that underlie every possible cooperation' (*TP*, 158). At first glance this seems unproblematic, since it claims simply that as soon as work enters the social context (intersubjective activity) it is subject to the conditions of communicative interaction. But recalling Habermas's point against Gadamer, that aside from being the matrix of our understanding, language is also the context of domination and coercion; and recalling his definition of work as governed by technical rules and aimed at dominating and manipulating nature; we are struck by the suggestion that instrumental action is embedded in language and hence dependent on the conditions of cooperation in communicative action. There seems to be a tension between Habermas's suggested distinction between the two kinds of action and his tendency to attribute priority and superiority to communicative action over purposive-rational action. This tension, as we shall see, will not go away in Habermas's further elaboration of the theory, but changes form and even intensifies. Indeed, determining the right boundary between theory and practice, between truth and virtue, and between facts and norms remains a constant feature of Habermas's philosophical work. See note 30 below.

17 *TRS*, 91.

18 *KHI*, 326.

19 Habermas, *Communication and the Evolution of Society*, trans. T. McCarthy (Boston: Beacon Press, 1979; hereafter *CES*), 1.

20 Peter Dews, in his introduction to *Habermas: A Critical Reader* (Oxford: Blackwell, 1999), states that in the postscript to *KHI* Habermas fully accepts the force of Apel's critique of his account of self-reflection, and claims that Habermas 'began to distinguish between two forms of "self-reflection," dividing critique into two distinct activities. One of these he still calls "critique," the other "reconstruction." The principal differences between these two activities, Habermas now suggests, are as follows:

(1) *Critique* is directed at objects whose "pseudo-objectivity" is to be revealed, whereas reconstruction deals with processes which are already acknowledged as the activity of the subject; (2) *Critique* deals with the deformation of particular identities, whereas reconstructions are concerned with anonymous systems of rules; (3) *Critique* makes conscious something unconscious, altering what determines a *false* consciousness with practical results, whereas reconstructions retrieve a correct but implicit know-how, and have no immediate practical effects' (11).

21 *CES*, 95.
22 Habermas, *The Theory of Communicative Action*, vol. 1 (Boston: Beacon Press, 1984; hereafter *TCA* 1), xiii.
23 *TCA* 1, 274.
24 *CEW*, 6.
25 *CES*, 29.
26 *TCA* 1, 277.
27 *TCA* 1, 332.
28 McCarthy, *The Critical Theory of Habermas*, 278–9.
29 *CES*, 8–9.
30 *TCA* 1, 287. This is a weakened form of his earlier thesis that other actions including purposive ones are embedded in, and hence dependent upon, the conditions of communicative action (*TP*, 158; see note 16). Here he is only saying that communicative action is prior to other actions, but does not repeat that other actions are conditioned by rules and presuppositions of communicative action.
31 *TCA* 1, 279, 288.
32 Jonathan Culler, 'Communicative Competence and Normative Force,' *New German Critique* 35 (Spring/Summer 1985): 133–45.
33 Erling Skjei, 'A Comment on Performative, Subject and Proposition in Habermas' Theory of Communication,' *Inquiry* 28 (1985): 87–104.
34 Allen Wood, 'Habermas' Defense of Rationalism,' *New German Critique* 35 (Spring/Summer 1985): 145–64.
35 James Bohman, 'Emancipation and Rhetoric: The Perlocutions and Illocutions of the Social Critic,' *Philosophy and Rhetoric* 21, no. 3 (1988): 188–9.
36 Ibid., 201.
37 For example, he writes: 'Through perlocutionary effects, the speaker gives the hearer something to understand which he cannot (yet) directly communicate. In this phase, then, the perlocutionary acts have to be embedded in contexts of communicative action. These strategic *elements* within a use of language oriented to reaching understanding can be distinguished from

strategic *actions* through the fact that the entire sequence of the stretch of talk stands – on the part of all the participants – under the presuppositions of communicative action' (*TCA* 1, 331).

38 *TCA* 1, 68.
39 *TCA* 1, 307.
40 Habermas believes that the interconnection of these worlds and the basic attitude of agents or the pragmatic function of utterances as complexes of rationality account for the constitution and progression of knowledge. See *TCA* 1, 238, figure 11.
41 *TCA* 1, 285.
42 *TCA* 1, 95.
43 Ibid.
44 Ibid.
45 *TCA* 1, 326–7.
46 *TCA* 1, 287.
47 *TCA* 1, 297.
48 *TCA* 1, 298.
49 *TP*, 18.
50 *TP*, 19.
51 *TCA* 1, 22.
52 *TCA* 1, 25.
53 *TCA* 1, 19.
54 Habermas, *Moral Consciousness and Communicative Action* (Cambridge: MIT Press, 1990; hereafter *MCCA*), 198.
55 Ibid., 122–3.
56 McCarthy, *Critical Theory of Habermas*, 348.
57 Ibid., 350.
58 As Habermas himself acknowledges, studies by Norma Haan, Carol Gillegan, and J.M. Murphy have raised serious questions about the main claims of Kohlberg's model (see *MCCA*, 175). The most immediate objections can be summed up in the following way: (a) even if we accept Kohlberg's different moral stages, it does not follow that a hierarchical order exists among them; (b) this model 'puts more than half of the population of the United States at some level below the postconventional in terms of their moral consciousness' (ibid.); (c) the indeterminacy of the transitional stage 4.5, is described as postconventional but not yet principled; and (d) the moral consciousness of female agents is put at stage 3, 'despite a presumption of a greater moral maturity' (ibid.). Habermas, however, believes that raising these objections demonstrates a failure to distinguish between moral and evaluative issues (*MCCA*, 181). See C. Gilligan, 'In a

Different Voice: Women's Conception of Self and Morality,' *Harvard Educational Review* 47 (1977) 481ff.; C. Gilligan and J.M. Murphy, 'Moral Development in Late Adolescence and Adulthood: A Critique and Reconstruction of Kohlberg's Theory,' *Human Development* 23 (1980): 159ff.; C. Gilligan and J.M. Murphy, 'The Philosopher and the Dilemma of the Fact,' in D. Kuhn, ed., *Intellectual Development beyond Childhood* (San Francisco: 1980); N. Haan, 'Two Moralities in Action Context,' *Journal of Personality and Social Psychology* 36 (1978): 28ff.; and J. Habermas, 'A Reply to My Critics,' in J.B. Thompson and D. Held, eds, *Habermas' Critical Debates* (Cambridge: MIT Press, 1982), 219–83.

59 *MCCA*, 130

60 *TCA* 1, 42.

61 *MCCA*, 120.

62 *MCCA*, 108.

63 *MCCA*, 26.

64 Habermas, *Legitimation Crisis* (Boston: Beacon Press, 1975; hereafter *LC*), 108.

65 *MCCA*, 71.

66 McCarthy, *Critical Theory of Habermas*, 313.

67 It is possible that all attempts at a consensus might fail at the end of a discourse. In this case Habermas suggests that we try for a legitimate compromise. Such a compromise has to be undistorted, non-deceptive, and non-manipulative and involve everyone. This means two things: (a) power is divorced from participants so as to prevent development of a strategic situation, and (b) no generalizable interest is possible. As Habermas explains: 'A normed adjustment between particular interests is called *compromise* if it takes place under conditions of a balance of power between the parties involved ... A compromise can be justified as a compromise only if both conditions are met; a balance of power among the parties involved and the non-generalizability of the negotiated interest exist. If even one of these *general* conditions of *compromise formation* is not fulfilled, we are dealing with pseudo-compromise [*Scheinkompromiss*]' (*LC*, 111–12).

68 *MCCA*, 89.

69 *MCCA*, 87.

70 *MCCA*, 88.

71 *MCCA*, 89.

72 *MCCA*, 93.

73 *MCCA*, 100.

74 *MCCA*, 95.

75 *MCCA*, 96–7.
76 Habermas, 'Wahrheitstheorien,' quoted in McCarthy, *Critical Theory of Habermas*, 310.
77 *MCCA*, 314.
78 *MCCA*, 108.
79 *MCCA*, 116.
80 Ibid.

3: The Communicative Ethics Controversy

1 *MCCA*, 196; emphasis added.
2 *MCCA*, 201.
3 *MCCA*, 203.
4 Ibid.
5 Immanuel Kant, *Prolegomena to Any Further Metaphysics* (Indianapolis: Hackett Publishing Co., 1977), 86.
6 *MCCA*, 203.
7 *MCCA*, 204.
8 *MCCA*, 203.
9 *MCCA*, 206.
10 *MCCA*, 204.
11 *MCCA*, 207.
12 Despite Habermas's effort, however, the charge of abstract universalization has persisted against his theory. The main contributors to this critique, made from a communitarian point of view, include C. Taylor, S. Benhabib, and J. Mendelson. The crux of their argument can be summarized as follows: the very idea of universalization arises out of a concrete practical context that itself bounds, and hence, gives meaning to the attempt to universalize. The concept of universalization, then, cannot be as abstract and as formal as Kantian moralities suggest.
13 See section II, 'The Spirit of Christianity and Its Fate,' and section III, 'Love,' in Hegel, *Early Theological Writings* (New York: Harper Torchbook, 1948); chap. 6, section C, 'The Spirit That Is Certain of Itself: Morality,' in Hegel, *The Phenomenology of Spirit* (Oxford: Oxford University Press, 1977); Hegel, *Philosophy of Right* (Oxford: Oxford University Press, 1952), # 40, addition.
14 For instance, Seyla Benhabib, in her insightful examination of the concept of 'critique' from Hegel to Habermas, claims that Hegel's critique of Kant's ethics does not point to ignoring the intersubjective dimension of human interaction but to a trans-subjective aspect that proves to be as problematic

as Kant's moral theory. See her *Critique, Norm, and Utopia* (New York: Columbia University Press, 1986; hereafter *CNU*), 84–95.

15 For more on this tension in Habermas see Gordon Finlayson's cogent article 'Does Hegel's Critique of Kant's Moral Theory Apply to Discourse Ethics?' in P. Dews, ed., *Habermas: A Critical Reader* (Oxford: Blackwell, 1999), 29–52.

16 See Benhabib, *CNU*, and her 'Communicative Ethics and Contemporary Controversies in Practical Philosophy,' in S. Benhabib and F. Dallmayr, eds, *The Communicative Ethics Controversies* (Cambridge: MIT Press, 1990); Jack Mendelson, 'The Habermas–Gadamer Debate,' *New German Critique* 18 (Fall 1979): 44–73; and Charles Taylor, 'Language and Society' and Martin Seel, 'The Two Meanings of Communicative Rationality,' in A. Honneth and H. Joas, eds, *Communicative Action* (Cambridge: MIT Press, 1991), 23–48. For a useful collection of essays with respect to the debate between Habermas and his communitarian critics see D. Rasmussen, ed., *Universalism versus Communitarianism: Contemporary Debates in Ethics* (Cambridge: MIT Press, 1990).

17 See Jean-François Lyotard, *The Postmodern Condition: A Report on Knowledge*, trans. G. Bennington and B. Massumi (Minneapolis: University of Minnesota Press, 1984); Michel Foucault, 'Politics and Ethics: An Interview,' in P. Rabinow, ed., *The Foucault Reader* (New York: Pantheon, 1984); Steven White, *Political Theory and Postmodernism* (Cambridge: Cambridge University Press, 1991); and Richard Rorty, 'Habermas and Lyotard on Postmodernity,' in Richard Bernstein, ed., *Habermas and Modernity* (Cambridge: MIT Press), 1985

18 See Seyla Benhabib, *Situating the Self: Gender, Community, and Postmodernism in Contemporary Ethics* (New York: Routledge, 1992); Carol Gilligan, *In a Different Voice: Psychological Theory and Women's Development* (Cambridge: Harvard University Press, 1982); Nancy Fraser, 'What Is Critical about Critical Theory? The Case of Habermas and Gender,' in S. Benhabib and D. Cornell, eds, *Feminism as Critique* (Minneapolis: University of Minnesota Press, 1987; Marie Fleming, *Emancipation and Illusion: Rationality and Gender in Habermas' Theory of Modernity* (University Park: Pennsylvania State University Press, 1997); and Johanna Meehan, ed., *Habermas and Feminism: Autonomy, Morality, and the Gendered Subject* (London: Routledge, 1995). See also Maeve Cooke's 'Habermas, Feminism and the Question of Autonomy,' in P. Dews, ed., *Habermas: A Critical Reader* (Oxford: Blackwell, 1999), 178–210.

19 For such critical commentary see R. Bernstein, ed., *Habermas and Modernity* (Cambridge: MIT Press, 1985); J. Thompson and D. Held, eds, *Habermas'*

Critical Debate (Cambridge: MIT Press, 1982); Axel Honneth, *The Critique of Power* (Cambridge: MIT Press, 1991); Thomas Rockmore, *Habermas on Historical Materialism* (Bloomington: Indiana University Press, 1989); C. Calhoun, ed., *Habermas and the Public Sphere* (Cambridge: MIT Press, 1992); T. McCarthy et al., eds, *Cultural-Political Interventions in the Unfinished Project of Enlightenment* (Cambridge: MIT Press, 1992); T. McCarthy et al., eds, *Philosophical Interventions in the Unfinished Project of Enlightenment* (Cambridge: MIT Press, 1992); S. White, ed., *The Cambridge Companion to Habermas* (Cambridge: Cambridge University Press, 1995); and M. Passerin d'Entrèves and S. Benhabib, eds, *Habermas and the Unfinished Project of Modernity* (Cambridge: MIT Press, 1997).

20 This critique has been chiefly made by Richard Rorty. See his *Philosophy and the Mirror of Nature* (Princeton: Princeton University Press, 1979); 'Habermas and Lyotard on Postmodernity,' in R.J. Bernstein, ed., *Habermas and Modernity* (Cambridge: MIT Press, 1985); and 'The Ambiguity of "Rationality,"' *Constellations* 3, no. 1 (1996): 73–82

21 *TCA* 1, xlii.

22 *MCCA*, 108.

23 *MCCA*, 46.

24 *MCCA*, 56.

25 *MCCA*, 198.

26 Habermas, 'Toward a Theory of Communicative Competence,' *Inquiry* 13 (1970), 372 (emphasis added).

27 *MCCA*, 202.

28 *MCCA*, 116.

29 Wolfgang Kuhlmann, 'Philosophie und Rekonstruktive Wissenschaft' (contribution to a symposium on the 'Theory of Communicative Action' held in the Center for Interdisciplinary Studies in Bielefeld, 1985), cited in Habermas, 'A Reply,' in A. Honneth and H. Joas, eds, *Communicative Action* (Cambridge: MIT Press, 1991), 230–3.

30 Habermas, 'A Reply,' 232.

31 Ibid.

32 *MCCA*, 97–8.

33 Habermas, *Postmetaphysical Thinking* (Cambridge: MIT Press, 1992), 120.

34 Ibid., 129–30.

35 *MCCA*, 43–115.

36 *MCCA*, 82. See Karl-Otto Apel, 'The Problem of Philosophical Fundamental Grounding in Light of a Transcendental Pragmatics of Language,' in K. Baynes, J. Bohman, and T. McCarthy, eds, *After Philosophy* (Cambridge: MIT Press, 1987) 277.

37 See Habermas, 'Philosophy as Stand-In and Interpreter,' in *After Philosophy*, 296–318, for an account of the role of philosophy among sciences.

38 *MCCA*, 106; emphasis added.

39 Habermas, 'Philosophy as Stand-In,' 310–11.

40 *MCCA*, 210.

41 *MCCA*, 211; emphasis added.

42 Benhabib, *CNU*, 298.

43 Habermas, *Autonomy and Solidarity*, ed. Peter Dews (London: Verso, 1986; hereafter referred to as *AS*), 201.

44 *AS*, 201.

45 *AS*, 249; emphasis added.

46 Habermas, 'Kohlberg and Neo-Aristotelianism,' *New Directions for Child Development*, 1988: 15; quoted in D. Rasmussen, *Reading Habermas* (Cambridge: Basil Blackwell, 1990), 72.

47 See Albercht Wellmer, 'Ethics and Dialogue: Elements of Moral Judgment in Kant and Discourse Ethics,' in Wellmer, *The Persistence of Modernity* (Cambridge: MIT Press, 1991), 113–231.

48 *MCCA*, 206.

49 *AS*, 250.

50 Habermas, 'Kohlberg and Neo-Aristotelianism,' quoted in Rasmussen, *Reading Habermas*, 72.

51 *AS*, 251.

52 Habermas, *Justification and Application: Remarks on Discourse Ethics* (Cambridge: MIT Press, 1993), 36.

53 Klaus Günther, *Der Sinn für Angemessenheit: Anwendungsdiskurse in Moral und Recht* (Frankfurt: Suhrkamp, 1988).

54 *Justification and Application*, 37.

55 *MCCA*, 207.

56 Thomas McCarthy acknowledges this Kantian residue and its significance for Habermas's conception of the public sphere. See Thomas McCarthy, *Ideals and Illusions: On Reconstruction and Deconstruction in Contemporary Critical Theory* (Cambridge: MIT Press, 1991), 181.

57 Habermas, 'Law and Morality,' in S.M. McMurrin, ed., *The Tanner Lectures on Human Values*, vol. 8 (Salt Lake City: University of Utah Press, 1988), 245.

58 *MCCA*, 99.

59 See G.W.F. Hegel, *Phenomenology of Spirit*, trans. A.V. Miller (Oxford: Oxford University Press, 1977), 259.

60 See Hegel, *Elements of Philosophy of Right*, ed. A. Wood (Cambridge: Cambridge University Press, 1991), sect. 135.

61 Finlayson, 'Does Hegel's Critique Apply?' (see note 15 above), 38–9.

62 Ibid., 47.
63 Benhabib, *CNU*, 319; she describes this problematic aspect of Habermas's theory as 'decisionism.' While theories of rationality – such as those of Lorenzen Apel, and Habermas – that *choose* different levels of justification for the normative grounding of their theory (either in the minimum rules of logic, or in universal pragmatics, or still in the context of the lifeworld) can be labelled as decisionist, for the sake of consistency I rather attribute the problem to a foundationalist tendency (as I described it on pages 66–7) that places the root of normative theory in the nature of humans as social beings capable of speech.
64 *MCCA*, 68.
65 McCarthy, *Critical Theory of Habermas*, 362.
66 See Agnes Heller, 'The Discourse of Habermas: Critique and Appraisal,' *Thesis Eleven* 10–11 (1984–5): 5–17; John B. Thompson, 'Universal Pragmatics,' in Thompson and David Held, eds, *Habermas' Critical Debates*, 116–33; Wellmer, 'Ethics and Dialogue'; and Otfried Höffe, 'Kantian Skepticism toward the Transcendental Ethics of Communication,' and Seyla Benhabib, 'Communicative Ethics and Contemporary Controversies in Practical Philosophy,' in Benhabib and Dallmyer, eds, *The Communicative Ethics Controversy*.
67 Benhabib, 'Communicative Ethics Controversies,' 345. Benhabib, however, goes too far in this direction when she claims that '(D) is actually redundant in Habermas' theory' (344) and that it gives the theory a *consequentialist* character and opens Habermas' view to anti-utilitarian critiques' (343). This is a mistaken criticism that results from misunderstanding the discursive situation as being open and possible only to those agents with the competence of stages 5 and 6 of moral development. Benhabib uses the example of a *sadist* and a *masochist* as participants in a discourse regarding the maxim 'Do not inflict unnecessary suffering,' and argues that it cannot win their assent. She neglects the important fact that, as the participants in discourse, they lack the required characteristics of agents who belong to the stages of postconventional morality.
68 Wellmer, 'Zur Kritik der Diskursethik,' in Wellmer, *Ethik und Dialog* (Frankfurt: Suhrkamp, 1986).
69 Benhabib, *CNU*, 315.
70 Benhabib, 'Communicative Ethics Controversies,' 346.

4: Discourse Ethics and Legitimation Problems in Advanced Capitalism

1 Mark E. Warren, 'The Self in Discursive Democracy,' in *The Cambridge Companion to Habermas* (New York: Cambridge University Press, 1995), 167.

2 *LC*, 120.
3 *CES*, 99.
4 Ibid.
5 *CES*, 156–7.
6 *CES*, 121.
7 *CES*, 130–76. I acknowledge the fact that many commentators (see Tom Rockmore, *Habermas and Historical Materialism* [Bloomington: Indiana University Press, 1989]), rightly, have questioned whether the remnants of Marxism and Historical Materialism left in Habermas are of any significance. Despite the validity of this question, I would like to point out that in so far as Habermas's project is oriented toward the attainment of social justice in an emancipated society free of domination, he shares this goal with the Marxist ideal of free society. And in so far as his theory of evolution supposes a linear progressive development toward a more sophisticated social and political formation, he shares the basic progressive assumption of Historical Materialism. These affinities, while they may be viewed as minimal, are sufficient for the purposes of my discussion.
8 Richard J. Bernstein and Kenley Dove, 'Comments on the Relationship of Habermas' Views to Hegel,' in D.P. Verene, *Hegel's Social and Political Theory* (New Jersey: Humanities Press, 1980), 238.
9 For further discussion of Habermas's connection and distance from his Marxist roots see Rick Roderick, *Habermas and the Foundation of Critical Theory* (New York: St Martin's Press, 1986); Julius Sensat, *Habermas and Marxism: An Appraisal* (Beverly Hills: Sage Publications, 1979); and Tom Rockmore, *Habermas and Historical Materialism*.
10 *CES*, 140.
11 *CES*, 153.
12 *LC*, 17–18.
13 *LC*, 16.
14 *LC*, 18.
15 *LC*, 20.
16 Ibid.
17 *LC*, 23.
18 *LC*, 3.
19 *LC*, 22.
20 *CES*, 193.
21 Ibid.
22 *LC*, 73,
23 *LC*, 97.
24 *CES*, 178.
25 Ibid.

26 *CES*, 180.
27 *CES*, 183.
28 Ibid.
29 *CES*, 184.
30 *CES*, 185.
31 *CES*, 186.
32 *LC*, 4.
33 Ibid.
34 *CES*, 154.
35 Ibid.
36 For a comprehensive and insightful survey of the debate concerning Habermas's theory of social evolution see Piet Strydom, 'The Ontogenetic Fallacy: The Immanent Critique of Habermas' Developmental Logical Theory of Evolution,' *Theory, Culture, and Society* 9 (1992): 65–93.
37 McCarthy, *Critical Theory of Habermas*, 261.
38 McCarthy, 'Rationality and Relativism: Habermas' Overcoming of Hermeneutics,' in Thompson and D. Held, eds, *Habermas' Critical Debates*, 73.
39 Ibid.
40 *CNU*, 292.
41 See Axel Honneth and Hans Joas, *Social Action and Human Nature* (Cambridge: Cambridge University Press, 1988); *Theory of Communicative Action*, ed. Honneth and Joas (Cambridge: MIT Press, 1991); and Honneth, *The Critique of Power* (Cambridge: MIT Press, 1991).
42 Klaus Eder, *Die Vergesellschaftung der Natur* (Frankfurt: Suhrkamp, 1988) quoted in Piet Strydom, 'The Ontogenetic Fallacy: The Immanent Critique of Habermas' Developmental Logical Theory of Evolution,' *Theory, Culture, and Society* 9 (1992): 82. For a more specific account of Eder's critique of Habermas also see Piet Strydom's informative article 'Sociocultural Evolution or the Social Evolution of Practical Reason?: Eder's Critique of Habermas,' *Praxis International* 13, no. 3 (October 1993): 304–22.
43 Michael Schmid, 'Habermas' Theory of Social Evolution,' in Thompson and Held, eds, *Habermas' Critical Debates*, 173–4.
44 Ibid., 176–7.
45 Piet Strydom, on this topic, writes: 'The main thrust of this immanent critique was three-fold. First, Honneth and Joas, but particularly Miller and, following him, Eder, clarified the problems attached to drawing conclusions from ontogenesis in respect of the change and development of culture and collective symbolic systems, and corrected the ontogenetic fallacy in this particular sense by the introduction of the concept of collec-

tive learning supported by a sociological learning theory. Next, Honneth, Frankenberg and Rödel, Arnason, and Eder exposed the implications of the ontogenetic fallacy in its second sense of extrapolation an epoch-transcendent theory of society and history from the model of ontogenetic development. Finally, the younger critical theorists each in his own way embarked on the development of a theoretical foundation to support these revisions. While they retained in some form or another the Habermasian idea of the theoretical significance of communication, this new departure invariably took the form of the philosophy or the theory of praxis, at times to the exclusion of evolution and at other times not' ('Sociocultural Evolution,' 308).

46 Habermas, *Eine Art Schadensabwicklung* (Frankfurt: Suhrkamp, 1987), 73; English trans. in *New Conservatism: Cultural Criticism and the Historians' Debate* (Cambridge: MIT Press, 1989), 261.
47 *TCA*, 2, 45.
48 Ibid.
49 *TCA* 2, 57.
50 *TCA* 2, 77.
51 Ibid.
52 *TCA* 2, 111.
53 Habermas and N. Luhmann, *Theorie der Gesellschaft oder Sozialtechnologie?* (Frankfurt, 1971).
54 Habermas, *Towards a Rational Society* (Boston: Beacon Press, 1970), 106.
55 'A Social-Scientific Concept of Crisis,' in *LC*, 7–33.
56 Habermas, 'Eine Auseinandersetzung mit Niklas Luhmann,' 484; quoted in Axel Honneth, *The Critique of Power* (Cambridge: MIT Press, 1991), 284.
57 *TCA* 2, 117.
58 *TCA* 2, 118.
59 *TCA* 2, 124.
60 *TCA* 2, 137.
61 *TCA* 2, 138.
62 *TCA* 2, 141–2.
63 *TCA* 2, 145.
64 *TCA* 2, 152.
65 *TCA* 2, 153.
66 *TCA* 2, 154.
67 *TCA* 2, 173.
68 *TCA* 2, 196.
69 *TCA* 2, 319–31.
70 *TCA* 2, 327.

71 *TCA* 2, 330.
72 *TCA* 2, 355.
73 It is obvious that Habermas's theory favours the tradition of European Enlightenment, which has brought the charge of ethnocentrism against him. I would like to point out, however, that in examining the heritage of modernity in Western democracies, Habermas's selectivity with respect to the great majority of his examples and case studies, taken from Germany and the United States, should be seen as the contextual origin of his theory rather than its normative application.
74 *TCA* 2, 374.
75 *TCA* 2, 375.
76 *TCA* 2, 376.
77 *TCA* 2, 378.
78 Ibid.
79 *TCA* 2, 382–3.
80 *TCA* 2, 383.
81 Ibid.
82 McCarthy, 'Complexity and Democracy, or the Seducements of Systems Theory,' in *Ideals and Illusions* (Cambridge: MIT Press, 1991: hereafter referred to as *II*), 180.
83 *II*, 130.
84 *II*, 131.
85 Honneth, *The Critique of Power*.
86 *CES*, 178.
87 McCarthy, 'Practical Discourse: On the Relation of Politics and Morality,' in *II*, 181–99.
88 *II*, 182.
89 *II*, 183.
90 This does not mean that compromise is not an acceptable means of treating the conflict situation. Indeed, even Habermas's early formulation of discourse theory included an account of negotiating a fair compromise (see *LC*, 111–12). However, as his critique of Ernst Tugendhat in *MCCA* (68–76) shows, compromise is only a second alternative to consensus, for while the former emphasizes the balance of power, the latter's focus is on the ideal of impartiality crystallized in the principle of universalization (U).
91 *II*, 191–2.
92 Habermas, 'On the Relationship of Politics, Law, and Morality,' quoted in McCarthy, *II*, 192.
93 See Habermas, 'Further Reflection on the Public Sphere,' in C. Calhoun, ed., *Habermas and the Public Sphere* (Cambridge: MIT Press, 1992).

94 Piet Strydom, 'The Ontogenetic Fallacy,' 90.

95 MCCA, 209.

96 Benhabib, *CNU*, 229.

97 *CNU*, 309.

98 Ibid.

99 *CNU*, 310.

100 Ibid.

101 Habermas, *Between Facts and Norms* (Cambridge: MIT Press, 1996), 114.

5: The Imperilment of Critical Theory

1 In *Wahrheitstheorien* (quoted in McCarthy's *Ideals and Illusions* [Cambridge: MIT Press, 1991], 187) Habermas writes: '[T]he result of practical discourses in which it is demonstrated that the validity claim of de facto recognized rules cannot be vindicated ... can stand in a critical relation to reality (i.e. the symbolic reality of society), while theoretical discourse can be directed not against reality itself (i.e. nature), but only against false assertions about it.' And in *MCCA* he adds: 'To use an ontological mode of expression, we might say that this asymmetry [between truth and rightness] is due to the fact that the orders of society, which we either conform to or deviate from, are not constituted *independently of validity*, as are the orders of nature, toward which we can assume an objectivating attitude. The social reality that we address in our regulative speech acts has by its very nature an *intrinsic* link to normative validity claims' (60–1).

2 See pages 92–3.

3 See Seyla Benhabib, *Critique, Norm, and Utopia* (New York: Columbia University Press, 1986), 229.

4 I recognize that these pairs need not be, and indeed are not, the same, or as tightly connected as I claim them to be, in other theories of morality (e.g., utilitarianism). Within a Kantian tradition, however, they are. In my view that is because the categorical imperative and the principle of human dignity in Kant are devised in such a way as to close the door to any scepticism or relativism, giving priority to the right over the good. This priority in turn defines the morality/ethics distinction and the rest of the dualisms that follow, and also decides the privileged elements of the dichotomies based on the original orientation of the theory. It is in this context that I see the above-mentioned binaries as related.

5 *II*, 196.

6 Klaus Günther, *Der Sinn für Angemessenheit* (Frankfurt: Suhrkamp/KNO 1992). A summary of his argument can be found in his article 'Impartial

Application of Moral and Legal Norms: A Contribution to Discourse
Ethics,' in D. Rasmussen, ed., *Universalism vs. Communitarianism* (Cambridge: MIT Press, 1990), 199–206.

7 *JA*, 89.
8 *JA*, 91.
9 *JA*, 90.
10 *JA*, 91.
11 Benhabib, *CNU*, 288.
12 *JA*, 92.
13 *JA*, 94.
14 John Rawls, 'Justice as Fairness: A Brief Restatement,' quoted in Habermas,
    JA, 94.
15 Rawls, *Political Liberalism* (New York: Columbia University Press, 1993;
    hereafter referred to as *PL*), 55.
16 *PL*, 58.
17 *PL*, 50.
18 Rawls's notion of reflective equilibrium has been charged with relativism
    since it gives up the strong concept of moral objectivity. But this contro-
    versy aside, I would like to call attention to a point raised by Thomas
    McCarthy in his 'Constructivism and Reconstructivism: Rawls and Ha-
    bermas in Dialogue,' where he writes: 'Philosophical accounts of reason
    have to pass what might be called a 'reflexivity test': they must be applica-
    ble to themselves without producing self-referential contradictions. On
    this score, I think there is a tension in *Political Liberalism* between the post-
    foundationalist line of argument meant to convince us, the readers, of a
    certain conception of public reason and the thesis that reasonable citizens
    may embrace it for whatever religious, metaphysical, or other comprehen-
    sive reasons they find acceptable' (*Ethics* 105 [October 1994]: 61).
19 Kenneth Baynes, *The Normative Grounds of Social Criticism* (Albany: State
    University of New York Press, 1992), 69.
20 *JA*, 93.
21 *PL*, 54.
22 *PL*, 58.
23 McCarthy, 'Kantian Constructivism,' 55.
24 Ibid.
25 'Kantian Constructivism,' 56; emphasis added.
26 See Max Horkheimer, 'Traditional and Critical Theory,' in *Critical Theory*
    (New York: Herder and Herder, 1972). Adorno and Horkheimer, however,
    remained pessimistic with respect to the possibility of the third element of
    the critique's task.

27 *JA*, 92.
28 *PL*, 399.
29 *PL*, 4.
30 For a further discussion of this matter see Ed Wingenbach, 'Unjust Context: The Priority of Stability in Rawls' Contextualized Theory of Justice,' *American Journal of Political Science* 43, no. 1 (January 1999): 213–32; and Brian Barry, 'John Rawls and the Search for Stability,' *Ethics* 105, no. 3 (1995): 874–915.
31 One cannot help but sympathize with E.A. Goerner's assessment that Rawls 'abandons all of the questioning, wondering, and thus subversive potential that has remained a part of the tradition [of political philosophy] since it got Socrates killed' ('Rawls' Apolitical Political Turn,' *Review of Politics* 55 [1993]: 138).
32 John Rawls, *The Law of Peoples* (Cambridge: Harvard University Press, 1999).
33 Thomas Pogge, 'An Egalitarian Law of People,' *Philosophy and Public Affairs* 23, no. 3 (1994): 224.
34 Habermas, 'Wie ist Legitimität durch Legalität möglich?' *Kritische Justiz* 20 (1987): 1–16; and 'The Rationalization of Law: Weber's Diagnosis of the Times,' in *TCA* 1, 243–71.
35 *TCA* 1, 260.
36 Habermas, 'Law and Morality,' in S.M. McMurrin, ed., *The Tanner Lectures on Human Values*, vol. 8 (Salt Lake City: University of Utah Press, 1988); 'The New Obscurity: The Crisis of the Welfare State and the Exhaustion of Utopian Energies,' in *New Conservatism: Cultural Criticism and the Historians' Debate* (Cambridge: MIT Press, 1989).
37 See notes 7 and 9 in chapter 4.
38 *MCCA*, 58.
39 *TCA* 2, 232.
40 Habermas, 'A Reply,' in Honneth and Joas, eds, *Communicative Action*, 257.
41 Axel Honneth, at the end of his *Critique of Power* (Cambridge: MIT Press, 1991; chap. 9), develops a critical analysis of Habermas's distinction between the domain of system, as norm-free interaction, and the realm of lifeworld, as power-free interaction, without fully drawing out the implication of his critique. Also see Günter Frankenberg, 'Disorder Is Possible: An Essay on System, Laws, and Disobedience,' in Axel Honneth et al., eds, *Cultural-Political Interventions in the Unfinished Project of Enlightenment* (Cambridge: MIT Press, 1992).
42 I will treat this appropriation later in the chapter.
43 Of course in his 'Hannah Arendt: On the Concept of Power' (in *Philosophical-*

Political Profiles [Cambridge: MIT Press, 1983], 171–88) Habermas already outlines Arendt's concept of communicative power and its opposition to the concept of *violence*, but he never attempts to connect the former with the notion of modern law so as to address the problem of political legitimacy. In fact, he criticizes Arendt's notion as restrictive in so far as she assumes a concept of politics that is independent from economic and social matters, for which 'Arendt pays the price of screening all strategic elements out of politics as "violence," severing politics from its ties to the economic and social environment in which it is embedded via administrative system' (179). Habermas charges that when Arendt equates strategic and instrumental action, and views them both as violence, she fails to see that there is a difference between the acquisition and maintenance of political power, its exercise, and its generation (180). Arendt's view of power, Habermas tells us here, only helps with the engendering of political power.

44 *BFN*, 132.
45 *TCA* 2, 173–4; *MCCA*, 209.
46 Habermas, 'A Reply to My Critics,' in Thompson and Held, eds, *Habermas' Critical Debates*, 262.
47 *BFN*, 132.
48 *BFN*, 493.
49 See, e.g., Leslie Mulholland, *Kant's System of Rights* (New York: Columbia University Press, 1990).
50 *BFN*, 107. It is worth noting that this understanding of the discourse principle (D), as Habermas himself acknowledges on page 108, is a new one. In previous works (e.g., *MCCA*, 93) it was understood as 'a principle of moral theory.'
51 The word 'all' in this formulation of the principle of democracy sets the standard so high that it makes satisfying the principle almost impossible, since in our diverse and pluralist society today it is rare that any claim meets with the assent of 'all.' This high standard already robs Habermas's new elaboration of the deliberative model of its substantive force, once again confronting it with a Hegelian charge of emptiness and ineffectiveness.
52 *BFN*, 110; emphasis added.
53 *BFN*, 128.
54 The claim that the unbalanced relation between private and public autonomy in liberalism can be resolved by discourse theory's move to view them as co-original is rejected by Rawls. Toward the end of his reply to Habermas in *PL*, Rawls writes, 'No special doctrine of co-originality is needed to explain this fact. It is hard to believe that all major liberal and

civic republican writers did not understand this. It bears on the age-old
question of how best to unite power with law to achieve justice' (417).
Despite Rawls's quick dismissal, however, in reading his *The Law of Peoples*
(Cambridge: Harvard University Press, 1999) one cannot help but observe
that he makes individual liberties more basic than democratic participatory rights. Indeed, one of the major arguments of French liberals like
Constant and Tocqueville against English liberals was that they did not see
the co-originality between public and private sovereignty clearly and thus
made the former secondary. Thus, the Rousseauan moment still had to be
integrated into liberalism.

55 *BFN*, 129.
56 *BFN*, 449.
57 *BFN*, 42.
58 *BFN*, 132.
59 *BFN*, xxviii.
60 *BFN*, 169.
61 Habermas, 'Three Normative Models of Democracy,' *Constellations*, 1, no. 1
    (1994): 8.
62 *BFN*, 45.
63 *BFN*, 482.
64 *BFN*, 147–8.
65 *BFN*, 149.
66 These new dimensions across which relations of power can flow coincide
    with a great deal of what Foucault had to say in his analysis of power/
    knowledge, which was severely criticized by Habermas in *The Philosophical
    Discourse of Modernity* (Cambridge: MIT Press, 1987). Here, Habermas's
    revisions concerning the concept of power seem to move towards encom-
    passing a more Foucauldean view of power. Indeed, throughout *BFN* one
    can find Habermas nodding his head at Foucault and using some of Fou-
    cault's terminology, such as 'normalization,' 'special power relations,' and
    'normalizing effects' in quotations (79, 420, 423). His description of com-
    municative power as resisting forms of repression (148) reads as follows:
    'when revolutionaries seize the power scattered through the streets; when
    a population committed to passive resistance opposes foreign tanks with
    their bare hands ...' This account is much closer to Foucault's 'agonism' in
    identifying the more productive power struggles than to anything that
    Habermas has written on power thus far. Accordingly, Habermas's and
    Foucault's debate regarding the question of modernity needs to be recon-
    structed. See chapter 6, section 2, below.
67 *BFN*, 483.

68 Bernhard Peters, 'On Reconstructive Legal and Political Theory,' in Mathieu Deflem, ed., *Habermas, Modernity, and Law* (London: Sage Publications, 1996), 122.

69 Habermas, 'The Entwinement of Myth and Enlightenment: Rereading *Dialectic of Enlightenment*,' *New German Critique* 26 (1982): 27.

70 Benhabib, *CNU*, 229.

71 Habermas, *Autonomy and Solidarity*, ed. Peter Dews (London: Verso, 1992), 264.

72 Habermas devotes chapter 6 of BFN to elaborating on the role of constitutional adjudication.

73 Habermas, 'Further Reflection on the Public Sphere,' in Graig Calhoun, ed., *Habermas and the Public Sphere* (Cambridge: MIT Press, 1992), 444.

74 *TCA* 2, 345.

75 Thomas McCarthy further questions the rigid way these dichotomies are maintained in Habermas in his penetrating essay 'Legitimacy and Diversity: Dialectical Reflections on Analytical Distinctions,' in Michel Resenfeld, ed., *Habermas on Law and Democracy* (Berkeley: University of California Press, 1998).

76 Criticizing the same aspect of Kant's moral theory, Hegel writes: '[T]o cling on to a merely moral point of view without making the transition to the concept of ethics reduces this gain [of the knowledge of the will as the root of duty] to an *empty formalism*, and moral science to an empty rhetoric of *duty for duty's sake*. From this point of view, no immanent theory of duties is possible' (G.W.F. Hegel, *Elements of Philosophy of Right*, ed. Allen Wood [Cambridge: Cambridge University Press, 1991], sect. 135).

77 *BFN*, 80.

78 Peter Dews, *The Limits of Disenchantment* (London: Verso, 1995), 200; emphasis added.

6: Recovering the Critical Impulse of Habernas's Theory of Democracy

1 William Scheuerman, 'Between Radicalism and Resignation: Democratic Theory in Habermas' *Between Facts and Norms*,' in P. Dews, ed., *Habermas: A Critical Reader* (Oxford: Blackwell, 1999), 155.

2 Simon Critchley and Axel Honneth, 'Philosophy in Germany,' *Radical Philosophy*, no. 89 (May 1998): 35.

3 Beginning in vol. 92 (March 1995): 109–80.

4 Habermas, *The Inclusion of the Other* (Cambridge: MIT Press, 1996; hereafter referred to as *IO*).

5 *IO*, 61.

6 Ibid.

7 *IO*, 63.

8 *IO*, 65.

9 *IO*, 50–1.

10 *PL*, 378–9. In his reply to Habermas, Rawls defines metaphysical theories as follows: 'I think of metaphysics as being at least a general account of what there is, including fundamental, fully general statements.' Hence, Habermas's theory is metaphysical in the following sense: 'it presents an account of what there is – human beings engaged in communicative action in their lifeworld' (379). At a high level of generality, I concur with Rawls's definition of metaphysics, but I find applying this definition to Habermas's theory to be imprecise. On this account of Habermas's view, everything belonging to the realm of nature does not exist. Thus, I don't find this passage to be consistent with the rest of Rawls's reply with respect to its thoughtfulness and rigour.

11 *PL*, 395. Rawls's method of justification in general has faced two kinds of questions: (1) To what extent is it different from traditional sorts of intuitionism? (2) Can it avoid the charge of relativism? Kenneth Baynes, in his illuminating discussion of Rawls and Habermas, contends that while 'Rawls can defend his position reasonably well against the first criticism, reflective equilibrium can adequately respond to the second only by moving in the direction of a discourse ethics.' *The Normative Grounds of Social Criticism* (Albany: State University of New York Press, 1992), 70.

12 *PL*, 375.

13 *IO*, 76.

14 *IO*, 77.

15 Ibid.

16 *IO*, 82–3.

17 *PL*, 94.

18 *IO*, 85.

19 *IO*, 83.

20 Rainer Forst, *Kontexte der Gerechtigkeit* (Frankfurt am Main: Suhrkamp, 1994), 159.

21 *IO*, 86.

22 Ibid.

23 In this respect Habermas detects an ambivalence in Rawls between the original strategy of *A Theory of Justice* and *PL*.

24 *IO*, 93.

25 *IO*, 98.

26 Ibid.

27 *IO*, 99.

28 John Rawls, 'Justice as Fairness: Political not Metaphysical,' *Philosophy and Public Affairs* 14 (Summer 1985).

29 Rawls, 'Justice as Fairness: A Brief Restatement,' 1989; quoted in Habermas, *JA*, 92.

30 For an insightful discussion of the proceduralist claims of both Habermas and Rawls see Cristina Lafont's 'Procedural Justice? Remarks on the Rawls-Habermas Debate' (unpublished manuscript presented at a panel entitled 'Critical Theory/Liberalism Debate,' Canadian Philosophical Association annual meeting, 25 May 2001, Quebec City); and her book *The Linguistic Turn in Hermeneutic Philosophy* (Cambridge: MIT Press, 1999 (esp. chap. 7).

31 *IO*, 72.

32 Thomas McCarthy, 'Liberal Theory and Racial Injustice: Toward a Critical Theory of Race,' unpublished manuscript, 18; emphasis added.

33 In the reading package used for Habermas's course on political theory at Northwestern University in the fall of 1999 (Phil. C68), a section entitled 'Blind Spots in Normative Theory: Class, Race, Gender' included N. Fraser's 'From Redistribution to Recognition' (from Cynthia Willett, ed., *Theorizing Multiculturalism*); T. McCarthy's 'Liberal Theory and Racial Injustice'; and C.W. Mills's *The Racial Contract* (Ithaca: Cornell University Press, 1997).

34 McCarthy, 'Liberal Theory and Injustice,' 33.

35 Despite the usual caution not to put their ideas into such an explicitly conclusive form, one still can find such statements. For example, Rawls in *The Law of Peoples* writes: 'The law of peoples assumes that every society has in its population a sufficient array of human capabilities, each in sufficient number so that the society has enough potential human re-sources to realize just institutions. *The final political end of society is to become fully just and stable for the right reasons. Once that end is reached* the law of peoples prescribes no further target such as, for example, to raise the standard of living beyond what is necessary to sustain those institutions' (*The Law of Peoples* [Cambridge Harvard University Press, 1999], 119; emphasis added).

36 McCarthy, 'Liberal Theory and Racial Injustice,' 31.

37 On Habermas's charge of irrationalism against post-structuralists see Gilles Deleuze, 'What Is Dispositif?' and Dominique Janicaud, 'Rationality, Force, and Power: Foucault and Habermas,' both in T.J. Armstrong, ed.,

Michel Foucault: Philosopher (New York: Routledge, 1992), 159–65 and 283–300, respectively.

38 Richard Bernstein, *The New Constellation* (Cambridge: MIT Press, 1991).

39 If we consider Martin Matuštík's statement, summing up his article in *Constellations* (vol. 1, no. 3, 1995: 383–421), that he has 'not sought a confrontation between modernism and postmodernism but rather an opening for a mutual corrective of Derrida's and Habermas' proposals for radical democracy after 1989,' along with the works by McCarthy, Lee, and Bernstein already cited here, one can see an emerging pattern of complementarity between critical theory and postmodernism.

40 Thomas McCarthy in two unpublished papers, 'Liberal Theory and Racial Injustice' and 'Purity and Impurity in Ethics: Kant on Race and Development,' probes the Kantian ideas of rationality and rational subject for hidden racial assumptions and prejudices.

41 McCarthy, 'Liberal Theory and Racial Injustice,' 32.

42 In addition to *PDM*, the same criticism has been voiced by the following critics: Nancy Fraser, *Unruly Practices: Power, Discourse and Gender in Contemporary Social Theory* (Minneapolis: University of Minnesota Press, 1989); Stephen White, *Political Theory and Postmodernism* (Cambridge: Cambridge University Press, 1991); Axel Honneth, *The Critique of Power* (Cambridge: MIT Press, 1991); Thomas McCarthy, *Ideals and Illusions* (Cambridge: MIT Press, 1991) and 'The Politics of the Ineffable: Derrida's Deconstruction,' in Michael Kelly, ed., *Hermeneutics and Critical Theory on Ethics and Politics* (Cambridge: MIT Press, 1991).

43 Habermas, *PDM*, 273.

44 I have dealt with this charge elsewhere: see Abdollah Payrow Shabani, 'Are All Critiques of Reason Irrational?' *Contemporary Philosophy* 20, nos. 1 and 2 (Jan./Feb. and March/April 1998): 19–30. But perhaps the most informative and well-balanced discussion of the Franco-German debate can be found in David Couzens Hoy and Thomas McCarthy, *Critical Theory* (Cambridge, Mass.: Blackwell, 1994); see also D. Janicaud, 'Rationality, Force and Power: Foucault and Habermas' Criticism,' in T. Armstrong, ed., *Michel Foucault: Philosopher* (New York: Routledge, Chapman and Hall Inc., 1992); and James Schmidt, 'Habermas and Foucault' in M. Passerin d'Entrèves and S. Benhabib, eds, *Habermas and the Unfinished Project of Modernity* (Cambridge: MIT Press, 1997).

45 See Habermas, 'Taking Aim at the Heart of the Present,' in D.C. Hoy, ed. *Foucault: A Critical Reader* (Cambridge, Mass.: Basil Blackwell, 1986), 103–8.

46 Michel Foucault, 'Foucault,' in J.D. Faubion and P. Rabinow, eds, *Michel*

Foucault: Aesthetics, Method, and Epistemology, vol. 2 (New York: New Press, 1999), 459.

47 Foucault's original plan to write the history of sexuality included six volumes, but by the time of his death he had penned only three volumes: *History of Sexuality* (New York: Vintage Books, 1980); *History of Sexuality: The Care of the Self* (New York: Vintage Books, 1988); and *History of Sexuality: The Use of Pleasure* (New York: Vintage Books, 1990).

48 See Habermas, *PDM,* 283–4; and Nancy Fraser, 'Foucault on Modern Power: Empirical Insight and Normative Confusion,' in *Unruly Practices,* 29.

49 McCarthy, 'Liberal Theory and Racial Injustice,' 15.

50 M. Foucault, *Foucault Reader,* ed. P. Rabinow (New York: Pantheon Books, 1984), 50.

51 Ibid., 49.

52 I owe this distinction between 'power' and 'Power' to Michael Hardt's foreword to Antonio Negri, *The Savage Anomaly: The Power of Spinoza's Metaphysics and Politics* (Minneapolis: University of Minnesota Press, 1991), xi–xvi.

53 On this suspicion he writes: '[O]ne runs the risk of falling back on the idea that there exists a human nature or a base that, as a consequence of certain historical, economic, and social processes, has been concealed, alienated, or imprisoned in and by mechanisms of repression. According to this hypothesis, all that is required is to break these repressive deadlocks and man will be reconciled with himself, rediscover his nature or regain contact with his origin, and reestablish a full and positive relationship with himself.' *Michel Foucault,* vol. 1, 282.

54 M. Foucault, 'The Ethics of the Concern for Self as a Practice of Freedom,' in P. Rabinow, ed., *Michel Foucault: Ethics, Subjectivity and Truth,* vol. 1 (New York: New Press, 1994), 284.

55 Ibid.

56 Indeed, as I already pointed out in note 66 of the last chapter, he uses some Foucauldean vocabulary, such as 'normalizing effects,' 'power relations,' and 'genealogical analysis'; and he describes his new model of power with an image most akin to Foucault's model: '[Power] emerges in its purest form in those moments when revolutionaries seize the power scattered through the streets; when a population committed to passive resistance opposes foreign tanks with their bare hands; when convinced minorities dispute the legitimacy of existing laws and engage in civil disobedience; when the sheer 'joy of action' breaks through in protest movements' (*BFN,* 148).

57 Foucault believes that there is a commonality between the juridical, or what he calls the liberal, conception of political power and the Marxist view of power, namely, 'an economism in the theory of power.' These theories view power as a concrete right that can be possessed or as an economic functionality that maintains the relations of production. See M. Foucault, *Power/Knowledge*, ed. Colin Gordon (New York: Pantheon Books, 1980; hereafter referred to as *PK*), 88.

58 *PK*, 122.

59 *PK*, 90.

60 *PK*, 92–3.

61 *PK*, 93.

62 M. Foucault, *Michel Foucault*, 1: 296.

63 Foucault interview with François Ewald, 'Le souci de la vérité,' *Magazine Littéraire*, no. 207 (1984): 18. For an informative debate on Foucault's view of truth see the exchange between Charles Taylor and William Connolly – Taylor, 'Foucault on Freedom and Truth' and Connolly, 'Taylor, Foucault, and Truth' – in *Political Theory* 12 (May 1984): 152–83 and 365–76, respectively; and C. Taylor, 'Connolly, Foucault, and Truth,' *Political Theory* 13 (August 1985): 377–85.

64 Ewald interview, 23.

65 *PK*, 94.

66 *PK*, 96.

67 Ibid.

68 Ibid.

69 Ibid.

70 *PK*, 97.

71 *PK*, 106.

72 Orville Lee, 'Culture and Democratic Theory: Toward a Theory of Symbolic Democracy,' *Constellations* 5, no. 4 (1998): 433.

73 M. Foucault, 'The Subject and Power,' in H.L. Dreyfus and P. Rabinow, eds, *Michel Foucault: Beyond Structuralism and Hermeneutics* (Chicago: University of Chicago Press, 1982), 212.

74 Lee, 'Culture and Democratic Theory,' 441.

75 Axel Honneth, 'The Social Dynamics of Disrespect: Situating Critical Theory Today,' in Dews, ed., *Habermas: A Critical Reader*, 321–37.

76 See L. Nicholson, ed., *Feminism/Postmodernism* (New York: Routledge, 1990) for a picture of the mutually informing relations between postmodernism and feminism. For example, Judith Butler's prolific appropriation of Foucault and Deleuze, in 'Gender Trouble, Feminist Theory and Psychoanalytic Discourse,' enables her to argue for a concept of subject as

the gendered body that is radically performative. Such a body is constantly inventing and reinventing its identity by engaging in discourse/ practices of society, gaining a fluid and fragmented character, as opposed to the fixed and unified character of the modern subject. See also J. Meehan, ed., *Feminists Read Habermas* (New York: Routledge, 1995); Jane Flax, *Disputed Subject* (New York: Routledge, 1993); Patricia Waugh, ed., *Postmodernism: A Reader* (London: Edward Arnold, 1992); S. Benhabib and D. Cornell, eds, *Feminism as Critique* (Minneapolis: University of Minnesota Press, 1987); Iana Sawicki, *Disciplining Foucault: Feminism, Power, and the Body* (New York: Routledge Press, 1991); and Jana Sawicki, *Feminism and Foucault: Reflections on Resistance*, ed. I. Diamond and L. Quinby (Boston: Northeastern University Press, 1988).

77 Lee, 'Cultural and Democratic Theory,' 434 (see note 72).

78 In relation to the felicitous convergence of direction of my argument with McCarthy's and Lee's papers, I would like to mention that I learned about their works when I was in the late stage of finishing my doctoral thesis (October–November 1999). So, while I welcome the weight they add to my argument, they did not have any formative influence on my thinking.

   With respect to this synthesizing approach, it is also worth noting that James Bohman too, appropriating Ian Hacking's work on Foucault's archaeology, sees the Foucauldean insight as capable of enriching Habermas's critical theory ('Two Versions of the Linguistics Turn: Habermas and Poststructuralism,' in Benhabib and Passerin d'Entrèves, eds, *Habermas and the Unfinished Project of Modernity*). Bohman believes that once Foucault's analysis is cleansed of its unnecessary anti-hermeneutic elements, it can be used to supplement Habermas's account of meaning and validity. Unlike Habermas's view on truth, which makes a strong connection between meaning and validity, Foucault's archaeology allows for indirectly connecting the revealing light of discursive formation with truth via 'cultural possibilities for making true-or-false statements' (p. 211). Bohman continues: '[B]y identifying this revised version of disclosure within discursive formations or styles of reasoning, Habermas can better account for the plurality of cultural worlds that his own hermeneutic perspective demands. In these cases, a less restrictive notion of disclosure enriches Habermas's own theory of meaning and interpretive methodology' (215).

79 Habermas, 'Modernity versus Postmodernity,' *New German Critique* 22 (Winter 1981): 13.

80 *PDM*, 161–210. For a variation on this critique of postmodernism see also Nancy Fraser, 'The French Derrideans: Politicizing Deconstruction or Deconstructing the Political,' in *Unruly Practices*, 69–92; Seyla Benhabib,

'Democracy and Difference: Reflections on the Metapolitics of Lyotard and Derrida,' *Journal of Political Philosophy* 2, no. 1 (1994): 1–23; and McCarthy, 'The Politics of the Ineffable,' 146–68.

81 Habermas, *PDM*, 210.

82 Stephen White, *Political Theory and Postmodernism* (Cambridge: Cambridge University Press, 1991), 14.

83 For an illuminating discussion of such critical resistance towards constructing a theoretical system see David Couzens Hoy, 'Conflicting Conception of Critique: Foucault versus Habermas,' in Hoy and McCarthy, *Critical Theory*, 144–71.

84 McCarthy, 'The Politics of the Ineffable,' 153.

85 Ibid.

86 Jacques Derrida, 'Force of Law: The Mystical Foundation of Authority,' in D. Cornell, M. Rosenfeld, and D.G. Carlson, eds, *Deconstruction and the Possibility of Justice* (New York: Routledge, 1992; hereafter referred to as 'FL'), 4.

87 'FL,' 6.

88 Ibid.

89 Ibid.

90 J. Derrida, 'Declaration of Independence,' *New Political Science*, Summer 1986: 7–15 (hereafter referred to as 'DI').

91 'DI,' 8.

92 Ibid.

93 'DI,' 9.

94 Ibid.

95 Benhabib, 'Democracy and Difference,' 15. However, Benhabib is very critical of Derrida's treatment of the declaration as indicative of an arbitrary and decisionist politics that does not have anything to offer to the political theory of democracy.

96 'DI,' 10.

97 Ibid.

98 'FL,' 16.

99 Ibid.

100 As Axel Honneth has shown in *Struggle for Recognition* (Cambridge: Polity Press, 1995), recognition of individuals as subjects of legal rights by itself is not enough for the purpose of subjects' self-constitution as moral agents. They also need to see that their contribution to society is acknowledged for its worth so that they are able to value and respect themselves as free and equal citizens. It is this reciprocal sense of recognition, then, that allows for social solidarity.

101 Michel Foucault, *Language, Counter-memory, Practice*, ed. D.F. Bouchard (Ithaca: Cornell University Press, 1977), 151.

102 McCarthy, 'The Politics of the Ineffable,' 155.

103 M. Foucault, 'Questions of Method,' in G. Burchell, C. Gordon, and P. Miller, eds, *The Foucault Effect* (Chicago: University of Chicago Press, 1991), 84; emphasis added.

104 See Derrida, 'FL'; *Politics of Friendship*, trans. George Collins (London: Verso, 1997); 'Remarks on Deconstruction and Pragmatism,' in C. Mouffe, ed., *Deconstruction and Pragmatism* (London: Routledge, 1996); and 'DI.'

105 Benhabib, 'Democracy and Difference,' 3.

106 In his 'Derrida and Habermas on ... Identity and Difference: Toward Radical Democratic Multiculturalism' (*Constellations* 1, no. 3 [1995]), Martin Matuštík argues along the same line when he writes that 'Derrida does not give up the Enlightenment project of human rights and deliberative democracy but intensifies their promise, first, in his "hope, fear, trembling" that the spell of a dominant center could be resisted and, second, in his critique of techno-capital' (387).

107 See Derrida, 'White Mythologies,' in *Margins of Philosophy*, trans. A. Bass (Chicago: University of Chicago Press, 1982).

108 'FL,' 27.

109 *Politics of Friendship*, 306.

110 Derrida presented a first sketch to the American Philosophical Association symposium on Law and Society on 30 December 1988, which was published in the *Journal of Philosophy* (see note 111). Later he developed this project into a book, *Politics of Friendship* (see note 104).

111 Derrida, 'The Politics of Friendship' [hereafter 'PF'], *Journal of Philosophy* 11 (November 1988): 635.

112 'PF,' 635–6.

113 'PF,' 638.

114 'PF,' 640.

115 'PF,' 641–2.

116 T. McCarthy, 'On the Margins of Politics,' *Journal of Philosophy* 11 (November 1988): 645.

117 Ibid., 648.

118 See above, chapter 2, sections 1, 2(b), and 3(c); and chapter 3, section 3.

119 See p. 111, above.

120 A. Wellmer, 'Zurkritik der Diskursethik,' in *Ethik und Dialog* (Frankfurt: Suhrkamp, 1986), 93.

121 J. Derrida, quoted in McCarthy, 'The Politics of the Ineffable,' 161.

122 Chantal Mouffe, 'Deconstruction, Pragmatism, and Democracy,' in C. Mouffe, ed., *Deconstruction and Democracy* (London: Routledge, 1996), 8.

7: Constitutional Patriotism and the Problems of Diversity and Solidarity

1 M. Ignatieff, *The Needs of Strangers* (New York: Penguin Books, 1986, 139–40).
2 R. Merkel, 'The Insanity of the Nation,' *Die Zeit*, 9 May 1990: 52; quoted in J. Habermas,' 'A Unified Nation of Angry DM-Burghers,' in H. James and M. Stone, eds, *When the Wall Came Down* (New York: Routledge, 1992), 99.
3 *Inclusion of the Other* (Cambridge: MIT Press, 1998; hereafter referred to as *IO*), 42, 40.
4 *IO*, 225.
5 In one of his earlier discussions of the topic, Habermas attributes the original use of the phrase 'constitutional patriotism' to Dolf Sternberger (Habermas, *New Conservatism: Cultural Criticism and the Historians Debate* [Cambridge: MIT Press, 1992], 193). Despite this origin Habermas has made the term his own by giving it a prominent role within his architectonic. The most extensive treatment of the topic appears in *IO*.
6 *IO*, 249.
7 *IO*, 257.
8 *IO*, 448–9.
9 *IO*, 225.
10 J. Habermas, *A Berlin Republic: Writings on Germany*, trans. Steven Rendall (Lincoln: University of Nebraska Press, 1997), 76.
11 *IO*, 118.
12 Ibid.
13 See Bernard Yack, 'The Myth of the Civic Nation,' *Critical Review* 10, no. 2 (Spring 1996): 193–211; and Thomas Mertens, 'Cosmopolitanism and Citizenship: Kant against Habermas,' *European Journal of Philosophy* 4, no. 3 (December 1996): 328–47; also W. Böckenförd, 'Die Nation,' *Frankfurter Allgemeine Zeitung*, 30 Sept. 1995; and Roger Scruton, 'In Defense of Nation,' in J.C.D. Clark, ed., *Ideas and Politics in Modern Britain* (London: Macmillan, 1990).
14 Yael Tamir, *Liberal Nationalism* (Princeton: Princeton University Press, 1993).
15 David Miller, *On Nationality* (Oxford: Oxford University Press, 1995).
16 Margaret Canovan, *Nationhood and Political Theory* (Cheltenham: Edward Elgar, 1996).
17 Ibid., 72.
18 M. Canovan, 'Patriotism Is Not Enough,' *British Journal of Political Science* 30, pt. 3 (July 2000): 413–32 (hereafter referred to as 'PE').
19 It is curious that Canovan frames her discussion in terms of an opposition between nationalism and constitutional patriotism, for it is one thing to argue that constitutional patriotism does not provide the necessary politi-

cal bond among members of a community, and quite another to argue that nationalism does so in a normatively desirable way. While constitutional patriotism may not be 'enough,' nationalism has repeatedly proved to be much more than 'enough.' Indeed, at the end of her article Canovan states that her criticism of new patriotism should not be taken as an endorsement of nationalism ('PE,' 431 note 76).

20 J. Habermas, 'Citizenship and National Identity,' in *BFN*, 500; Attracta Ingram, 'Constitutional Patriotism,' *Philosophy of Social Criticism* 22, no. 6 (1996): 2.

21 'PE,' 419.

22 *IO*, 225.

23 *IO*, 221.

24 Immanuel Kant, *The Metaphysics of Morals* (New York: Cambridge University Press, 1991), § 43, p. 123.

25 Ibid.

26 'PE,' 419.

27 'PE,' 422.

28 Kant, *Metaphysics of Morals*, § 47, p. 127.

29 Thomas McCarthy, in a cogent article entitled 'On Reconciling Cosmopolitan Unity and National Diversity' (*Public Culture* 11, no. 1 [1999]), explores this Kantian root and proposes ways in which Kantian cosmopolitanism needs to be altered in order to be of service to the problem of diversity.

30 *IO*, 156, 159.

31 *IO*, 118.

32 *IO*, 131.

33 'PE,' 423.

34 *IO*, 159.

35 'PE,' 424.

36 Against the criterion of 'birth and blood' one can argue that postwar Germany took a special path toward constitutional democracy, a move that resulted from the realization, made possible by defeat and the Basic Law of 1949, that the earlier mode of belonging, the *Volksgemeinschaft*, had proved itself undesirable. For accounts of the German political culture see D.P. Conradt, 'Changing German Political Culture,' in G.D. Almond and S. Verba, eds, *The Civic Culture Revisited* (Boston: Little, Brown, 1980), 212–72.

37 For a study of the question of identity in Switzerland, see J. Steinberg, *Why Switzerland?* (Cambridge: Cambridge University Press, 1996).

38 See J. Fitzmaurice, *The Politics of Belgium: A Unique Federalism* (London: Hurst & Co., 1996).

39 'PE,' 424–6; emphasis added. In the remaining part of the paper, Canovan criticizes what she calls 'rooted republicanism,' found in Maurizio Viroli's *For Love of Country: An Essay on Patriotism and Nationalism* (Oxford: Clarendon Press, 1995), as falling short of its goal of patriotism based on a critical love of country.

40 I recognize that one might argue that there is a strong racial component in the actual functioning of Swiss and American political institutions, even if this is not explicit in the legal texts (see the cantonal referenda on accepting new citizens into Switzerland). It is, for example, extremely difficult to acquire Swiss citizenship and regional chauvinisms are strong in that country. As for the U.S., one might argue that the subjugation of African and native Americans still constitutes the substratum of much of American identity, while the ideology of the melting pot is closely related to the country's *linguistic* identity (see the adamant refusal of bilingualism by many Americans in the face of the huge growth in the Hispanic population).

41 Speech by Abraham Lincoln on 10 July 1858, quoted in Viroli, *For Love of Country*, 180.

42 Canada admits 1 per cent of its population in new immigrants every year. Such immigration policy bestows a very transient and diverse character on the idea of Canadian identity.

43 A. Ingram, 'Constitutional Patriotism,' 2.

44 Ibid.

45 Martha Nussbaum, *For Love of Country: Debating the Limits of Patriotism* (Boston: Beacon Press, 1996).

46 In his *On Nationality* (see note 15), David Miller comes close to advocating such a position.

47 Walker Connor, 'Nation Building or Nation Destroying?' *World Politics* 24 (1972): 319–55.

48 W. Kymlicka and C. Straehle, 'Cosmopolitanism, Nation-State, and Minority Nationalism: A Critical Review of the Recent Literature,' *European Journal of Philosophy* 1, no. 1 (1999): 78.

49 C. Taylor, 'Cross-Purposes: The Liberal-Communitarian Debate,' in *Philosophical Arguments* (Cambridge: Harvard University Press, 1995).

50 This clarification allows Taylor to show a richer range of positions on the spectrum of the liberal-communitarian debate, which sees not only 'atomist individualists like Nozick and holist collectivists like Marx, but also holist individualists like Humboldt and atomist collectivists like B.F. Skinner.' 'Cross-purposes,' 185.

51 Ibid., 189.

52 Ibid., 191.
53 C. Taylor, 'Why Do Nations Have to Become States?' in G. Laforest, ed., *Reconciling the Solitudes: Essays on Canadian Federalism and Nationalism* (Montreal: McGill University Press, 1993), 45.
54 M. Ignatieff, *The Needs of Strangers*, 138.
55 For a insightful and critical reading of Taylor's paper see Kenneth Baynes, 'Communitarian and Cosmopolitan Challenges to Kant's Conception of World Peace,' in J. Bohman and M. Lutz-Bachmann, eds, *Perpetual Peace: Essays on Kant's Cosmopolitan Ideal* (Cambridge: MIT Press, 1997), 219–34.
56 M. Viroli, *For Love of Country*, 14.
57 M. Viroli, 'On Civic Republicanism: Reply to Xenos and Yack,' *Critical Review* 12, nos. 1–2 (Winter/Spring 1998): 190.
58 Ibid., 189–90.
59 See *Who Is This We?* ed. E.M. Godway and G. Finn (Montreal: Black Rose Books, 1994); Gayatri Spivak, *The Post-Colonial Critic*, ed. S. Harasym (New York: Routledge, 1990); Iris Marion Young, 'The Ideal of Community and the Politics of Difference,' in L.J. Nicholson, ed., *Feminism/Postmodernism* (New York: Routledge, 1990); Maurice Blanchot, *La communauté inavouable* (Paris: Minuit, 1983), Eng. trans. P. Joris, *The Unavowable Community* (Barrytown, NY: Station Hill Press, 1988); and Giorgio Agamben, *The Coming Community*, trans. M. Hardt (Minneapolis: University of Minnesota Press, 1993).
60 Habermas, *New Conservatism* (Cambridge: MIT Press, 1989), 193.
61 B. Yack, 'Myth of the Civic Nation,' 196. He is sympathetic to the ideal of constitutional patriotism, but is sceptical about a series of contrasts – i.e., Western/Eastern, rational/emotive, voluntary/inherited, and good/bad – that the civic/ethnic dichotomy parallels.
62 To see views opposite to the claim that the transition of East Germany from communism to liberal democracy could have taken the shape of a confederation based on liberal principles of human rights and democracy, as opposed to unification based on shared nationality, see James and Stone, eds, *When the Wall Came Down* and R.T. Gray and S. Wilke, eds, *German Unification and Its Discontent* (Seattle: University of Washington Press, 1996).
63 Yack, 'Myth of the Civic Nation,' 209. I would like to point out that the cultural inheritance itself was partly forged by the nation-state in its ongoing self-constitution and consolidation. In France, this meant suppressing non-French linguistic and ethnic groups (e.g., the Bretons under the Revolution and Napoleon 1st) and building national monuments and symbols (through most of downtown Paris!). In the U.S., similarly, Aboriginal peoples were exterminated, while the founding myths of the

American Revolution were created and built up, as were the monuments, in Washington, DC, and elsewhere.

64 H. Putnam, 'Why Reason Cannot Be Naturalized,' in *Realism and Reason: Philosophical Papers*, vol. 3 (Cambridge: Cambridge University Press, 1983), 234.

65 Ibid.

66 Ibid.

67 *IO*, 132.

68 T. McCarthy, 'On Reconciling Cosmopolitan Unity and National Diversity,' 195.

69 For a detailed account of developmental psychology and moral identities see Habermas, *TCA* 2, 175 and *MCCA*, 122–4; T. McCarthy, *Critical Theory of Habermas*, 344–5; and Lawrence Kohlberg, *Essays on Moral Development*, vols. 1, 2 (New York: Harper & Row, 1981, 1984).

70 Jan-Werner Müller, *Prospect*, March 2001, at http://www.prospect-magazine.co.uk/highlights/portrait_muller_mar01/index.html.

71 See Habermas, 'Kant's Idea of Perpetual Peace: At Two Hundred Years' Historical Remove,' in *IO*, 165–202, where he defends the idea of cosmopolitan democracy on the basis of appropriating, and differentiating between, law and morality in the concept of human rights.

72 Immanuel Kant, 'Perpetual Peace,' in H. Reiss, ed., *Kant's Political Writing* (Cambridge: Cambridge University Press, 1970), 102.

73 Baynes, 'Communitarian and Cosmopolitan Challenges to Kant's Conception of World Peace,' 219.

74 Michael Ignatieff, 'Identity Parades,' *Prospects*, April 1998, at http://www.prospect-magazine.co.uk/highlights/identity_parades/index.html.

75 Habermas, 'Reply to Symposium Participants, Benjamin N. Cardozo School of Law,' in M. Rosenfeld and A. Arato, eds, *Habermas on Law and Democracy* (Los Angeles: University of California Press, 1998), 399.

76 *IO*, 161.

77 Patchen Markell, 'Making Affect Safe for Democracy? On Constitutional Patriotism,' *Political Theory* 28, no. 1 (2000) 54. I find his argument that Habermas's constitutional patriotism should not be understood as what 'renders affect safe for liberal democracies by redirecting our attachment and sentiment from one subset of objects (the "ethnic") to another subset of objects (the "civic")' attractive. He argues that there are notable elements in Habermas's work that resist what he calls the 'strategy of redirection.'

78 'PF,' 295.

79 M. Ignatieff, *The Needs of Strangers*, 141.

80 T.S. Elliot, 'East Coker,' from *Four Quartets* (London: Faber, 1944), 31.
81 Ignatieff, *The Needs of Strangers*, 141.
82 S. Rushdie, 'In Good Faith,' in *Imaginary Homelands* (London: Granta Books, 1981), 394.

Bibliography

Adorno, Theodor. *Minima Moralia: Reflections from Damaged Life.* Trans. E.F.N. Jephcott. London: NLB, 1974.
- *Negative Dialectic.* Trans. E.B. Ashton. New York: Seabury Press, 1973.
Adorno, Theodor, and Max Horkheimer. *Dialectic of Enlightenment.* Trans. John Cumming. New York: Continuum Publishing Co., 1987.
Agamben, Giorgio. *The Coming Community.* Trans. Michael Hardt. Minneapolis: University of Minnesota Press, 1993.
Almond, G.D., and S. Verba, eds. *Civic Culture Revisited.* Boston: Little, Brown, 1980.
Alway, Joan. *Critical Theory and Political Possibilities.* Westpoint, Conn.: Greenwood Press, 1995.
Apel, Karl-Otto. *Towards a Transformation of Philosophy.* London: Routledge and Kegan Paul, 1980.
Arato, Andrew. 'Constitution and Continuity in the East European Transitions.' *Constellations* 1, no. 1 (1994): 92–112.
- 'Slouching toward Philadelphia?' *Constellations* 3, no. 2 (1996): 225–47.
Arato, Andrew, and Jean Cohen. *Civil Society and Social Theory.* Cambridge: MIT Press, 1991.
Arendt, Hannah. *The Human Condition.* Chicago: University of Chicago Press, 1958.
- *Lectures on Kant's Political Philosophy.* Ed. Ronald Beiner. Chicago: University of Chicago Press, 1982.
Armstrong, Timothy. *Michel Foucault: Philosopher.* New York: Routledge, 1992.
Austin, J.L. *How to Do Things with Words.* Cambridge: Harvard University Press, 1979.
Bader, Veit. 'Citizenship and Exclusion: Radical Democracy, Community, and Justice. Or, What Is Wrong with Communitarianism?' *Political Theory* 23, no. 2 (1995): 211–46.

Bailey, Leon. *Critical Theory and the Sociology of Knowledge*. New York: Peter Lang, 1994.

Balibar, Etienne. 'Is European Citizenship Possible?' *Public Culture* (1996): 355–76.

Barry, Brian. 'John Rawls and the Search for Stability.' *Ethics* 105, no. 3 (1995): 874–915.

Baynes, Kenneth. *The Normative Grounds of Social Criticism*. Albany: State University of New York Press, 1992.

Baynes, Kenneth, James Bohman, and Thomas McCarthy, eds. *After Philosophy: End or Transformation?* Cambridge: MIT Press, 1993.

Beiner, Ronald. *What's the Matter with Liberalism?* Berkeley, Los Angeles: University of California Press, 1992.

– *Philosophy in a Time of Lost Spirit: Essays on Contemporary Theory*. Toronto: University of Toronto Press, 1997.

Bellamy, Richard, and Alex Warleigh. 'From an Ethics of Integration to an Ethics of Participation: Citizenship and the Future of the European Union.' *Millennium* 27, no. 3 (1998): 447–68.

Benhabib, Seyla. 'Modernity and Aporias of Critical Theory.' *Telos*, no. 49 (Fall 1981): 38–60.

– 'Epistemologies of Postmodernism: A Rejoinder to Jean-François Lyotard.' *New German Critique* 33 (Fall 1984): 103–26.

– *Critique, Norm, and Utopia: A Study of the Foundations of Critical Theory*. New York: Columbia University Press, 1986.

– *Situating the Self: Gender, Community, and Postmodernism in Contemporary Ethics*. New York: Routledge, 1992

– 'Deliberative Rationality and Models of Democratic Legitimacy.' *Constellations* 1, no. 1 (1994): 26–52.

– 'Democracy and Difference: Reflections on the Metapolitics of Lyotard and Derrida.' *The Journal of Political Philosophy* 2, no. 1 (1994): 1–23.

– 'The Local, the Contextual and/or Critical.' *Constellations* 3, no. 1 (1996): 83–94.

– A Book review of Habermas's *Between Facts and Norms* in *American Political Science Review* 91, no. 3 (Spring 1997): 725–6.

– 'The Embattled Public Sphere: Hannah Arendt, Jürgen Habermas and Beyond.' *Theoria*, December 1997: 24.

– 'Citizens, Residents, and Aliens in a Changing World of Political Membership in the Global Era.' Unpublished manuscript, presented to the colloquium series at the School of Criticism and Theory, Cornell University, 1999.

Benhabib, Seyla, ed. *Democracy and Difference*. Princeton, NJ: Princeton University Press, 1996.

Benhabib, Seyla, and Fred Dallmayr, eds. *The Communicative Ethics Controversy.* Cambridge: MIT Press, 1990.

Bernard-Henry, Levy. 'Power and Sex: An Interview with Michel Foucault.' *Telos*, no. 32 (1977).

Bernauer, James. *Michel Foucault: Force of Flight.* New Jersey: Humanities Press, 1990.

Bernstein, J.M. *Recovering Ethical Life.* New York: Routledge, 1995.

Bernstein, Richard. *The Restructuring of Social and Political Theory.* University of Pennsylvania Press, 1976.

– 'Serious Play: The Ethical-Political Horizon of Jacques Derrida.' *Journal of Speculative Philosophy* 1, no. 2 (1987): 93–115.

– *The New Constellation.* Cambridge: MIT Press, 1991.

Bertilsson, Margareta. Book review of Habermas's *Faktizität und Geltung* in *Contemporary Sociology* 23 (January 1994): 156–9.

Böckenförd, W. 'Die Nation.' *FrankfurterAllgemeine Zeitung*, 30 September 1995.

Bohman, James. 'Emancipation and Rhetoric: The Perlocutions and Illocutions of the Social Critic.' *Philosophy and Rhetoric* 21, no. 3 (1988): 185–204.

– 'Complexity, Pluralism, and the Constitutional State: On Habermas' *Faktizität und Geltung.*' *Law and Society Review* 28, no. 4 (1994): 897–929.

– 'Citizenship and Norms of Publicity: Wide Public Reason in Cosmopolitan Societies.' *Political Theory* 27, no. 2 (April 1999): 176–202.

– *Public Deliberation: Pluralism, Complexity, and Democracy.* Cambridge: MIT Press, 1996.

Bohman, James, and Matthias Lutz-Bachmann, eds. *Perpetual Peace: Essays on Kant's Cosmopolitan Ideal.* Cambridge: MIT Press, 1997.

Bohman, James, and William Rehg, eds. *Deliberative Democracy: Essays on Reason and Politics.* Cambridge: MIT Press, 1997.

Booth, James. 'Communities of Memory: On Identity, Memory, and Debt.' *American Political Science Review* 93, no. 2 (June 1999): 249–63.

Braaten, Jane. *Habermas' Critical Theory of Society.* Albany: State University of New York Press, 1991.

Bronner, Stephen Eric, and Douglas Kellner, eds. *Critical Theory and Society: A Reader.* New York: Routledge, 1989.

Brown, Wendy. 'Democracy's Lack.' *Public Culture* 10, no. 2 (1998): 425–9.

Calhoun, Craig, ed. *Habermas and the Public Sphere.* Cambridge: MIT Press, 1992.

Canovan, Margret. *Nationhood and Political Theory.* Cheltenham: Edward Elgar, 1996.

– 'Patriotism Is Not Enough.' *British Journal of Political Science* 30, pt. 3 (July 2000): 413–32.

Carens, Joseph, ed. *Is Quebec Nationalism Just? Perspective from Anglophone Canada.* Montreal and Kingston: McGill-Queen's University Press, 1995.

Chambers, Simone. *Reasonable Democracy: Jürgen Habermas and the Politics of Discourse.* Ithaca: Cornell University Press, 1996.

– 'Critical Theory and Civil Society.' Forthcoming in W. Kymlicka and S. Chambers, eds, *Alternative Perspectives on Civil Society.* Princeton: Princeton University Press.

Christiano, Thomas. 'Freedom, Consensus, and Equality in Collective Decision Making.' *Ethics* 101 (October 1990): 151–81.

Cohen, Jean. 'Why More Political Theory?' *Telos,* no. 40 (1979): 70–94.

Cohen, Jean, and Andrew Arato. *Civil Society and Political Theory.* Cambridge: MIT Press, 1992.

Cohen, L.J. 'Do Illocutionary Forces Exist?' *Philosophical Quarterly* 14 (1964): 118–37.

Connolly, William. 'Taylor, Foucault, and Truth.' *Political Theory* 12 (May 1984): 365–76.

Connor, Walker. 'Nation Building or Nation Destroying?' *World Politics* 24 (1972): 319–55.

Cooke, Maeve. 'Authenticity and Autonomy.' *Political Theory* 25, no. 2 (1997): 258–88.

Couture, Jocelyne, Kai Nielsen, and Michel Seymour, eds. *Rethinking Nationalism.* Calgary: University of Calgary Press, 1998.

Critchley, Simon. *Ethics, Politics, Subjectivity: Essays on Derrida, Levinas and Contemporary French Thought.* London: Verso, 1999.

Critchley, Simon, and Peter Dews, eds. *Deconstructive Subjectivities.* Albany: State University of New York Press, 1996.

Critchley, Simon, and Axel Honneth. 'Philosophy in Germany: An Interview.' *Radical Philosophy,* no. 89 (May 1998): 27–39.

Culler, Jonathan. 'Convention and Meaning: Derrida and Austin.' *New Literary History,* 1981: 15–30.

– *On Deconstruction: Theory and Criticism after Structuralism.* Ithaca: Cornell University Press, 1982.

– 'Communicative Competence and Normative Force.' *New German Critique* 35 (Spring/Summer 1985): 133–45.

Dallmayr, Fred. *Twilight of Subjectivity: Contributions to a Post-individualist Theory of Politics.* Amherst: University of Massachusetts Press, 1981.

– *Polis and Praxis.* Cambridge: MIT Press, 1984.

– 'Democracy and Postmodernism.' *Human Studies* 10, no. 1 (1986): 144–67.

Daniels, Norman, ed. *Reading Rawls: Critical Studies of a Theory of Justice.* New York: Basic Books, 1975.

Darwall, Stephen, ed. *Equal Freedom*. Chicago: University of Chicago Press, 1995.

Deflem, Mathieu. *Habermas, Modernity, and Law*. London: Sage Publications, 1996.

Deleuze, Gilles. *Foucault*. Minneapolis: University of Minnesota Press, 1988.

– *Logic of Sense*. New York: Columbia University Press, 1990.

– *Nietzsche and Philosophy*. London: Athlone Books, 1992.

– *Essays Critical and Clinical*. Trans. Daniel Smith and Michael Greco. Minneapolis: University of Minnesota Press, 1997.

Derrida, Jacques. *Speech and Phenomena, and Other Essays on Husserl's Theory of Signs*. Trans. David Allison. Evanston: Northwestern University Press, 1973.

– *Of Grammatology*. Trans. Gayatri Chakravorty Spivak. Baltimore: Johns Hopkins University Press, 1974.

– 'Limited Inc. abc.' *Glyph* 2 (1977): 162–254.

– *Writing and Difference*. Trans. Alan Bass. London: Routledge and Kegan Paul, 1978.

– *Margins of Philosophy*. Trans. Alan Bass. Chicago: University of Chicago Press, 1982.

– 'The Principle of Reason: The University in the Eyes of Its Pupils.' *Diacritics*. 19 (1983): 3–20.

– 'Of an Apocalyptic Tone Recently Adopted in Philosophy.' Trans. John P. Leavey. *Oxford Law Review* 6, no. 2 (1984): 3–37.

– 'Declaration of Independence.' *New Political Science*, Summer 1986: 7–15.

– *The Post Card: From Socrates to Freud and Beyond*. Trans. Alan Bass. Chicago: University of Chicago Press, 1987.

– 'The Politics of Friendship.' *Journal of Philosophy* 11 (November 1988): 632–44.

– 'Force of Law: The Mystical Foundation of Authority.' In D. Cornell, M. Rosenfeld, and D.G. Carlson, eds, *Deconstruction and the Possibility of Justice*. New York: Routledge, 1992.

– *Specters of Marx*. Trans. Peggy Lamuf. New York: Routledge, 1994.

– *Politics of Friendship*. Trans. George Collins. London: Verso, 1997.

Dews, Peter, *Logic of Disintegration: Poststructuralist Thought and the Claims of Critical Theory*. London: Verso, 1987.

– *The Limits of Disenchantment: Essays on Contemporary European Philosophy*. London: Verso, 1995.

Dews, Peter. ed. *Habermas: A Critical Reader*. Oxford: Blackwell, 1999.

Dreyfus, Hurbert L., and Paul Rabinow. *Michel Foucault: Beyond Structuralism and Hermeneutics*. Chicago: University of Chicago Press, 1982.

Dworkin, Ronald. *Taking Rights Seriously*. Cambridge: Harvard University Press, 1978.

– *Law's Empire*. Cambridge: Harvard University Press, 1986.
– 'Liberal Community.' *California Law Review* 77, no. 3 (1989): 479–504.
Estlund, David. 'Who Is Afraid of Deliberative Democracy? On the Strategic/ Deliberative Dichotomy in Recent Constitutional Jurisprudence.' *Texas Law Review* 71 (1993): 1437–77.
Ewald, François. 'Michel Foucault: Le souci de la vérité.' *Magazine Littéraire*, no. 207 (1984): 16–23.
Famia, Joseph. 'Complexity and Deliberative Democracy.' *Inquiry* 39 (1996): 357–97.
Feder, Kittay, and Diana Meyers, eds. *Women and Moral Theory*. Totowa, NJ: Rowman and Littlefield, 1987.
Ferry, Luc, and Alain Renaut. *French Philosophy of the Sixties: An Essay on Anti-humanism*. Amherst: University of Massachusetts Press, 1990.
– *From the Rights of Man to the Republican Idea*. Trans. Franklin Philip. Chicago: University of Chicago Press, 1992.
Fichte, Johann Gottlieb. *Science of Knowledge*. Trans. P. Heath and J. Lachs. Philadelphia: Meredith Corporation, 1970.
– *Critique of All Revelation*. Trans. Garrett Green. Cambridge: Cambridge University Press, 1978.
Forester, John, ed. *Critical Theory and Public Life*. Cambridge: MIT Press, 1988.
Forst, Rainer. 'Justice, Reason, and Critique: Basic Concepts of Critical Theory.' Paper presented at the University of Ottawa, Fall 1995.
Foucault, Michel. *The Archaeology of Knowledge*. New York: Routledge, 1972.
– *The Order of Things*. Ed. R.D. Laing. New York: Vintage Books, 1973.
– *Madness and Civilization*. New York: Vintage Books, 1973.
– 'Michel Foucault on Attica: An Interview.' *Telos* no. 19 (Spring 1974): 154–61.
– 'Human Nature: Justice versus Power.' In Fons Elders, ed., *Reflexive Water: The Basic Concerns of Mankind*. London: Souvenir Press, 1974.
– *Language, Counter-memory, Practice*. Ed. Donald F. Bouchard. Ithaca: Cornell University Press, 1977.
– *Discipline and Punish*. Trans. Alan Sheridan. New York: Vintage Books, 1979.
– *History of Sexuality Volume 1: An Introduction*. Trans. Robert Hurley. New York: Vintage Books, 1980.
– *Power/Knowledge*. Ed. Colin Gordon. New York: Harvester Press, 1980.
– 'Omnes et Singulatim.' In S.M. McMurrin, ed., *The Tanner Lectures on Human Values*, vol. 2. London: Cambridge University Press, 1981.
– *The Foucault Reader*. Ed. Paul Rabinow. New York: Pantheon, 1984.
– 'Technologies of the Self.' In Luther Martin, Huck Gutman, and Patrick Hutton, eds, *Technologies of the Self*. Amherst: University of Massachusetts Press, 1988.

- *The Final Foucault*. Ed. James Bernauer and David Rasmussen. Cambridge: MIT Press, 1988.
- *History of Sexuality, Volume 3: The Care of the Self*. Trans. Robert Hurley. New York: Vintage Books, 1988.
- *Foucault Live: Interviews, 1964–84*. Ed. Sylvere Lotringer. New York: Semiotext Foreign Agents Series, 1989.
- *History of Sexuality Volume 2: The Use of Pleasure*. Trans. Robert Hurley. New York: Vintage Books, 1990.
- Fraser, Nancy. 'Toward a Discourse Ethic of Solidarity.' *Praxis International* 5 (1986): 427–9.
- *Unruly Practices: Power, Discourse and Gender in Contemporary Social Theory*. Minneapolis: University of Minnesota Press, 1989.
- Gilligan, Carol. *In a Different Voice*. Cambridge: Harvard University Press, 1982.
- Godway, Eleanor M., and Geraldine Finn, eds. *Who Is This We?* Montreal: Black Rose Books, 1994.
- Gray, Richard T., and Sabine Wilke, eds. *German Unification and Its Discontent*. Seattle: University of Washington Press, 1996.
- Gutmann, Amy, and Dennis Thompson. *Democracy and Disagreement*. Cambridge: Harvard University Press, 1996.
- Gutting, Gary. *Michel Foucault: Archaeology of Scientific Knowledge*. Cambridge: Cambridge University Press, 1989.
- Habermas, Jürgen. *Towards a Rational Society*. Trans. Jeremy Shapiro. Boston: Beacon Press, 1970.
- 'Toward a Theory of Communicative Competence.' *Inquiry* 13 (1970): 360–75.
- *Knowledge and Human Interest*. Trans. Jeremy Shapiro. London: Heinemann, 1971.
- 'A Postscript to Knowledge and Human Interest.' *Philosophy of Social Science* 3 (1973): 157–89.
- *Theory and Practice*. Trans. John Viertel. Boston: Beacon Press, 1973.
- 'Moral Development and Ego Identity.' *Telos*, no. 24 (Spring 1974): 41–55.
- 'On Social Identity.' *Telos*, no. 19 (Spring 1974): 112–35.
- *Legitimation Crisis*. Trans. Thomas McCarthy. Boston: Beacon Press, 1975.
- 'Some Distinctions in Universal Pragmatics.' *Theory and Society* 3 (1976): 155–67.
- 'A Review of Gadamer's Truth and Method.' In F. Dallmayr and T. McCarthy, eds, *Understanding Social Inquiry*, 361. Notre Dame, Ind.: The University Press, 1977.
- 'Una Intervista con Jürgen Habermas.' *Rinascita*, nos. 30 and 31, 28 July and 4 August 1978.

– *Communication and the Evolution of Society*. Trans. Thomas McCarthy. Boston: Beacon Press, 1979.
– 'History and Evolution.' *Telos*, no. 39 (Spring 1979): 5–44.
– 'Aspects of Rationality of Acton.' In T. Getaets, ed., *Proceeding of the International Symposium on 'Rationality Today*,' 185–205. Ottawa: University of Ottawa Press, 1979.
– 'The Dialectics of Rationalization: An Interview with Jürgen Habermas.' By Axel Honneth, Eberhard Knödler-Bunte, and Arno Widmann. In *Telos*, no. 49 (Fall 1981): 5–32
– 'New Social Movements.' *Telos*, no. 49 (Fall 1981): 33–8.
– 'Modernity versus Postmodernity.' *New German Critique* 22 (Winter 1981): 3–14.
– 'The Entwinement of Myth and Enlightenment: Re-Reading *Dialectic of Enlightenment*.' *New German Critique* 32 (1982): 13–30.
– *Philosophical-political Profiles*. Trans. Frederick G. Lawrence. Cambridge: MIT Press, 1983.
– *The Theory of Communicative Action*. Vol. 1. Trans. Thomas McCarthy. Boston: Beacon Press, 1984.
– 'The French Path to Postmodernity: Bataille between Eroticism and General Economics.' *New German Critique* 33 (Fall 1984): 79–102.
– *Autonomy and Solidarity: Interviews with Jürgen Habermas*. Ed. Peter Dews. London: Verso, 1986.
– *The Theory of Communicative Action*. Vol. 2. Trans. Thomas McCarthy. Boston: Beacon Press, 1987.
– 'Wie ist Legitimität durch Legalität möglich?' *Kritische Justiz* 20 (1987): 1–16.
– *Philosophical Discourse of Modernity*. Cambridge: MIT Press, 1987.
– 'Law and Morality.' In S.M. McMurrin, ed., *The Tanner Lectures on Human Values*, vol. 8. Salt Lake City: University of Utah Press.
– *Nachmetaphysisches Denken*. Frankfurt: Suhrkamp Verlag, 1988.
– *On the Logic of the Social Sciences*. Trans. Shierry Weber Nicholsen and Jerry A. Stark. Cambridge: MIT Press, 1988.
– *On Society and Politics: A Reader*. Ed. Steven Seidman. Boston: Beacon Press, 1989.
– 'Justice and Solidarity: On the Discussion Concerning "Stage" 6.' *The Philosophical Forum* 21, no 2. 1/2 (Fall/Winter 1989–90): 32–53.
– *The New Conservatism: Cultural Criticism and the Historians' Debate*. Trans. Shierry Weber Nicholsen. Cambridge: MIT Press, 1990.
– *Moral Consciousness and Communicative Action*. Trans. Christian Lenhardt and Shierry Weber Nicholsen. Cambridge: MIT Press, 1990.

- *The Structural Transformation of the Public Sphere.* Trans. Thomas Burger. Cambridge: MIT Press, 1991.
- *Postmetaphysical Thinking.* Trans. William Mark Hohengarten. Cambridge: MIT Press, 1992.
- *Justification and Application.* Trans. Ciaran P. Cronin. Cambridge: MIT Press, 1993.
- 'Three Normative Models of Democracy.' *Constellations* 1, no. 1 (1994).
- 'Human Rights and Popular Sovereignty: The Liberal and Republican Versions.' *Ratio Juris* 7, no. 1 (1994): 1–13.
- 'Multiculturalism and the Liberal State.' *Stanford Law Review* 47, no. 5 (May 1995): 849–53.
- *Between Facts and Norms.* Trans. William Rehg. Cambridge: MIT Press, 1996.
- 'Paradigms of Law.' *Cardozo Law Review* 17, nos. 4/5 (March 1996): 771–84.
- 'George Simmel on Philosophy and Culture: Postscript to a Collection of Essays.' *Critical Inquiry* 22 (1996): 403–14.
- *A Berlin Republic: Writings on Germany.* Trans. Steven Rendall. Lincoln: University of Nebraska Press, 1997.
- *The Inclusion of the Other.* Trans. Ciaran Cronin and Pablo De Greiff. Cambridge: MIT Press, 1998.
- 'Learning by Disaster: A Diagnostic Look Back on the Short 20th Century.' *Constellations* 5, no. 3 (1998): 307–20.
- 'Frank Michelman and "Democracy vs. Constitutionalism."' Unpublished manuscript, 1999.
- 'Bestiality and Humanity: A War on the Border between Legality and Morality.' *Constellations* 6, no. 3 (1999): 263–72.
- Habermas, Jürgen, ed. *Observations on 'The Spiritual Situation of the Age.'* Trans. Andrew Buchwalter. Cambridge: MIT Press, 1985.
- Habermas, Jürgen, and N. Luhmann, *Theorie der Gesellschaft oder Sozialtechnologie?* Frankfurt: Suhrkamp, 1971.
- Hegel, G.W.F. *Philosophy of Right.* London: Oxford University Press, 1952.
- *On Christianity.* Trans. T.M. Knox and Richard Kroner. New York: Harper and Brothers, 1961.
- *The Difference between Fichte's and Schelling's System of Philosophy.* Trans. and ed. H.S. Harris and Walter Cerf. Albany: State University of New York Press, 1977.
- *Faith and Knowledge.* Trans. Walter Cerf and H.S. Harris. Albany: State University of New York Press, 1977.
- *Phenomenology of Spirit.* Trans. A.V. Miller. Oxford: Oxford University Press, 1977.

Held, David. *Introduction to Critical Theory*. Los Angeles: University of California Press, 1980.

Holub, Robert. *Jürgen Habermas: Critic in the Public Sphere*. New York: Routledge, 1991.

Honig, Bonnie. 'Difference, Dilemmas, and the Politics of Home.' In Seyla Benhabib, ed., *Democracy and Difference*. Princeton: Princeton University Press, 1996.

– 'Immigrant America? How Foreignness "Solves" Democracy's Problems.' *Social Text* 56 (1998): 1–28.

Honneth, Axel. 'Communication and Reconciliation: Habermas' Critique of Adorno.' *Telos*, no. 39 (Spring 1979): 45–61.

– 'Work and Instrumental Action.' *New German Critique* 26 (1982): 31–54.

– 'An Aversion against the Universal.' *Theory, Culture, and Society* 2, no. 3 (1985): 147–57.

– *The Critique of Power*. Trans. Kenneth Baynes. Cambridge: MIT Press, 1991.

Honneth, Axel, and Hans Joas. *Social Action and Human Nature*. Cambridge: Cambridge University Press, 1988.

Honneth, Axel, and Hans Joas, eds. *Communicative Action*. Trans. J. Gaines and D.L. Jones. Cambridge: MIT Press, 1991.

Honneth, Axel, Thomas McCarthy, Claus Offe, and Albrecht Wellmer, eds. *Cultural-Political Interventions in the Unfinished Project of Enlightenment*. Cambridge: MIT Press, 1992.

Horkheimer, Max. *Eclipse of Reason*. New York: Continuum Publishing Company, 1947.

– *Critical Theory*. Trans. Matthew O'Connell. New York: Herder and Herder, 1972.

Hoy, David. 'Debating Critical Theory.' *Constellations* 3, no. 1 (1996): 104–14.

Hoy, David, and Thomas McCarthy. *Critical Theory*. Cambridge: Blackwell, 1994.

– *Foucault: A Critical Reader*. Oxford: Blackwell, 1986.

Ignatieff, Michael. *The Needs of Strangers*. New York: Penguin Books, 1986.

– *Blood and Belonging*. New York: Penguin Books, 1994.

Ingram, Attracta. 'Constitutional Patriotism.' *Philosophy and Social Criticism* 22, no. 6 (1996): 1–18.

Ingram, David. 'Rawls and Habermas on the Law of Peoples.' Unpublished manuscript, 15 September 2000.

James, Harold, and Marla Stone, eds. *When the Wall Came Down*. New York: Routledge, 1992.

Jameson, Fredric. *The Ideologies of Theory*. Vol. I. Minneapolis: University of Minnesota Press, 1988.

– *The Ideologies of Theory*. Vol. II. Minneapolis: University of Minnesota Press, 1988.

Jay, Martin. *The Dialectical Imagination*. Berkeley, Los Angeles: University of
   California Press, 1973.
– *Marxism and Totality: The Adventures of a Concept from Lukács to Habermas*.
   Berkeley, Los Angeles: University of California Press, 1984.
Jay, Martin. 'Review of Habermas.' *History and Theory* 28, no. 1 (1989): 94–112.
Kant, Immanuel. *Critique of Judgment*. Trans. J.C. Meredith. Oxford: Clarendon,
   1952.
– *Critique of Practical Reason*. Trans. L.W. Beck. Indianapolis: Bobbs-Merrill,
   1956.
– 'An Answer to the Question: What Is Enlightenment.' In *Foundation of the
   Metaphysics of Morals*. Trans. L.W. Beck. Indianapolis: Bobbs-Merrill, 1959.
– *The Doctrine of Virtue*. Trans. Mary Gregor. New York: Hamper and Row,
   1964.
– *Groundwork of the Metaphysics of Morals*. Trans. H.J. Paton. New York: Harper
   Torchbooks, 1964.
– *Critique of Pure Reason*. Trans. N. Kemp Smith. New York: St Martin's Press,
   1965.
– *The Metaphysical Elements of Justice*. Trans. J. Ladd. Indianapolis: Bobbs-
   Merrill, 1966.
– *The Metaphysics of Morals*. New York: Cambridge University Press, 1991.
– 'Perpetual Peace.' In Hans Reiss, ed., *Kant's Political Writings*. Cambridge:
   Cambridge University Press, 1970.
– *Prolegomena to Any Further Methaphysics*. Trans. Paul Carus. Hackett Publish-
   ing Company, 1977.
Kavoulakos, Konstantinos. 'Constitutional State and Democracy: On Jürgen
   Habermas' *Between Facts and Norms*.' *Radical Philosophy* 96 (1999).
Kearney, Richard, ed. *Dialogue with Contemporary Continental Thinkers: The
   Phenomenological Heritage*. Manchester: Manchester University Press, 1984.
Kellner, Douglas. *Critical Theory, Marxism, and Modernity*. Cambridge: Polity
   Press, 1989.
Kelly, Michael, ed. *Critique and Power: Recasting the Foucault/Habermas Debate*.
   Cambridge: MIT Press, 1994.
Kohlberg, Lawrence. *Essays on Moral Development*. Vols. 1 and 2. New York:
   Harper and Row, 1981, 1984.
Kortian, Garbis. *Metacritique*. Cambridge: University of Cambridge Press,
   1980.
Kristeva, Julia. *Nations without Nationalism*. Trans. Leon S. Roudiez. New York:
   Columbia University Press, 1993.
Kymlicka, Will. *Liberalism, Community, and Culture*. New York: Oxford Univer-
   sity Press, 1989.
– *Contemporary Political Philosophy*. New York: Oxford University Press, 1990.

- 'An Emerging Consensus?' *Ethical Theory and Moral Practice* 1 (1998): 143–57.
- 'The Ethics of Inarticulacy' *Inquiry* 34 (1991): 155–182.
- *Multicultural Citizenship.* New York: Oxford University Press, 1995.
- *Politics in the Vernacular.* Oxford: Oxford University Press, 2001.

Kymlicka, Will, and Wayne Norman. 'Return of the Citizen: A Survey of Recent Work on Citizenship Theory.' *Ethics* 104 (January 1994): 352–81.

Laclau, Ernesto, ed. *The Making of Political Identities.* London: Verso, 1994.

Laclau, Ernesto, and Chantal Mouffe. *Hegemony and Social Strategy: Toward a Radical Democratic Politics.* London: Verso, 1985.

- 'Post-Marxism without Apologies.' *New Left Review*, no. 166 (November/December 1987): 79–106.

Lafont, Cristina. *The Linguistic Turn in Hermeneutic Philosophy.* Cambridge: MIT Press, 1999.

Laforest, Guy, ed. *Reconciling the Solitudes: Essays on Canadian Federalism and Nationalism.* Montreal and Kingston: McGill-Queen's University Press, 1993.

Larmore, Charles. *Patterns of Moral Complexity.* Cambridge: Cambridge University Press, 1987.

- *The Morals of Modernity.* Cambridge: Cambridge University Press, 1996.

Lee, Benjamin. 'Peoples and Publics.' *Public Culture* 10, no. 2 (1998): 371–94.

Lee, Orville. 'Culture and Democratic Theory: Toward a Theory of Symbolic Democracy.' *Constellation* 5, no. 4 (1998).

Lüdtke, Martin. 'The Utopian Motif Is Suspended: Conversation with Leo Lowenthal.' *New German Critique* 38 (Spring/Summer 1986): 105–11.

Lukács, Georg. *History and Class Consciousness.* Cambridge: MIT Press, 1971.

Lyotard, Jean-François. *The Postmodern Condition.* Minneapolis: University of Minnesota Press, 1984.

- 'Interview.' *Diacritics* 14, no. 3 (1984): 16–21.

- *The Differend.* Minneapolis: University of Minnesota Press, 1988.

Macedo, Stephen. *Deliberative Politics: Essays on Democracy and Disagreement.* New York: Oxford University Press, 1999

MacIntyre, Alisdair. *After Virtue.* Notre Dame: University of Notre Dame Press, 1984.

- *Whose Justice? Which Rationality?* Notre Dame: Notre Dame University Press, 1989.

Manin, Bernard. 'On Legitimacy and Political Deliberation.' *Political Theory* 15 (1987): 338–68.

Mansbridge, Jane. 'Using Power / Fighting Power.' *Constellations* 1, no. 1 (1994): 53–73.

Marcuse, Herbert. *Negation: Essays in Critical Theory.* Trans. Jeremy Shapiro. Boston: Beacon Press, 1968.

Markell, Patchen. 'Contesting Consensus: Rereading Habermas on the Public Sphere.' *Constellations* 3, no. 3 (1997): 377–400.
– 'Making Affect Safe for Democracy? On Constitutional Patriotism.' *Political Theory* 28, no. 1 (2000).
Mason, Andrew. 'Political Community, Liberal-Nationalism, and the Ethics of Assimilation.' *Ethics* 109 (January 1999): 261–86.
Marx, Karl. *A Contribution to the Critique of Political Economy.* Ed. Maurice Dobb. New York: International Publishers, 1970.
– *Grundrisse.* New York: Vintage Books, 1973.
– *The Portable Karl Marx.* Ed. Eugene Kamenka. New York: Viking Penguin, 1983.
Marx, Karl, and Frederick Engels. *The German Ideology.* Ed. C.J. Arthur. New York: International Publishers, 1970.
– *Collected Works.* New York: International Publishers, 1975.
Matuštík, Martin. 'Derrida and Habermas on the Aporia of the Politics of Identity and Difference: Towards Radical Democratic Multiculturalism.' *Constellations* 1, no. 3 (1995): 383–98.
McCarthy, Thomas. *The Critical Theory of Jürgen Habermas.* Cambridge: MIT Press, 1981.
– *Ideals and Illusions: On Reconstruction and Deconstruction in Contemporary Critical Theory.* Cambridge: MIT Press, 1991.
– 'Kantian Constructivism and Reconstructivism: Rawls and Habermas in Dialogue.' *Ethics* 105 (October 1994): 44–63.
– 'On the Margins of Politics.' *Journal of Philosophy* 11 (November 1988): 645–8.
– 'Philosophy and Critical Theory: A Reply to Richard Rorty and Seyla Benhabib.' *Constellations* 3, no. 1 (1996): 95–103.
– 'On Reconciling Cosmopolitan Unity and National Diversity.' *Public Culture* 11, no. 1 (1999): 175–209.
Meeham, Johanna, ed. *Habermas and Feminism: Autonomy, Morality, and the Gendered Subject.* London: Routledge, 1995.
Mellos, Koula. *Rationalité, Communication, Modernité.* Ottawa: Les Presses de l'Université d'Ottawa, 1991.
Mertens, Thomas. 'Cosmopolitanism and Citizenship: Kant against Habermas.' *European Journal of Philosophy* 4, no. 3 (December 1996): 328–47.
Michelman, Frank. 'Law's Republic.' *Yale Law Journal* 97 (1988): 1493–1537.
– 'Can Constitutional Democrats Be Legal Positivists? Or Why Constitutionalism?' *Constellations* 2, no. 3 (1996): 293–308.
– Review of Habermas's *Between Facts and Norms* and *The Journal of Philosophy* 93 (1996): 307–15.
Miller, David, *On Nationality.* Oxford: Oxford University Press, 1995.

Moggach, Douglas. 'Hegel and Habermas.' *The European Legacy* 2, no. 3 (1997): 548–54.

Mouffe, Chantal. 'Radical Democracy: Modern or Postmodern?' In Andrew Ross, ed., *Universal Abandon*, 46–62. Minneapolis: University of Minnesota Press, 1988.

Negri, Antonio. *Marx beyond Marx*. Trans. Harry Cleaver. South Hadley. Mass.: Routledge, 1984.

– *The Savage Anomaly: The Power of Spinoza's Metaphysics and Politics*. Trans. Michael Hardt. Minneapolis: University of Minnesota Press, 1991.

Newey, Glen. 'Gassing and Bungling.' *London Review of Books* 14, 8 May 1997: 14–15.

Nietzsche, Friedrich. *Thus Spoke Zarathustra*. Trans. R.J. Hollingdale. New York: Penguin Books, 1961.

– *On the Genealogy of Morals* and *Ecce Homo*. Trans. Walter Kaufmann. New York: Vintage Books, 1969.

– *Beyond Good and Evil*. Trans. R.J. Hollingdale. New York: Penguin Books, 1973.

– *The Gay Science*. Trans. Walter Kaufmann. New York: Vintage Books, 1974.

Nicholson, L.J., ed. *Feminism/Postmodernism*. New York: Routledge, 1990.

Norris, Christopher. *Derrida*. Cambridge: Harvard University Press, 1987.

Nussbaum, Martha. *For Love of Country: Debating the Limits of Patriotism*. Ed. Joshua Cohen. Boston: Beacon Press, 1996.

Osborne, Peter, ed. *A Critical Sense: Interviews with Intellectuals*. London: Routledge, 1996.

Outhwaite, William. *Habermas: A Critical Introduction*. Cambridge: Polity Press, 1994.

Payrow Shabani, Omid A. 'Are All Critiques of Reason Irrational?' *Contemporary Philosophy* 20, nos. 1 and 2 (1998): 19–30.

Philips, Anne. 'Dealing with Difference: A Politics of Ideas or a Politics of Presence?' *Constellations* 1, no. 1 (1994): 74–91.

Pippin, Robert. B. *Modernism as a Philosophical Problem*. Cambridge: Basil Blackwell, 1991.

Pogge, Thomas. 'An Egalitarian Law of People.' *Philosophy and Public Affairs* 23, no. 3 (1994): 195–224.

Post, Robert C. 'The Constitutional Concept of Public Discourse.' *Harvard Law Review* 103 (1990): 603–86.

Poster, Mark, ed. *Foucault, Marxism and History*. Cambridge: Polity Press, 1984.

– *Critical Theory and Poststructuralism: In Search of a Context*. Ithaca: Cornell University Press, 1989.

– *Politics, Theory, and Contemporary Culture*. New York: Columbia University Press, 1993.

Preuss, Ulrich. 'Prospect of a Constitution for Europe.' *Constellations* 3, no. 2 (1996): 207–24.

Putnam, Hillary. *Realism and Reason: Philosophical Papers*. Vol. 3. Cambridge: Cambridge University Press, 1983.

– 'Why Reason Cannot Be Naturalized.' In Putnam, *Realism and Reason*, vol. 3.

Rancière, Jacques. 'After What?' *Topoi* 7, no. 2 (September 1988): 181–5.

– Democracy Means Equality.' *Radical Philosophy* 82 (1997): 29–36.

– 'Politics, Identification, and Subjectivization.' In John Rajchman, ed., *The Identity in Question*. New York: Routledge, 1995.

– *Disagreement*. Trans. Julie Rose. Minneapolis: University of Minnesota Press, 1999.

Rasmussen, David. *Reading Habermas*. Cambridge: Basil Blackwell, 1990.

Rasmussen, David, ed. *Universalism versus Communitarianism: Contemporary Debates in Ethics*. Cambridge: MIT Press, 1990.

– *The Handbook of Critical Theory*. Cambridge: Blackwell Publishers, 1996.

Rawls, John. *A Theory of Justice*. Cambridge: Harvard University Press, 1971.

– 'Kantian Conservatism in Moral Philosophy.' *Journal of Philosophy* 77 (1980): 515–72.

– 'The Basic Liberties and Their Priority.' In S. McMurrin, ed., *The Tanner Lectures on Human Values*, vol. 3, 1–87. Salt Lake City: University of Utah Press, 1982.

– 'Justice as Fairness: Political not Metaphysical.' *Philosophy and Public Affairs* 14 (1985): 227–51.

– *Political Liberalism*. New York: Columbia University Press, 1993.

– *Collected Papers*. Ed. Samuel Freeman. Cambridge: Harvard University Press, 1999.

– *The Law of Peoples*. Cambridge: Harvard University Press, 1999.

Rehg, William. 'Discourse and the Moral Point of View: Deriving a Dialogical Principle of Universalization.' *Inquiry* 34 (1990): 27–48.

Remer, Gary. 'Political Oratory and Conversation: Cicero versus Deliberative Democracy.' *Political Theory* 27, no. 1 (February 1999): 39–64

Rockmore, Thomas. *Habermas on Historical Materialism*. Bloomington: Indiana University Press, 1989.

Roderick, Rick. *Habermas and the Foundation of Critical Theory*. St Martin's Press, 1986.

Rorty, Richard. *Philosophy and the Mirror of Nature*. Princeton: Princeton University Press, 1979.

– 'Habermas and Lyotard on Postmodernity.' In R.J. Bernstein, ed., *Habermas and Modernity*. Cambridge: MIT Press, 1985.

– 'The Ambiguity of "Rationality."' *Constellations* 3, no. 1 (1996): 73–82.

Ruddick, Sara. *Maternal Thinking*. New York: Ballantine Books, 1989.

Rushdie, Salman. *Imaginary Homeland*. London: Granta Books, 1981.

Sallis, John, ed. *Deconstruction and Philosophy*. Chicago: University of Chicago Press, 1987.

Sandel, Michael. *Liberalism and the Limits of Justice*. Cambridge: Cambridge University Press, 1982.

Savelsberg, Joachim. Review of Habermas's *Between Facts and Norms*. *American Journal of Sociology* 102 (May 1997): 1736–9.

Scheuerman, William. 'Neumann v. Habermas: The Frankfurt School and the Case of the Rule of Law.' *Praxis International* 13 (1993): 50–67.

– *Between the Norm and the Exception*. Cambridge: MIT Press, 1997.

Scruton, Roger. 'In Defense of Nation.' In J.C.D. Clark, ed., *Ideas and Politics in Modern Britain*. London: Macmillan, 1990.

Sensat, Julius Jr. *Habermas and Marxism: An Appraisal*. Beverly Hills: Sage Publications, 1979.

Shklar, Judith. 'Giving Injustice Its Due.' *Yale Law Journal* 98 (April 1989): 1135–51.

Skjei, Erling. 'A Comment on Performative, Subject and Proposition in Habermas' Theory of Communication.' *Inquiry* 28 (1985): 87–104.

Smith, Nick. 'The Spirit of Modernity and its Fate: Jürgen Habermas.' *Radical Philosophy* 60 (Spring 1992): 23–9

Spinoza, Benedict. *Ethics*. Indianapolis: Hackett Publishing Co., 1992.

Sprinker, Michael, ed. *Ghostly Demarcation*. London: Verso, 1999.

Steel, Meili. 'The Ontological Turn and Its Ethical Consequence: Habermas and the Poststructuralists.' *Praxis International* 11, no. 4 (1992): 428–45.

Stein, Tine. 'Does the Constitutional and Democratic System Work?' *Constellations* 4, no. 3 (1998): 420–49.

Strydom, Piet. 'The Ontogenetic Fallacy: The Immanent Critique of Habermas' Developmental Logical Theory of Evolution.' *Theory, Culture, and Society* 9 (1992): 65–93.

– 'Sociocultural Evolution or the Social Evolution of Practical Reason?: Eder's Critique of Habermas.' *Praxis International* 13, no. 3 (1993): 304–32.

Tamir, Yael. *Liberal Nationalism*. Princeton: Princeton University Press, 1993.

Taylor, Charles. 'Foucault on Freedom and Truth.' *Political Theory* 12 (1984): 152–83.

– 'Connolly, Foucault and Truth.' *Political Theory* 13 (August 1985): 377–85.

– *Philosophical Papers*. New York: Cambridge University Press, 1985.

– *Sources of the Self: The Making of Modern Identity*. Cambridge: Harvard University Press, 1989.

– *Reconciling the Solitudes: Essays on Canadian Federalism and Nationalism*.

Ed. Guy Laforest. Montreal, Kingston: McGill-Queen's University Press, 1993.
- *Multiculturalism.* Ed. Amy Gutmann. Princeton: Princeton University Press, 1994.
- 'Cross-Purposes: The Liberal-Communitarian Debate.' In *Philosophical Arguments.* Cambridge: Harvard University Press, 1995.
- 'Why Democracy Needs Patriotism.' In Joshua Cohen, ed., *For the Love of Country: Debating the Limits of Patriotism.* Boston: Beacon, 1996.
- 'Nationalism and Modernity.' In R. McKim and J. McMahan, eds, *The Morality of Nationalism.* Oxford: Oxford University Press, 1997.
Therborn, Goran. 'Jürgen Habermas: A New Eclecticism.' *New Left Review* 67 (1971): 69–83.
Thompson, John and David Held, eds. *Habermas' Critical Debates.* Cambridge: MIT Press, 1982.
Tuori, Kaarlo. 'Discourse Ethics and the Legitimacy of Law' *Ratio Juris* 2 (1989): 125–43
Van der Burg, Wibren. 'Jürgen Habermas on Law and Morality: Some Critical Comments.' *Theory, Culture, and Society* 7 (1990): 105–11.
Vatimo, Gianni. *The End of Modernity.* Trans. Jon R. Snyder. Baltimore: Johns Hopkins University Press, 1991.
Viroli, Maurizio. *For Love of Country: An Essay on Patriotism and Nationalism.* Oxford: Oxford University Press, 1995.
- 'On Civic Republicanism: Reply to Xenos and Yack.' *Critical Review* 12, nos. 1–2 (Winter/Spring 1998).
Walzer, Michael. *Spheres of Justice: A Defense of Pluralism and Equality.* New York: Basic Books, 1983.
- 'What Does It Mean to Be an "American"?' *Social Research* 57 (1990): 591–614.
Wellmer, Albrecht. 'On the Dialectic of Modernism and Postmodernism.' *Praxis International* 4, no. 4 (1985): 337–62.
- *Ethik und Dialog.* Frankfurt: Suhrkamp, 1986.
- *The Persistence of Modernity.* Trans. David Midgley. Cambridge: MIT Press, 1991.
White, Stephen, K. 'Foucault's Challenge to Critical Theory.' *American Political Science Review* 80, no. 2 (June 1986): 419–32.
- *The Recent Work of Jürgen Habermas.* Cambridge: Cambridge University Press, 1988.
- *Political Theory and Postmodernism.* Cambridge: Cambridge University Press, 1991.
White, Stephen K., ed. *Lifeworld and Politics: Between Modernity and Postmodern-*

ity: Essays in Honor of Fred Dallmayr. Notre Dame: University of Notre Dame Press, 1989.

– *The Cambridge Companion to Habermas.* Cambridge: Cambridge University Press, 1995.

Wood, Allen. 'Habermas' Defense of Rationalism.' *New German Critique* 35 (Spring/Summer 1985): 145–64.

Wood, David. *Derrida: A Critical Reader.* Cambridge, Mass.: Blackwell, 1992.

Wieviorka, Michel. 'Violence, Culture and Democracy: A European Perspective.' *Public Culture* 8 (1996): 329–54.

Wingenbach, Ed. 'Unjust Context: The Priority of Stability in Rawls' Contextualized Theory of Justice.' *American Journal of Political Science* 43, no. 1 (1999): 213–32.

Xenos, Nicholas. 'Questioning Patriotism.' *Critical Review* 12, nos. 1–2 (Winter/Spring 1998): 197–201.

Yack, Bernard. 'The Myth of the Civic Nation.' *Critical Review* 10, no. 2 (Spring 1996): 193–211.

– 'Can Patriotism Save Us from Nationalism: A Rejoinder to Viroli.' *Critical Review* 12, nos. 1–2 (Winter/Spring 1998): 203–6.

Young, Iris. 'Asymmetrical Reciprocity: On Moral Respect, Wonder, and Enlarged Thought.' *Constellations* 3, no. 3 (1997): 340–63.

Zimmermann, Rolf. 'Emancipation and Rationality: Foundational Problems in the Theories of Marx and Habermas.' *Ratio* 26 (1984): 143–65.

Index